C000025918

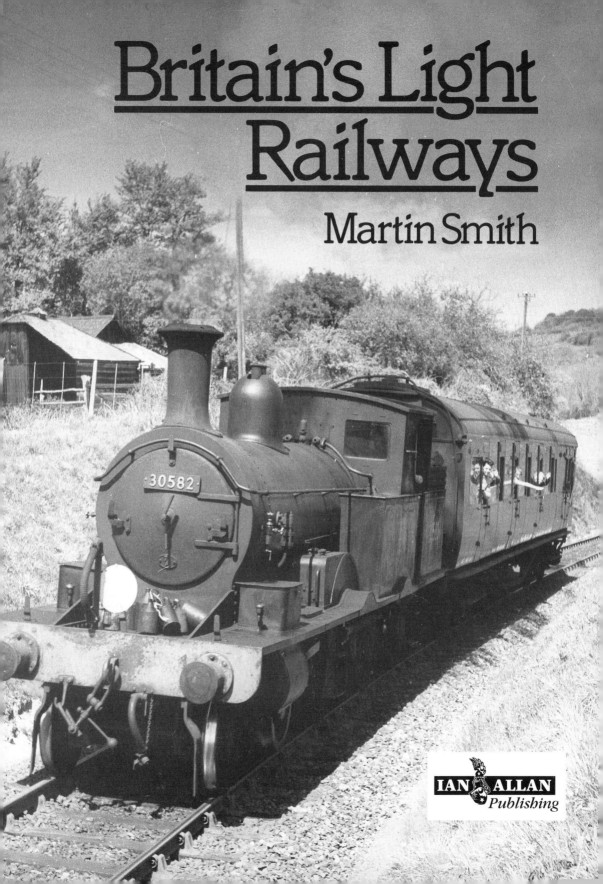

Britain's Light Railways

Martin Smith

Ian Allan Publishing

First published 1994

ISBN 0 7110 2223 2

All rights reserved. No part of this book may be reproduced or transmitted in any form or by any means, electronic or mechanical, including photo-copying, recording or by any information storage and retrieval system, without permission from the Publisher in writing.

© Martin Smith 1994

Designed by Ian Allan Studio

Published by Ian Allan Publishing

an imprint of Ian Allan Ltd, Terminal House, Station Approach, Shepperton, Surrey TW17 8AS; and printed by Ian Allan Printing Ltd, Coombelands House, Coombelands Lane, Addlestone Weybridge Surrey KT15 1HY.

Front cover, top: **The former Southern Railway branch to Lyme Regis started life as the Axminster & Lyme Regis Light Railway. The Adams 'Radial Tanks' were synonymous with the line, and this picture shows Nos 30583 and 30584 leaving Axminster on 11 July 1959 with through coaches from Waterloo.** R. C. Riley

Front cover, below left: **A regular visitor to the Derwent Valley Light Railway in the 1950s was ex-NER 'J25' class 0-6-0 No 65700, seen here taking on water at Wheldrake.** Ian Allan Library

Front cover, below right: **One of the Campbeltown & Machrihanish Light Railways' Barclay 0-6-2Ts, probably *Atlantic*, pulls away from Hall Street in Campbeltown.** Bucknall Collection/Ian Allan Library

Back cover: **The Sand Hutton Light Railway in Yorkshire used War Surplus 0-4-0WTs, and here *Esme* stands outside the engine shed in the summer of 1927.** Rail Archive Stephenson

Title page: **Many light railways eventually became, in effect, conventional rural branches and one of the most charismatic was the old Axminster & Lyme Regis Light Railway on the Somerset/Dorset border. For most of its life, the line was worked by the legendary 'Radial Tanks', and this classic picture shows No 30582 hauling a rather lightweight train in the 1950s.** Ian Allan Library

Contents

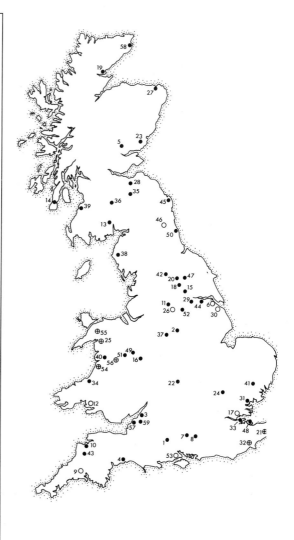

● CLOSED
○ OPEN (PART OR WHOLE)
⊕ PRESERVED LINE

MAP OF GREAT BRITAIN SHOWING THE SITES OF LIGHT RAILWAYS

Acknowledgements

As always, the biggest thank-you goes to my ever-tolerant wife, Micky, a founder member of the 'Save the Semi-Colon Society'.

During the preparation of this book, practical assistance and invaluable advice was kindly provided, often in very generous helpings, by: Mr D. W. Allan (Welsh Highland Railway), Stephen Batty, Paul Burkhalter, Alan Butcher, Ian S. Carr, Richard Casserley, Peter Cookson (Pontefract Railway Society), Andrew J. Cooper, Steve Daly (Welsh Railways Research Circle), Jack Davis, Stuart Dixon (British Coal), John Dodds, Lt Frank Drebin, Mrs R. Duncan, Mr C. T. Goode, Colin Hall, David Hay, Mr A. Hodson, Peter Horne (BR, Eastleigh), Alastair Ireland (Lowthers Railway Society), Keith Jones (GNoSR Association), Andrew Kennedy, Rex Kennedy, Colin Judge, Fred Landery (Caledonian Railway Association), Mr G. Lindsay, Bob Ling (Mobil Oil, Coryton), Frank Lismore, Sandy Maclean, Andrew McCracken (Strathspey Railway), Charles Meacher, Richard Mellor (Esso Petroleum, Fawley), Mr D. G. Morgan (Trainload Freight), Mr J. M. Orchiston, Colin Palmer (BR, South Humberside), Stuart Rankin (G&SWR Association), John Redfern, Bill Robertson, Graham Robinson (G&SWR Association), Eric Sawford, W. Marshall Shaw (North British Study Group, Mr C. Roy Skinner, Mr J. Smith (Lens of Sutton), Graham Stacey (LCGB/RAS), Andrew Stephen, Mr A. Sunderland, Charles S. Taylor, Paul Taylor (Tyne & Wear Metro), Neil Thompson (Vale of Rheidol Railway), Gordon Thomson (Ayrshire Railway Preservation Group), Arnold Tortorella (G&SWR Association), Mark Toynbee (Kent & East Sussex Railway), Peter Waller, Frank Winter (the Pipe Society), Mr Eric Youldon, and the staff at numerous county libraries, local history libraries and records offices. To all of you, sincere thanks.

Martin Smith
Coleford,
Somerset.
June 1993.

Bibliography

Much useful information has been gleaned from the following sources:

Bradshaw's Manual

British Locomotive Catalogue, (B. & D. Baxter), Moorland Publishing.

Clinker's Register, (C. R. Clinker), Avon Anglia.

Great Central, (George Dow), Locomotive Publishing Co.

Light Railways: their rise and decline, (W. J. K. Davies), Ian Allan.

Locomotives of the Great Western Railway, RCTS.

Locomotives of the LB&SCR, (D. L. Bradley), RCTS.

Locomotives of the LNER, RCTS.

L&SWR Locomotives, (D. L. Bradley), Wild Swan.

L&SWR Engine Sheds, (Chris Hawkins & George Reeve), Irwell Press.

Narrow Gauge Railways in North/South Caernarvonshire, (J. I. C. Boyd), Oakwood Press.

Private and Untimetabled Railway Stations, (G. Croughton, R. W. Kidner, A. Young), Oakwood Press.

The Railways of Southern England, (Edwin Course), Batsford.

Railways of South Shields, (Neil T. Sinclair & Ian S. Carr), Tyne and Wear Museums.

Railways of the South Yorkshire Coalfield from 1880, (A. L. Barnett), RCTS.

Sou' West Journal (The magazine of the Glasgow & South Western Railway Association), articles by Ian Kirkpatrick (Issues 21/22) and Arnold Tortorella (Issue 19).

Various ageing periodicals including *Railway Magazine, Railway Observer, Railway World* and *Trains Illustrated,* and also assorted public and working timetables.

Introduction

For those of us who have yet to qualify for a bus pass, first-hand experience of independent light railways will, almost certainly, be confined to the Derwent Valley, East Kent, Kent & East Sussex and the Shropshire & Montgomeryshire Light Railways. Throughout Britain, however, there were around 60 locomotive-operated railways which were either born out of, or later applied for, Light Railway Orders, and this book is about those lines. In order to see why light railways came into being, one has to look back to earlier railway history.

By the late 19th century, railways had reached almost every major town and city in Britain. Furthermore, many rural areas had reaped the benefits from lines which passed through on their way from one sizeable community to another. In contrast, however, there were numerous small towns which because of their geographical locations, had eluded the attentions of the major railway companies. If those towns had any sort of railway at all, it was often one which had been promoted by a consortium of local businessmen, with the harsh economics of running a railway having been ignored in favour of local pride. From necessity, the majority of localised independent railway companies had, eventually, sold out to one of the big boys. Those which had insisted on going it alone had, almost invariably, become well used to letters from the bank manager.

There were many reasons why small local railway companies of the mid Victorian era seldom succeeded as independents, but one of those reasons was hardly the fault of the companies themselves. The construction and the operating methods of every one of

Britain's public railways had to meet the stringent standards set down by the Board of Trade before one single farthing could be extracted from fare-paying passengers and, although the Government's standards prevented rogue or naive promoters building potentially dangerous railways, those standards were totally inflexible. Therefore, even the most rural of branch lines had to be built to what were virtually main line standards, complete with elaborate signalling arrangements, separate goods yards, raised platforms and fully-manned level crossings. The outcome was that, even if enough money could be raised to build a rural railway, the potential traffic very rarely justified the comparatively large construction and legal bills. Often, however, local pride demanded that the construction went ahead; the almost inevitable outcome being a bout of 'told-you-so' from the hard-nosed realists.

A further hindrance to the promotion of rural railways was that each company had to be incorporated by an Act of Parliament. This was an extremely costly business even when the legal procedures went

Below: **The Easingwold Railway in Yorkshire was authorised by an Act of Parliament but was granted revised powers under the terms of a Light Railway Order in 1928, 37 years after the line had opened. When the company's own locomotive was out of action a replacement was hired from the LNER, but the sight of 'J71' class 0-6-0T No 1758 in the Easingwold bay of Alne station on 19 July 1927 provides few clues of the light railway status of its temporary user.**
Real Photographs/Ian Allan Library

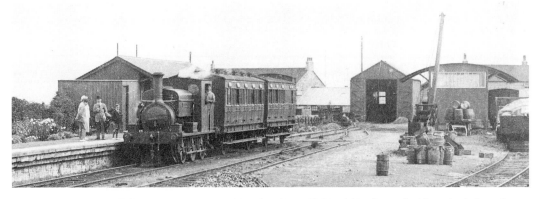

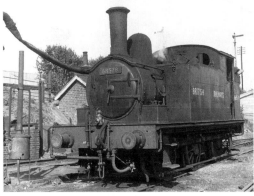

Above: **Lightweight rails, ancient four-wheeled coaches, an industrial-style saddle tank locomotive and a general air of under-use...it all adds up to a typical latter-day light railway scene. This is Seahouses, the terminus of the North Sunderland Railway in Northumberland.**
Lens of Sutton

Left: **The Kelvedon, Tiptree & Tollesbury Pier Light Railway in Essex was worked, at first, by the Great Eastern and, later, the LNER. Traditional motive power continued to be used after Nationalisation, as evidenced in the sight of 'J69' class 0-6-0T No 68578 taking water at Kelvedon on 17 September 1949. The main line station is visible on the higher level behind.**
R. E. Vincent

smoothly, but when opposition from main line railway companies or landowners reared its head, as it usually did, the most well-considered financial projections could be consigned to the waste-paper bin, and shareholders would be required to dig even deeper into their pockets.

The problems facing the builders of small rural railways had first been addressed in 1864. In that year, the Railway Construction Facilities Act was passed and this made provision for plans to be authorised by a Board of Trade certificate, provided that there was no opposition. Perhaps predictably, the number of proposals which were free from opposition were virtually nil, and so in 1868 that legislation was superseded by the Regulation of Railways Act. Contained in part of the Act were the words '...to construct and work or to work as a light railway...', and this is believed to be the first official recognition in this country of the term 'light railway'.

In order to qualify under the 1868 Act, however, railway promotions still had to be free from opposition, and so very few companies were to benefit. Among the few were the Great Yarmouth & Stalham Light Railway in East Anglia, and the Culm Valley Light Railway in Devon. Despite their corporate titles, those companies were built more as lightweight branch lines rather than as the type of light railway

which started to materialise some 30 years later; therefore, they are not included in this book.

Despite its good intentions, the 1868 Act failed to encourage the widespread promotion and construction of rural railways. The passing of the Tramways Act in 1870 was also well-meaning but, significantly, it failed to obviate the sizeable hurdle of a full-blooded Act of Parliament being required for even the most lightweight of railways. The classic example of high legal costs involved the Easingwold Railway in Yorkshire which, in the pre-light railway days of the mid-1880s, incurred Parliamentary expenses of £1,267 for the authorisation of its 2½-mile line. Furthermore, the word 'tramways' was not a good selling point for the Act in this country as the traditional British concept of a tramway was that of a means of urban passenger transportation or a horse-worked freight line. Nevertheless, a few celebrated little lines were born as a result of the Act. One was the standard gauge Wisbech & Upwell Tramway in East Anglia, which opened throughout in 1884 and was worked by the Great Eastern Railway with Worsdell's distinctive enclosed 'G15' (later LNER 'Y6') class 0-4-0Ts. Others were the 2ft 4½ in gauge Glyn Valley Tramway in north-east Wales, which was rebuilt from a horse-worked mineral line, and the Wantage Tramway of 1875.

It was 1894 before any further serious thought was

Above: **The LNER's 'J69' 0-6-0Ts were ideal for lightly-laid branches, and the Elsenham & Thaxted Light Railway in Essex was one such line which made use of the class. No 7193 (later BR No 68600) waits at Elsenham with the 4.25pm to Thaxted on 22 April 1935.** LCGB/Ken Nunn Collection

given to improving rural communication by the use of light railways. In that year, the Board of Trade held a conference and called on engineers and inspectors who had witnessed the usefulness of light railways abroad. The outcome was the Light Railways Act of 14 August 1896. The act did much to simplify the mechanics of promoting and constructing secondary railways, its main advantage being that lines could be built under Light Railway Orders rather than fully-fledged Acts of Parliament. Another significant part of the the Act was that, for the first time in British railway history, local authorities were entitled to operate light railways either solely or in collaboration with private companies. Active encouragement of this was offered by the availability of Treasury subsidies, a grant of up to 25% of a light railway's construction costs being payable if a local authority chipped in as well. In the case of lines which, in the opinion of the Board of Agriculture or the Board of Trade, would *'benefit agriculture in any district'* or where *'a necessary*

means of communication would be established between a fishing harbour or fishing village and a market, or that such railway is necessary for the development of or maintenance of some definite industry', up to 50% of the cost of construction could be covered by a grant or a loan. The Government put its money where its mouth was, and made available a total of £1,000,000 to cover the grants.

Three Light Railway Commissioners were appointed by the Board of Trade: The Earl of Jersey (Chairman), Colonel George Ottley Boughey and Henry Allan Steward. They were given considerable powers of discretion, but one aspect beyond their control was that of land costs. Although the 1896 Act made provision for compulsory purchase of land, disputes had to be settled under the 1889 Arbitration Act which was administered independently. In the Light Railways Act itself, the most significant omission was any real definition as to what constituted a light railway. As a rule, however, conventional railways were built with rails of not less than 75lb/yd and ballast of at least 24in thick; by comparison, light railways tended to use rails of around 50-60lb/yd and ballast of between 9in and 14in, thereby reducing the cost of construction from an average of £4,500-£5,000 per mile to some £3,000-£3,500 per mile.

In practice, some companies such as the Corring-

ham Light Railway managed to reduce those costs even further by dispensing with earthworks almost completely. By contrast, part of the Kent & East Sussex was laid with 80-90lb/yd rails which, in view of its future use of a 0-8-0T weighing 46¾ tons, proved to be a wise move. Other features which were usually acceptable for the operation of light railways were unmanned and ungated level crossings, minimal station buildings and an absence of lineside fencing. Furthermore, signals were required only at connections with main lines or if the 'one engine in steam' principle was not used. As their part of the bargain, the light railway companies were obliged to enforce a maximum speed limit of 25mph (reduced to 10mph near unguarded crossings and on curves sharper than 9 chains radius), and to heed the relevant axle-weight limits for locomotives and rolling stock.

Another restriction placed on light railway companies was that their trains should not encroach on main-line tracks at any junction stations. That effec-

tively prevented through running between a light and a main-line railway, although through coaches were not altogether unknown. Among the few recorded exceptions were sleeping carriages from Euston, which were taken off at The Mound, in Scotland, to travel to Dornoch by means of the Dornoch Light Railway, and the Southern Railway's running of through coaches from Cannon Street to Tenterden in conjunction with the Kent & East Sussex Light Railway.

The Light Railways Act made no stipulations regarding locomotives but, of course, the lightweight construction of the lines and corporate bank balances of the operators placed their own restrictions. As the years progressed, many opted for standard industrial designs, often 0-6-0STs, from the likes of Manning Wardle or Hudswell Clarke, those types being well tried and tested for economy of operation, sturdiness and ease of repair. Other companies preferred to pick up second-hand bargains. Ex-London & South Western Railway 'Ilfracombe Goods' 0-6-0s were pur-

Above: **Lt-Col Holman Frederick Stephens often experimented with alternative forms of motive power in an attempt to reduce operating costs to the absolute minimum. This Shefflex 'twin-car' railbus was purchased in 1930 for use on the Kent & East Sussex Light Railway but, considering that this picture was taken at Rolvenden just five years later, little need be said about the machine's popularity.**
Rail Archive Stephenson

Above left: **A few light railways were still fully operational in British Railways days and one of the most scenic was, arguably, the old Dornoch Light Railway in Sutherland. Ex-Highland Railway 0-4-4T No 55053 hauls a typical mixed train near The Mound in July 1954.**
Ian Allan Library

Left: **In common with several of its contemporaries, the Weston, Clevedon & Portishead Light Railway made use of ex-LB&SCR 'Terriers' 0-6-0Ts. Here, WC&P No 2 *Portishead* pulls away from Clevedon with a Weston-bound train. The loading of six coaches was untypically heavy for the WC&P, the first three carriages appearing to be the 'Triplet' set which was purchased from the Southern Railway in 1924 and, usually, more than adequate to meet all demands on their own. The neck of the shed yard at Clevedon can be seen on the right of the picture.**
Real Photographs/Ian Allan Library

chased for the Kent & East Sussex and the Shropshire & Montgomeryshire Light Railways after 30-40 years main line service; former London, Brighton & South Coast 'Terrier' 0-6-0Ts went to, among others, the Weston, Clevedon & Portishead Light Railway, whereas the Nidd Valley Light Railway purchased two ex-Metropolitan Railway Beyer Peacock 4-4-0Ts, which had been ousted from London by the spread of electrification.

It was a similar story with rolling stock. The carriage and wagon lists of Britain's independent light railways provided a fair old lesson on the nation's railway history, coaches being obtained from countless main line companies, both large and small. Coaches of the Metropolitan, North London and District Railways, in particular, came on the market at knockdown prices after electrification had rendered them redundant and, during the 1920s, the Southern's electrification schemes also made many coaches surplus to requirements. The independent light railways proved

to be excellent customers for surplus stock. Furthermore, cancelled orders for overseas railways also resulted in surprise bargains for the ever-impecunious light railways and, consequently, coaches looking like something out of Hoot Gibson's Wild West films became far from unknown on quiet British rural branch lines. It did much to add to the overwhelming character of those railways.

Even in 1921, when a lengthy report on Britain's light railways was made for the newly-formed Ministry of Transport, the subject of locomotives and rolling stock was not raised. However, recommendations were made for officially reducing the requirements (signalling, platforms etc.) imposed on light railways provided that, in some cases, a 15mph speed limit could be enforced. But by then, interest in light railways was on the wane.

In 1912, a revised Light Railways Act had entered the statute books, this, ironically, being more attractive to the promoters of urban tramways than those of conventional railways. By 1918 a total of 687 applications, involving 5,051 route miles, had been made for Light Railway Orders, but those figures were not as impressive as they seemed. Of the 687 applications, 124 had been merely amendments to pre-1896 proposals, the Light Railways Act having permitted existing proposals to be amended to light railway specifications. Furthermore, although 2,101 route miles had been authorised, only 860 had actually been constructed and, of that figure, some 350 miles had been for urban tramways such as the Kinver Light Railway in the West Midlands and those of Middlesex County Council. Of the remaining 510 miles of genuine light railways, over 300 miles had been accounted for by main line railway companies which, being well seasoned in the art of negotiating and exploiting official legislation, found that nominal subsidiary companies could easily be 'guided' to promote and construct rural branches with, of course, the aid of Government grants. The main line companies' practice of setting-up thinly-disguised subsidiaries, and either working or leasing the lines when they were completed was, however, far from new; the Light Railways Acts merely enabled that established practice to qualify, in some cases, for financial assistance.

The most blatant examples of 'working the loopholes' were performed by the London & South Western Railway and concluded, after the Grouping, by the Southern Railway. The Order for the Totton, Hythe & Fawley Light Railway in Hampshire was revived in 1921 and to nobody's surprise, its powers were transferred to the Southern Railway at the Grouping, while construction of the line had hardly got under way. In the West Country, the North Devon & Cornwall Junction Light Railway was opened in 1925 and, with remarkably little raising of eyebrows, was immediately leased to the Southern. Furthermore, the intention of the Light Railways Acts had been to bring secondary lines into close con-

Above: **Not only the 'Colonel Stephens' railways made economies. Witness the style of the waiting room at Tolleshunt Knights station on the Kelvedon, Tiptree & Tollesbury Pier Light Railway.**
D. Trevor Rowe

Right: **Few light railways could have been more rural (or ramshackle) than the Shropshire & Montgomeryshire, one of the 'Colonel Stephens' lines. This was Chapel Lane station on the S&M's Criggion branch...and no comments are offered about the passenger.**
Lens of Sutton

tact with rural communities but, once again, the L&SWR was behind one of the more conspicuous departures from that intention. The Basingstoke & Alton Light Railway, which was worked by the L&SWR from the outset, had three intermediate station. The distances of these stations from the communities which they allegedly served were 1 mile, 1½ miles and 2½ miles. Remarkably, the Basingstoke & Alton was the very first light railway to be sanctioned under the 1896 Act, and so it might have been expected that the Commissioners would have looked very closely indeed at the company's involvement with the L&SWR., Out of earshot from Waterloo, the word's 'smell' and 'rat' were voiced with considerable frequency.

The figures quoted above, and the tactics of the L&SWR/SR, sadly confirm that the Light Railways Acts did not always benefit those whom they had been aimed. Further confirmation is offered by the fact that, of the free grants paid to assist a total of 80 route miles of light railways, all went to lines which were either owned or worked by main line companies; 22 miles of loan-assisted construction were accounted for by the same sources. By comparison, just 23 route miles of light railway construction undertaken by totally independent concerns were loan-assisted. The minnows constantly alleged that access to the much-heralded grants and loans was constantly hampered. The fact that by the end of 1918 only £203,000 of the £1,000,000 had been used, did much to support their protests. Of the light railways featured in this book, only about half could be regarded as having started life as true independents, ie with their own locomotives, rolling stock and staff; the remainder were, despite their wonderful charisma, little more than tentacles of main line companies.

The Light Railways Acts might have been controversially administered, but they at least succeeded in raising the status of narrow gauge lines. Prior to 1896, any railway built to a gauge of less than 4ft 8½ in was considered, by most, to be more a toy than a real railway, but there were of course, exceptions. The Fes-

tiniog Railway in North Wales, for example, was regarded as an excellent feast of engineering and, due to the terrain it crossed, could not realistically have been built to the standard gauge. In some quarters, it was pointed out that Isambard Brunel had, in the mid-1800s, engineered two 7ft gauge mineral lines across the mountains of South Wales but on the whole, the Festiniog was, unlike most of its narrow gauge counterparts, viewed as a 'proper' railway. The Light Railways Acts brought an air of respectability to narrow gauge railways and, by 1920, a total of 280 route miles of public narrow gauge lines were operating in Britain.

Despite the mixed effects of the 1896 Act in England, light railways were viewed with greater favour in remote parts of Scotland although, admittedly, the only real independent north of the border was the 2ft 3in gauge Campbeltown & Machrihanish Light Railway. In 1921, however, the Scottish Rural Transport Committee advocated 381 miles of new railways in Scotland, including 156 miles of narrow gauge in Argyll, Skye and the Outer Hebrides, compared to the 225 miles of new roads which were proposed for that area at the same time.

The promoter of some 130 miles of narrow gauge lines in Scotland was the Hebridean Light Railway, a London-based consortium which solicited the support of the North British Railway. On the Isle of Skye, the HLR planned a line from Isleornsay, where a

steamer pier was proposed, to Uig with a branch from Portree to Dunvegan; on the Isle of Lewis, the company's proposals were for lines from Stornoway to Tarbet and Carloway with a branch from Carloway to Breasclet. As things turned out, a combination of local opposition and a lack of capital put paid to all of those schemes.

One interesting, albeit hypothetical, aspect of the Hebridean Light Railway's proposals is that, in view of the intended backing of the North British Railway, one of the strongest opponents of the schemes would almost certainly have been the NBR's staunch rival, the Highland Railway. The Highland Railway itself was the thinly-disguised backer of many light railways schemes and, in 1897, it had proposed a light railway from the steamer pier at Kyle Akin, on the Isle of Skye, to Torrin, and one from Stornoway to Carloway on Lewis. Had all the parties insisted on fighting to get their own schemes passed, fur would positively have flown.

Among the Scottish standard gauge light railways which were proposed but never built were the 14-mile Forsinard, Melvich & Port Skerra Light Railway, planned to run from the Highland Railway's line at Forsinard to a remote harbour on the north Sutherland coast. Another proposal which would have required the assistance of the Highland Railway was for an eight-mile light railway from Inverness to the head of Loch Ness. The Cromarty Light Railway, which was intended to link the community of its

name to Dingwall, actually had some six miles of its track laid and a further two miles of earthworks finished before work was abandoned in 1914.

The 1921 report on light railways for the Ministry of Transport (mentioned earlier) concluded that, in England and Wales, the needs of rural communities would best be served by integrated road and rail transport. Although the 1920s were well before the days of mass car-ownership, motor-buses and lorries were around in adequate numbers to offer, not integration, but stiff competition for rural business. At the Grouping in 1923, many eternally-insolvent light railways became positively unwanted by any of the 'Big Four', whereas those which had been promoted and worked by main line companies logically passed to the appropriate new 'group'. For example, the North Lindsey Light Railway, which was worked by the Great Central Railway, was grouped along with its parent in the LNER, while the Highland-worked Wick & Lybster Light Railway became just another small component of the mighty LMSR. From the Grouping onwards, the 'worked' light railways became little more than conventional branches, and although those lines lost much of their character as a result, the backing of financially-sound parents did much to secure their immediate futures.

A total of 15 independent light railway companies were left to go it alone after 1923. Perhaps predictably, their corporate coffers, which had been only precariously filled to start with, did not contain

Above: **The Derwent Valley Light Railway in Yorkshire remained independent until its demise in the 1980s. In its later years, however, the line was gradually truncated and, as is evident in this picture, not exactly kept in first-class condition. The photograph of 17 May 1968 shows the last train to Wheldrake passing the ungated crossing near Elvington.** Rodney Wildsmith

Right: **In many cases, light railways remained open for freight or specialised traffic for a considerable time after the cessation of passenger services, although one line has had a much higher-profile existence in recent years. The old Ponteland Light Railway in Northumberland, which closed to passengers in 1929, served two industrial concerns until 1988 and, nowadays, much of the line forms part of the Tyne & Wear Metro's route to Newcastle Airport. This picture of 24 August 1983 shows Class 31 No 31324 waiting to leave Rowntree's factory, from where it would have continued its journey via the old light railway route, passing 'under the wires' of the Metro.** Ian S. Carr

enough to replace worn-out equipment and, of course, there was no 'big brother' to subsidise the lean years. As road transport took an increasing quantity of their trade, their chances of ever gaining a firm financial foothold lessened. Their only chances of survival were to cut overheads to the bone and, to the delight of historians and enthusiasts, that frequently resulted in wonderful eccentricities. Familiar scenes included weed-infested tracks, ramshackle station buildings (assuming that there had been any to start with), rolling stock whose liveries depended on the cheapest paint currently available and, in many cases, a motley assortment of veteran locomotives which had gleefully been sold off by main line companies some 20 or 30 years earlier.

As early as 1925, the ailing condition of most independent light railways was apparent. Apart from the Nidd Valley Light Railway which, for that year, showed receipts of £7,112 against expenditure of just £2,999, the balance sheets of other light railways showed expenditures ranging from 78% to 118% of receipts. The most common figure was around 95% which, although indicating a profit, left virtually nothing for investment. Seven of those 15 independents were to close completely by 1940, and they included the Nidd Valley, which had in 1925 revealed comparatively healthy figures; furthermore, two other independents were by 1940 to consist of little more than freight sidings. Despite this, six former light railways are still use today, in whole or in part, as freight lines; a section of another light railway boasts a scheduled BR passenger service, and a further line remains completely intact and fully operational

under private ownership. Perhaps the most secure futures belong to the routes of the Totton, Hythe & Fawley and the Ponteland Light Railways, much of the latter now being incorporated in the Tyne & Wear Metro's line to Newcastle Airport.

A great irony about the closures of the 1930s was that one of the casualties was the 2ft 6in gauge Leek & Manifold Valley Light Railway in Staffordshire, which had benefitted from the expertise of Everard Richard (E. R.) Calthrop, one of the most well-respected names in light railway engineering. Calthrop's theory was to construct a line to suit not only the local terrain but also the potential traffic, and he argued that no rural light railways had the need for any gauge other than 2ft or 2ft 6in. For the 2ft 6in gauge, Calthrop calculated that by using rails of 30-35lb/yd and restricting axle weights to a maximum of five tons, wear and tear to the permanent way would be minimised. In that respect, he had the last laugh as, when the L&MVLR closed in 1934, it still retained its original rails after 30 years of operation. One of Calthrop's great innovations on the L&MVLR was transporter wagons, these being used successfully to convey standard gauge trucks from the interchange point at Waterhouses to the narrow gauge terminus at Hulme End.

Another great proponent of light railways was Arthur (later Sir Arthur) Heywood who, in the 1870s, constructed a 15in gauge railway at his home, Duffield Bank in Derby, and at Eaton Hall. Heywoods railways were a mixture of conventional estate railways, serving the needs of a sizeable country home and its expansive grounds, and pleasure railways. The cost of transporting goods on his railways worked out at 11d (4¾p) per ton per mile, and that included interest on capital, depreciation etc; furthermore, that figure was for a line which included gradients of up to 1 in 11 and was worked in all weathers with loads of up to 46 tons on the level. Needless to say, Heywood was a vociferous supporter of the 1896 Light Railways Act, but expressed amazement that promoters of such railways stuck slavishly to the standard gauge. Like E. R. Calthrop, Heywood had little time for those who persisted with a 'main-line' mentality when narrow gauge was clearly more suitable.

The names of Calthrop and Heywood might have been closely linked with the world of light railways, but the most synonymous of all was, without any doubt whatsoever, Lt-Col Stephens. In the post-Grouping years, Stephens's empire comprised seven separate railways, known as the 'Associated Companies', and all were run with extreme economy in mind. The practice of penny-pinching was not intended to fill Stephens's pockets but simply out of necessity to keep the lines open.

Holman Frederick Stephens was born in 1868 and was educated at University College, London. From 1888 to 1891, he was a pupil of J. J. Hanbury, the superintendent of the Metropolitan Railway, at Neasden Works, and later worked in the Met's running department. His first administrative appointment was as Resident Engineer on the Cranbrook & Paddock Wood Railway in Kent; later, he became Inspector of Accidents (Railway) for the Board of Trade and, during the Great War, he served in the Royal Engineers where he attained the rank of Lieutenant-Colonel.

Stephens's first direct involvement with light railways came in 1897 when he supervised the construction of the Rother Valley (Light) Railway, better known today as the Kent & East Sussex. Two years later, he became the company's General Manager and, a year after that, the Managing Director. Despite his management of other lines over ensuing years, Stephens's personal favourite was always the K&SELR due, in part, to its proximity to his office at Salford Terrace in Tonbridge. Stephens went on to manage, among others, the Shropshire & Montgomeryshire, the East Kent and the Weston, Clevedon & Portishead Light Railways, and also the Rye & Camber and the Selsey Tramways. Furthermore, he was the Chief Engineer for the Sheppy Light Railway and such projects as the rebuilding of the Burry Port & Gwendraeth Valley and the Plymouth, Devonport & South Western Junction Railways, and the construction of Britain's last standard gauge light railway, the North Devon & Cornwall Junction.

During the 1920s, Stephens pioneered the use of internal combustion engines for traction on rural railways. He persevered with Drewry railcars, which could return in excess of 16mpg on level runs, Muir-Hill 'rail tractors' for light freight, and even road omnibuses fitted with flanged railway wheels. The buses were usually used in pairs mounted back-to-

back, Ford- and Shefflex-powered vehicles appearing on the Kent & East Sussex, and one with Wolseley-Siddeley engines being used on the Shropshire & Montgomeryshire. Stephens's railways were universally remarkable for their miscellany of motive power but, no matter how decrepit some of his contraptions might have seemed, they often bore imposing names. Stephens had a great interest in classical mythology, possibly inherited from his father who had

Maximum
rates for
conveyance
of passen-
gers.

41. The maximum rate of charge to be made by the Company for the conveyance of passengers upon the railway including every expense incidental to such conveyance shall not exceed the following (that is to say) :—

For every passenger conveyed in a first-class carriage the sum of three pence per mile ;

For every passenger conveyed in a second-class carriage the sum of two pence per mile ;

For every passenger conveyed in a third-class carriage the sum of one penny per mile ;

For every passenger conveyed on the railway for a less distance than three miles the Company may charge as for three miles and every fraction of a mile beyond three miles or any greater number of miles shall be deemed a mile.

12

spent some years working as the art critic of the *Athenaeum,* and he used imposing names such as *Hecate, Thisbe* and *Hesperus* for even the most ancient or under-powered locomotives. Stephens had no qualms about using the same name on different locomotives simultaneously, and this has since caused much head-scratching in those cases where locomotives were transferred from one of his outposts to another.

Lt-Col Holman Frederick Stephens passed away on 23 October 1931 at the comparatively young age of 63, a succession of strokes having left him paralysed. Comparatively little is known about his personal life, but of recorded descriptions of the man himself, this writer likes this much-repeated one: *'A huge man of commanding presence and, seemingly, poured in liquid form into his suit'.* Stephens had been described as 'kind but not always loved', the former attribute being backed up by reports that, if a week's takings from a particular line were inadequate to pay the staff wages, Stephens was not averse to extracting his own wallet on the spot, provided that there was no evidence of slacking.

After Stephens's death, the uphill task of trying to keep the Associated Railways going fell to his former assistant, W. H. Austen. Even the Stephens-inspired economies couldn't perform miracles for ever; nevertheless, three 'Colonel Stephens' railways survived as locomotive-owning independents until Nationalisation in 1948, when they passed to British Railways. The last ex-'Colonel Stephens' locomotive to survive in BR service was former-K&ESLR 0-6-0T No 3, which had started life as a standard LB&SCR 'Terrier' in 1872, and had been purchased by the K&ESLR in 1901. As BR No 32670, it was retired from service in November 1963 but, happily, was quickly earmarked for preservation.

Leaving the dear Lt-Col to rest in peace and returning to the 1920s, four completely new light railways were constructed during that decade, and two others which were formerly privately-used freight lines were upgraded for public use after gaining the necessary Light Railway Orders. However, this does not indicate that some succeeded where others were failing fast, as two of the four new lines were

Above: **The official authorisation for light railways invariably laid down stipulations regarding fares. This extract refers to the Cawood, Wistow & Selby Light Railway, but is representative of similar lines elsewhere in Britain.** Author's files

the Southern Railway's thinly veiled subsidiaries at Fawley and Torrington. The remaining two were both narrow gauge affairs, one being the Ashover Light Railway in Derbyshire which closed completely in 1950, 14 years after passenger services had ceased. The other was the Romney, Hythe & Dymchurch Light Railway which might be considered more of a miniature/pleasure line than a true light railway.

For the purpose of this book, lines such as the RH&DLR will be excluded, as will electric tramways such as the Llandudno & Colwyn Bay Light Railway and the Kinver Light Railway. Furthermore, pre-served railways which have blossomed under Light Railway Orders during the last 20-odd years will also be omitted. Other charismatic and rural independents such as the Garstang & Knott End in Lancashire, the West Sussex and the narrow gauge Lynton & Barnstaple in Devon are also excluded because, quite simply, they neither owned their origins to, nor subsequently obtained, Light Railway Orders.

A number of lines featured were up and running well before the days of any Light Railway Act, only to have their powers transferred to a Light Railway Order at a later date. Those lines are nevertheless included with, to the best of this writer's knowledge, only one exception, that being the 3ft 6in gauge Southwold Railway, the delightful 8¾ mile-long line in Suffolk which had opened in 1879. The company obtained the necessary Order in 1913 for a one-mile extension to Southwold Harbour, but in view of the extension's minimal contribution to the overall history of the railway company, it has reluctantly been decided not to include the Southwold in this book. Despite the exclusion of the Southwold Railway, it is hoped that this book will offer a refreshing change of subject matter from such mundane or over-exposed items as 'Black Fives' and BR '4MT' tanks.

1 Amesbury & Military Camp Light Railway

The London & South Western Railway and its successor, the Southern Railway, were quite adept at exploiting the loopholes in the Light Railways Acts. Their favoured method usually involved setting up a so-called subsidiary company for the purpose of obtaining a Light Railway Order and, when everything was up and running, the 'subsidiary' would conveniently be absorbed by big brother. This resulted in the relevant light railways becoming little more than conventional branches but, in almost all cases, they redeemed themselves in the interest stakes by having individualistic forms of motive power. Unfortunately, that did not hold true for the Amesbury & Military Camp Light Railway. The A&MCLR was one of the L&SWR's subsidiaries but, to be perfectly honest, it had an uneventful existence, and furthermore did not even have the saving grace of an interesting locomotive history. Therefore, it is somewhat unfortunate that it heads the alphabetical list of Britain's light railways.

The A&MCLR's principal purpose was to serve Army camps on the eastern fringe of Salisbury Plain. The War Department had purchased extensive tracts of land around the Amesbury area and, in 1897, it encouraged the L&SWR to build a 10¾-mile branch from the Basingstoke-Salisbury main line to Amesbury, Bulford and Shrewton, where Army camps were to be established. The necessary Light Railway Order was obtained in September 1898 in the name of the A&MCLR. While the railway was under construction, the Army requested that the Amesbury-Shrewton section of the railway be diverted in order to avoid an area which would be required for manoeuvres but, instead, the partly-finished section was abandoned.

Consequently, only the section as far as Amesbury was completed and, when it opened on 1 October 1901, it was used only by military traffic. Public passenger services did not commence until 2 June 1902. At first, the single track branch diverged from the main line at Newton Toney Junction, the spelling of which was altered to Newton Tony in October 1903, but a separate third track for the branch trains was laid parallel to the main line between Grateley and the junction in April 1902. In August 1904, the branch was doubled as far as Newton Tony and a connecting spur was unveiled at Newton Tony Junction. That work was undertaken to enable through running on to the branch from the Salisbury direction, as a change of heart had resulted in plans for the branch to be extended to Bulford, where a sizeable camp had recently been completed.

Below: **Drummond's '700' class 0-6-0s regularly appeared on the Amesbury branch, particularly during the later years. This picture of a '700' at Bulford station is undated, but the general air of dilapidation suggests that closure was not far off.** Lens of Sutton

The Bulford extension eventually opened on 1 June 1906. In its entirety the public section of the line was 5¾ miles long, the section from Bulford station to the Camp and beyond being for Army use only. The intermediate stations on the branch were at Newton Tony (½-mile from the junction with the main line) and Amesbury (4¼ miles), the latter being an expansive three-platform affair which had a turntable in its yard so that tender engines could work the branch. Between Amesbury and Bulford, the Larkhill Military Railway opened a branch from Ratfyn to Rollestone Camp in 1914, that line later being extended to Fargo Hospital and Lake Down Airfield with sidings to Handley Page aircraft hangers and Stonehenge Airfield. However, the LMR's lines were solely for military use and the last sections closed in October 1929. The three locomotives which worked the military railway were War Department 0-6-0STs, the first being a Peckett 'X' class, the second a 'B2' class from the same maker, and the third a Manning Wardle 'M' class of 1875 which had previously belonged to the Isle of Wight Railway.

The loading restriction for single-headed trains on the Amesbury branch was eight bogie coaches, while double-heading permitted 15 bogie coaches. In the down direction between Newton Tony and Amesbury, freight trains were restricted to 18 wagons plus a 20-ton brake van, the limit in the up direction being 20 wagons plus the brake. For the entire length of the branch, a 16-ton axle weight limit prevailed and speeds were restricted to the usual light railway maximum of 25mph. By May 1909, the doubling of the Newton Tony-Bulford section had been completed, thereby upgrading the entire branch to double-track status.

By the early 1920s, the summer schedules usually comprised seven passenger trains each way on weekdays and one on Sundays, all originating or terminating at Salisbury. Branch trains used No 6 bay at Salisbury station, and a turn of duty for engine crews consisted of three return trips on the branch. In the branch's early days, Adams 0-4-4Ts had usually looked after the passenger workings while '395' class 0-6-0s had handled the freight services. However, Adams 4-4-2Ts (the celebrated 'Radial Tanks'), were known to have appeared on the line, the sighting of No 0429 being recorded in 1911. By the 1920s, the usual branch locomotives were the ubiquitous 'M7' class 0-4-4Ts, but one scheduled daily freight working during the 1920s and 1930s required the combined attentions of an 'M7' and a 'Jubilee' class 0-4-2. During that period, Salisbury-based 'Jubilees' Nos 606/49/53 appeared on the Amesbury branch at one time or another. On arrival at Amesbury, it was normal practice for the 'Jubilee' to shunt at the yard while the

Left: **Ex-LSWR '700' class 0-6-0 No 30317 is in charge of the 9.40am Bulford-Salisbury train on 28 June 1952, the last day of public passenger services on the Amesbury branch. The location is near Newton Tony, and evidence of recent re-sleepering can be seen.** Ian Allan Library

Below left: **On 14 May 1955, an enthusiasts' special hauled by Beattie '0298' class 2-4-0WT No 30587 worked through to Bulford Camp and, here, the locomotive is being turned at Amesbury. Despite the cessation of scheduled passenger services three years earlier, it is very clear that the spacious station was still well used for freight traffic.** H. C. Casserley

Below: **This extract from the L&SWR working timetable of 1909 shows speed restrictions which were very typical of most light railways.**

1st JUNE to 30th SEPTEMBER, 1909, or until further notice.   B

PERMANENT SPEED RESTRICTIONS.

THE UNDERMENTIONED SPEED RESTRICTIONS MUST BE STRICTLY ADHERED TO.

AMESBURY BRANCH LINE.

10	NEWTON TONY AND AMESBURY JUNCTIONS ... ... Trains passing over Roman Road East and West Level Crossings.	10
10	NEWTON TONY AND AMESBURY, 77 MILES 76 CHAINS ... Trains approaching, and within a distance of 300 yards of Level Crossing.	10
25	AMESBURY JUNCTION AND GRATELEY TO BULFORD ... ... Trains over other portions of Line.	25

For continuation see next page.

'M7' returned to Salisbury with a passenger train. By the late 1930s, however, 'T1' class 0-4-4Ts were the favoured steeds for Amesbury duties, Nos 10, 16 and 361 being allocated to Salisbury shed during that period principally for working the branch. When No 16 was withdrawn in January 1946, classmate No 13 was transferred from Eastleigh as a replacement.

The timetables for March 1940 show a similar passenger service to that of 1922, but by then the average journey times were a mite faster at 30-35min. During the war years, 'K10' 4-4-0 No 394 was loaned to the War Department for shunting duties at Bulford Camp. After the war, most branch duties were given back to the 'M7' class 0-4-4Ts, and Salisbury's allocation lists during that year showed Nos 41/60/243/675 as the resident representatives of the class.

The timetables which were issued for the period commencing 30 June 1952 indicated that the entire passenger service on the Amesbury branch was to consist of just one train in each direction on weekdays, but it seems that a lack of communication between the Southern Region's operating and printing departments had prevailed, as the branch was closed to passengers on that very date. The branch reverted to single-track status and the loop near Newton Tony Junction, which had provided through running to and from Salisbury, was dismantled in the late 1950s. Freight services continued, however, and three trains usually ran to and from Grateley each week until total closure of the branch on 4 March 1963.

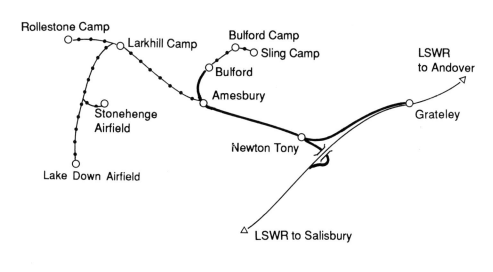

2 Ashover Light Railway

In 1837, when excavation work was being undertaken for the construction of a tunnel near Clay Cross on the North Midland Railway, the consulting engineer, a certain George Stephenson, took note of coal seams which the work revealed. Knowing a good thing when he saw one, Stephenson founded the Clay Cross Co for the purpose of tapping the area's natural resources. Over the years, deposits of limestone, gritstone and fluorspar were discovered in the area and, in 1918, the Clay Cross Co purchased additional land so that it could extend its sphere of operations. Although horse-worked tramways had sufficed for the coal mining, the proposed new workings were considered extensive enough to warrant a locomotive-operated railway.

The line was promoted under the banner of the Ashover Light Railway, and obtained the necessary Order in December 1919. Negotiations with local landowners were minimal as, most conveniently, much of the railway's route was over land belonging to the Clay Cross Co itself. To reduce construction costs, it was decided to build the line to a gauge of 2ft, and as the town of Ashover was a popular haunt for weekend visitors, it was considered that a narrow gauge railway would also become something of a tourist attraction. The consulting engineer engaged to oversee the work was one Lt-Col Holman Stephens, a gentleman whose name will crop up frequently throughout this book.

The Ashover Light Railway held its formal opening ceremony on 6 April 1925, the event being presided over by the chairman, 91 year-old Thomas Hughes Jackson. Public traffic commenced the following day, and the line thereby became one of the very last light railways to be unveiled in Britain. It has also proved to be a saviour in another way as, after the less-than-gripping story of the Amesbury & Military Camp Light Railway (above), this writer can quickly redeem himself with the tale of a totally independent light railway, and a narrow gauge one to boot.

The ALR's single-track line commenced at Clay Cross & Egstow station, almost directly above the northern portal of Clay Cross tunnel on the LMSR's main Derby-Sheffield route. The ALR station comprised a single low platform with a wooden shelter, and was on a spur to the west of the yard. In the yard were the engine and carriage sheds and also freight sidings; one of the sidings was on an incline which was worked by an electric-powered winch, where the contents of narrow gauge wagons could be tipped into standard gauge trucks for onward transportation. Just beyond Clay Cross & Egstow station were reception sidings. The usual practice for mixed trains arriving from Ashover was for the wagons to be detached on the gradient approaching the sidings and, after the passenger carriages had safely arrived at the station, the wagons would then be allowed to run into the sidings under gravity.

A little under ½-mile from the terminus was Chesterfield Road halt, from where a frequent bus service was available to take passengers to Chesterfield; beyond the halt, at the top of the 1 in 37 climb from the terminus, was a passing loop. There were three further halts in quick succession, Holmgate (1¼ miles from Clay Cross & Egstow), Springfield (1½ miles) and Clay Lane (1¾ miles), before the line reached the most important intermediate station at Stretton (2½ miles). In a cutting below the ALR's station at Stretton was the LMSR's main line station, and the ALR's trains were often held for up to 20min in order to connect with LMSR services.

Beyond Stretton were two passing loops, the second of which marked the start of the scenic section of the route through the valley of the River Amber. The next halts were at Hurst Lane (4 miles), which was equipped with a passing loop and facilities for trains in both directions to take water simultaneously, Woolley (4¾ miles), which had a goods siding, Dale Bank (5½ miles) and Milltown (5¾ miles). Fallgate station (6 miles) had sidings to accommodate traffic from the numerous local quarries, and engine and carriage sheds; about ¼-mile beyond Fallgate was a siding serving an electric power station. The line then passed through Salter Lane halt (6¾ miles) which, in fact, was better situated for the main part of Ashover than the actual terminus at Ashover (Butts), 7¼ miles from Clay Cross & Egstow. On the approach to the terminus there was a triangle used for turning purposes, and a spur to Butts Quarry.

In true light railway fashion, the line had been built with economy in mind. There were no semaphore signals, Wise's patent train staff being used, but telephone boxes were provided at strategic locations along the line so that crews could report to the office in cases of emergency. The permanent way was secondhand 30lb/yd flat-bottomed rails which had been obtained from the War Surplus Disposals Board, the very source from which the locomotives had been purchased.

There were six locomotives, all 4-6-0PTs which had been built for the War Department in 1916/17 by the Baldwin Locomotive Works in Philadelphia, USA. They had 1ft 11½ in coupled wheels, outside cylinders of 9in x 12in, Walschaerts valve gear, and were fitted with vacuum brake equipment. At first

Above: **Fallgate station on the Ashover Light Railway merged into the magnificent Derbyshire countryside.** Ian Allan Library

Left: **One of the ALR's 4-6-0PTs hauls a train of empty stone wagons away from Ashover during the late 1940s.** Ian Allan Library

the livery was Midland red, but that was later dropped in favour of black. The locomotives were named after the children of the managing director, *Bridget, Georgie, Guy, Hummy, Joan* and *Peggy,* but it remains unknown whether that name theme was adopted out of nepotism or as a boast about the gentleman's breeding habits. It has been suggested that few children could have been so inestimably honoured as to have War Surplus hardware named after them, but it should be pointed out that two of the family worked for the Clay Cross company.

There seems to be some dispute as to whether the nameplate of *Georgie* was ever carried, some reports suggesting that the locomotive was, in fact, named *Guy.* The question of duplicated names would not, however, have resulted as the locomotive in question was withdrawn before performing any revenue-earning tasks, and before the arrival of the other one named *Guy.*

For the opening of the line, four passenger coaches were purchased from the Gloucester Wagon Works, their bogies being, in the line's best traditions, war surplus items. In later years, a number of open-sided bogie coaches were purchased for use during the summer season and, at its peak, the Ashover Light Railway's stud of carriages numbered 12. In its heyday, the company owned 59 freight wagons, most being of the open bogie type obtained from that ever-popular source, the Disposals Board.

At first, the weekday service on the Ashover Light Railway comprised seven trains each way on weekdays, eight on Saturdays and four on Sundays; the weekday trains were usually mixed but the Sunday ones carried only passengers. Journey times between Clay Cross and Ashover were usually 45-55min. The company's directors were delighted by the line's popularity as, during its first full week of operation, some 5,000 passengers were carried. On Wednesdays, Saturdays and Sundays, cheap day returns were available, the fare between Clay Cross and Ashover being 6d (2½p). Despite the plethora of stations and halts along the line, trains also stopped for passengers where public roads were crossed, that being a comparatively easy undertaking since all but one of the level crossings on the line were ungated.

The ALR's initial burst of popularity was, however, short lived. Although freight traffic showed a marked

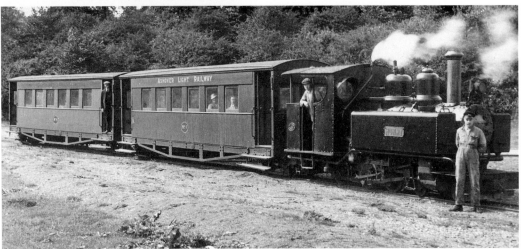

Left: **The locomotives of the 2ft gauge Ashover Light Railway might have been small, but they nevertheless looked very workmanlike. This undated picture shows** *Bridget* **at Clay Cross.** Rail Archive Stephenson

Below: **In the heyday of the Ashover Light Railway, great pride was taken in the appearances of the locomotives and carriages. The well-polished 4-6-0PT** *Hummy* **was photographed in charge of two of the original Gloucester coaches, probably very soon after the opening of the line in 1925.** Bucknall Collection/Ian Allan Library

increase as industries in the area developed, the passenger figures plummeted as road transport offered increasingly stiff competition. During the 12 months of 1930, 23,384 passengers were carried for fares totalling just £361, both figures being about one-third of those for the eight-month period of April-December 1925. At the end of September 1931, passenger services were suspended, and during the next five years were reinstated only during the holiday periods. Even then, passenger trains ran only on three days of the week. The only intermediate stopping place on the line to retain any air of usage was Stretton station, the other stations and halts being stripped of many fitments and reduced to the status of request stops.

Passenger traffic failed to pick up, and on 13 September 1936 all scheduled passenger services were withdrawn for good. It was a little under 11½ years since the line had opened in the traditional blaze of glory. Nevertheless, the ALR remained open for freight and was used reasonably regularly through the 1940s, the main commodity carried being ballast which was quarried at Ashover. Early in 1950, however, British Railways cancelled its order for ballast and so the ALR was left without a purpose. The inevitable total closure followed on 31 March 1950.

After the cessation of scheduled passenger services,

there had been a few excursions and special workings. Those of June 1940 had hardly been full-blooded enthusiasts' specials, as they had been to provide a means of transport for visitors to Ogston Hall, where a garden fete had been held in aid of the Red Cross and Women's Home Missions. The final special working had been in August 1947, when members of the Stephenson Locomotive Society had been conveyed in a train of open wagons hauled by the locomotive *Joan*.

During the line's freight-only days a small 0-4-0 diesel locomotive, a tiny petrol-electric machine named *Amos*, and a Muir-Hill Fordson petrol rail-tractor had been acquired to replace the steam locomotives. As if to maintain one tradition until the end, *Amos* had been constructed from the remains of an ex-WD locomotive. There could surely have been no other British public railway which was so reliant on Army Surplus equipment. As for the Army Surplus 4-6-0PTs, four had been withdrawn or scrapped by 1945; *Joan* was retired in 1948 thereby leaving *Peggy* to fly the flag until the line's demise in 1950.

AXHOLME JOINT RAILWAY
see (29) GOOLE & MARSHLAND LIGHT RAILWAY

3 Avonmouth Light Railway

The community of Avonmouth lies some eight miles west of Bristol, and in 1877 a sizeable dock was opened at Avonmouth to ease the burden on the older docks in the heart of Bristol. Before long, the new dock at Avonmouth became over-subscribed and so, in 1902, the first sod was cut for the Royal Edward Dock on an adjacent site. By then, the Avonmouth area had acquired many of the industries and much of the paraphernalia which were synonymous with a port-orientated community, and although Avonmouth had been served by railways since 1865, the prospect of the new Royal Edward Dock triggered a minor flurry of proposals for additional lines in the area.

One of these was the Avonmouth Light Railway which had, in fact, been incorporated on 12 December 1893, almost three years before the Light Railways Act entered the statute books. The use of the words 'light railway' in the company's title was, at first, purely cosmetic, but the plans for the ALR lay dormant for over eight years and when, on 1 December 1902, the company was formally reincorporated, assent was for construction as a bona fide light railway under the terms of the 1896 Act.

With the backing of the prominent local business family, the Miles's, construction of the ALR commenced later in 1902, but it was 1908 before the first ¾-mile section eventually opened for business. The ALR left the joint GWR/Midland (originally Bristol Port Railway & Pier) Bristol-Avonmouth line near Avonmouth Sidings Signalbox, just to the east of the old dock, and swung northwards to cross what is now the A4 Portway trunk road by means of an ungated level crossing. Then, on curves of five chains radius, the ALR snaked towards St Andrew's Road. A ¼-mile long extension serving an electricity generating station and, in theory at least, providing access to the National Smelting Co, was opened in 1913, but that is as far as the ALR ever went. Its original plans for a 2⅛-mile line linking up with the GWR at Holesmouth, to the north of Avonmouth Docks, were never realised.

The intention of the ALR had been solely to serve industrial concerns in the rapidly-expanding estates on the fringes of the docks, passenger traffic never having featured in the company's plans. The ALR's activities are sparsely documented and, regarding motive power, the only educated guess ever put forward is that the company possibly had two Manning Wardle 0-6-0STs. It is, however, most unlikely that both locomotives were used simultaneously despite the fact that the engine shed, which was situated near the junction with the Bristol-Avonmouth line, was capable of housing two engines.

In 1926, the ALR was purchased jointly by the GWR and the LMSR. The ALR's powers to complete its line to Holesmouth were due to expire in 1927, but it remains a matter of speculation whether the new joint proprietors had any serious intention of constructing the extension. No such extension was ever built and, by 1931, most of the ALR's existing route had fallen into disuse. The precise date of the line's total demise remains unconfirmed, but the general concensus is circa 1932/33.

AVONMOUTH LIGHT.

DIRECTORS:

Chairman—PHILIP NAPIER MILES, Esq., King's Weston, Henbury.

Alexander B. Carter, Esq., King's Weston Estate Office, Shirehampton. | Thomas Kirkland, Esq., 6, Balham Park Road, Balham, S.W.

OFFICERS.—Sec., W. H. Pretty ; Auditor, Frank N. Tribe, F.C.A. ; Solicitors, Osborne, Ward, Vassall & Co.

Offices—King's Weston Estate Office, Shirehampton, Bristol.

Incorporated as a Light Railway 1st December. 1903, to construct a light railway 2 miles 1 furlong in length, from a junction at Shirehampton with the Bristol Port and Pier Railway of the Great Western and Midland to a junction at Henbury with the Avonmouth and Severn Tunnel Railway of the Great Western.

CAPITAL.—Authorised, 21,000*l.* in shares of 10*l.* Issued, 14,800*l.*; received, 13,330*l.* Loans authorised but not issued, 7,000*l.* Expenditure, 12,033*l.*; balance, 1,297*l.*

Accounts made up to 31st December.

Line is in course of construction.

Left: **No matter how obsure a railway company was, it was unlikely to escape a listing in** *Bradshaw's Shareholders' Guide.* **This extract from the 1915 edition gives the corporate details for the Avonmouth Light Railway.** Author's files

4 Axminster & Lyme Regis Light Railway

From 1845 onwards, proposals for a branch line to the historic and picturesque fishing village of Lyme Regis in west Dorset surfaced with unsurprising regularity, but only one of the early contestants went as far as cutting its first sod. With the coming of the Light Railways Act in 1896, the prospect of financial assistance for the construction of a railway to a fishing community awakened many local businessmen and also, somewhat predictably, the London & South Western Railway whose Waterloo-Exeter main line was little more than the proverbial stone's throw away. With the blessing of, and the offer of a working agreement from, the L&SWR, the Axminster & Lyme Regis Light Railway was born.

The single-track 6¾-mile branch was opened on 24 August 1903. It left the main line at Axminster where branch trains used a bay at the rear of the up platform, and crossed the main line west of the station by means of a bridge. On the down side of the main line, a spur was laid between the main line and the branch in order to facilitate through freight workings, but the spur was only rarely used and was lifted in 1915. The terminus at Lyme Regis comprised a single platform, a modest goods yard and a wooden single-road engine shed; that shed was destroyed by fire in 1913 and its replacement was an asbestos structure which set the L&SWR back the princely sum of

£400. Due to the steep hills surrounding Lyme Regis, even the most ambitious civil engineer would have blanched at the prospect of bringing the line into the centre of the village, and so the terminus was sited about ½-mile outside the village and some 250ft up on a hill. It was a fair compromise.

The branch's only intermediate station was at Combpyne, 4½ miles from Axminster; perched 500ft up on the hills, it had a passing loop and a 14-lever signalbox which, in 1930, was sold to a local farmer. Combpyne was the best station for sightseers who wished to view the site of a distant landslip on the coast, and they arrived in significant enough numbers to warrant suffixing the station nameboard with the words 'For the Landslip'. Despite causing acute anxiety among unsuspecting strangers to the area, that wording was to be displayed until 1939. For many years, a vintage ex-LC&DR carriage was used as a camping coach at Combpyne, its more modern replacement lasting almost as long as the branch itself. South of Combpyne was the line's most famous engi-

Below: **The Adams 'Radial Tanks' were synonymous with the Lyme Regis branch, and this fine picture shows No 3520 (later BR No 30584) ready to leave Axminster with a branch working in 1934.** Ian Allan Library

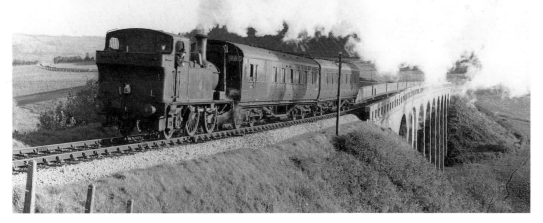

Above: **On 11/12 November 1958, ex-GWR '14XX' class 0-4-2T No 1462 underwent unsuccessful trials on the Lyme Regis branch; it was photographed at Cannington Viaduct with the 10am Lyme Regis-Axminster service on 12 November.** S. C. Nash

neering work, the 10-arch viaduct at Cannington, which at the time of its construction was one of the largest in England to have been built in concrete.

The L&SWR was well aware that the ferocious gradients and sharp curves on the branch would severely restrict the options for motive power, particularly in view of the axle-weight limit of 12 tons. Consequently, two LB&SCR 'Terrier' 0-6-0Ts, No 646 *Newington* and No 669 *Clapham*, were purchased five months before the opening of the branch. However, soon after commencing their designated duties, they were found to be severely underpowered for the increasingly heavy holiday trains. In 1907 the Axminster & Lyme Regis Light Railway was officially absorbed by the L&SWR, and the new owners relaid the tracks so that they could introduce alternative types of motive power. Later that year, 'O2' 0-4-4Ts Nos 202 and 208 were drafted in but, even with the precautionary measure of half-filled tanks and bunkers, their axle weights were precariously close to the limits. Moreover, the sharp curvatures of the branch took a severe toll on their frames and flanges.

The L&SWR's problem of having an almost unworkable line persisted until 1913 when, after a bout of lateral thinking, the company's new locomotive superintendent, Robert Urie, came up with the idea of modifying two of the Adams '415' class 4-4-2Ts, better known as the 'Radial Tanks'. The locomotives were, by then, already on the duplicate list and carried Nos 0125/0419. During surgery they received smaller tanks of just 800gal capacities and had the play in their bogies increased. The modifications extracted the company from its predicament, and in 1914, '415' class No 521 was similarly treated and sent along to join its classmates. For the next 47

years, the 'Radial Tanks' were synonymous with the branch.

Traffic figures on the line were healthy, with over 60,000 passengers using the branch annually; freight made a significant contribution, with farm produce generating much of the outward traffic. To meet the demand, the original service of six weekday trains each way had by 1914 been increased to eight, and a number of those were mixed. By the last summer before the Grouping, nine trains plied each way on weekdays, with a usual journey time of 20min.

At the Grouping in 1923, the Southern Railway took control of the line. By then, the regular trio of 'Radial Tanks' were Nos 0125/0486/0521; one of the original pair, No 0419, had been put to sleep in 1921, and the 1914 arrival, No 521, had been numbered on the duplicate list in 1922. However, No 0486 was retired in 1928 and, as possible long-term replacements for the other two veteran 'Radials', ex-SE&CR 'P' class 0-6-0T No A558 and former-LB&SCR 'D1' class 0-4-2T No B612 were transferred to the parent shed at Exmouth Junction for trials on the Lyme Regis branch.

The 'P' class 0-6-0T proved quite useless, but the 'D1' 0-4-2T seemed promising and, after its trials, was sent back to Brighton Works so that its bunker and tank capacities could be reduced in order to lessen its weight. In its new slimline guise, it returned to Dorset while three classmates, Nos B276/359/633, were earmarked for similar treatment at Brighton in preparation for Lyme Regis duties. As the quartet of 0-4-2Ts settled down nicely to their new tasks, things looked grim for the 'Radial Tanks', but the coincidence of three of the four 0-4-2Ts requiring urgent attention simultaneously in 1930 necessitated the removal of the two sidelined 'Radials' from storage.

Rather than go straight into the fray, the two 'Radial Tanks' were dispatched to Eastleigh for extensive modernisation. The cost of £2,620 proved to be money well spent, as the 1930s saw a significant increase in traffic on the branch. By the late 1930s, summer services comprised 11 or more trains each way on weekdays, and the Sunday services had done very nicely since their introduction in 1930. After the war, an additional locomotive became essential and, in 1946, the Southern located another 'Radial Tank', formerly L&SWR No 488, in store on the East Kent Light Railway; it had been sold for Government service in 1917 and had subsequently been purchased by the EKLR. A total of £1,638 was spent on restoring it to pristine condition. Come Nationalisation in 1948, the three 'Radial Tanks' became BR Nos 30582/83/84 and carried on quite happily. Throughout the mid-1950s two-coach trains were still the norm, although the occasional six-coach trains were required in peak summer. Six coaches were the maximum that could be accommodated at the platforms and, of course, those trains were worked double-headed.

By the late 1950s, the question of the 'Radial Tanks' age again reared its head, and so in 1958 GWR '14XX' class 0-4-2T No 1462 was tried on the branch. It proved totally unsuitable. The following year, some sections of the track were renewed and two curves were slightly straightened so that ex-LMS 2-6-2T No 41297 could be put through its paces. The outcome was reasonably successful and, despite doubts about their weights, the 2-6-2Ts were viewed as the most likely permanent replacements for the 'Radial Tanks'. No 30584 was withdrawn in January 1961, Nos 30582/83 following suit six months later. The 2-6-2Ts took over and with sporadic summer-time assistance from Standard '2MT' 2-6-2Ts in 1961 carried on until the introduction of DMUs in November 1963, by which time the branch had passed to Western Region control. However, occasional diesel failures in 1964 and 1965 resulted in brief reapparances of the 2-6-2Ts. Single-cars replaced the DMUs in March 1965 and remained until the closure of the line on 29 November that year, the last scheduled service having worked two days earlier. Freight facilities had been withdrawn in February 1964.

Since the Grouping, or even well before, the Lyme Regis line had been more of a conventional country branch than a 'proper' light railway. Nevertheless, the 'Radial Tanks' did much to give the line a real air of individuality and, unsurprisingly, most of the branch's appeal went when they were retired. One remarkable statistic about the three 'Radials' is that they outlived all of their classmates by a minimum of 32 years.

Below: **From 1961, ex-LMSR 2-6-2Ts took over the working of the Lyme Regis branch, and No 41291 is seen arriving at the well-kept terminus on 4 June 1963.** Ian Allan Library

Right: **On this 25in Ordnance Survey map of 1905, the short-lived connection between the down platform of Axminster station and the Lyme Regis branch is evident.** Crown Copyright

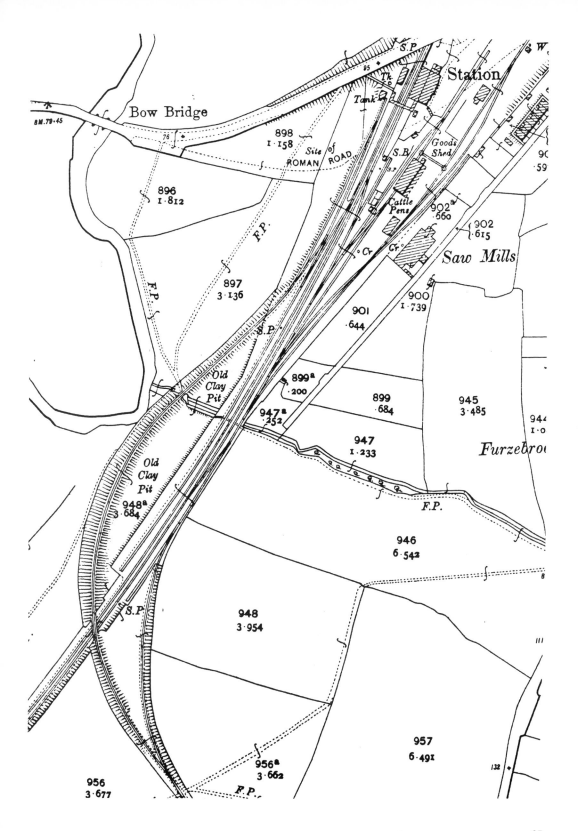

Bow Bridge

BM.79.45

Station

S.P.

S.W.

Tk

Tank

Site of
ROMAN ROAD

S.B.

Goods
Shed

S.P.

90

898
1.158

896
1.812

897
3.136

Cattle
Pens

902ᵃ
.660

902
.615

Saw Mills

Cr

Cr

900
1.739

901
.644

945
3.485

944
1.0

S.P.

Old
Clay
Pit

899ᵃ
.200

899
.684

947
1.233

Furzebro

947ᵃ
.252

F.P.

Old
Clay
Pit

948ᵃ
3.684

946
6.542

8

S.P.

948
3.954

111

957
6.491

132

956ᵃ
3.662

956
3.677

F.P.

25

5 Bankfoot Light Railway

In November 1908, a Light Railway Order was obtained for the construction of a branch from Strathord, five miles north of Perth on the Alyth line, to the small village of Bankfoot. The three-mile branch, which had no intermediate stations, opened to freight traffic on 5 March 1906 and for passengers on 14 May.

From the outset, the branch was worked by the Caledonian Railway, Drummond '171' class 0-4-4Ts being the usual locomotives. A total of 24 members of this class were built between 1884 and 1891 for light branch work, their most distinctive feature being their solid trailing wheels. Most of the class were withdrawn in the early 1920s but one, by then LMSR No 15103 which was classified '1P', soldiered on until November 1945 and was not actually scrapped until August the following year.

In February 1912, the Caledonian bought out the Bankfoot Light Railway for the sum of £5,250, part of the agreement being that the creditors of the impe-

cunious little company undertook not to pursue any claims. At the Grouping the branch passed to the LMSR, passenger services at that time comprising seven trains each way on weekdays plus additional ones on Saturdays, almost all workings running through to or from Perth. During the 1920s many of the branch's passengers defected to the roads and, in an attempt to achieve economies, an LMSR Sentinel-Cammell steam railcar was introduced. The railcar's duties involved seven or eight trips each way between Strathord and Bankfoot, with services spaced at intervals of 60-90min and timed to connect with main line trains to and from Perth. Sadly, even the railcar could not restore the branch to profitability and passenger services were withdrawn on 13 April 1931, although public freight traffic continued to be handled until total closure on 7 September 1964.

On 18 June 1962, an RCTS Scottish Railtour had negotiated the line, the locomotive in charge of the two ex-Caley coaches on that special working having been '2P' 0-4-4T No 55260, built by the LMSR in 1925 to a design which had originated with John McIntosh in 1897. It seems that the designs which emerged from St Rollox stood the test of time rather better than some of the Caley's branch services.

BANKFOOT LIGHT RAILWAY COMPANY.

Schedule of Liabilities referred to in and signed as relative to and of even date with minute of agreement between the Caledonian Railway Company and the Bankfoot Light Railway Company.

	£	s.	d.
Mortgage holders as per Bankfoot Light Railway Company's register of mortgages	5,072	0	0
Roderick Fraser—Bill held by Bank of Scotland	550	0	0
Do. Debt	10	0	0
Cash balance due to secretary	50	0	0
Rates and taxes unpaid	29	0	0
Auditor's fees unpaid	89	10	0
Miscellaneous small accounts amounting to	45	0	0
Secretary's remuneration for salary clerks and writings since incorporation of Company modified to	600	0	0
Balance of law expenses since incorporation of the Company to 31st January 1912 unpaid	420	0	0
Caledonian Railway Company balance on revenue	645	0	0
	£7,510	10	0

NOTE.—The above do not include interest accrued to 31st January 1912.

J. BLACKBURN Secy.
THOMAS DEMPSTER Secy.

Left: **The Caledonian Railway's Confirmation Act of 1913 referred to the purchase of the Bankfoot company the previous year.** Author's files

Below: **Ex-Caledonian '2F' 0-6-0 No 57243 takes a break from shunting duties at Bankfoot in July 1957, the station yard appearing well-maintained despite the cessation of passenger services 26 years previously. The angles of the shadows will enable expert photographers to determine that the time of day is around 3.55pm, but those with an interest in church architecture will find a simpler way of ascertaining the time.** W. J. V. Anderson

6 Barton & Immingham Light Railway

Above: **Goxhill station was the point at which the Barton & Immingham Light Railway joined the Ulceby-New Holland line. In this undated picture, the light railway can be seen diverging to the left in the distance.**
Lens of Sutton

The port of Grimsby in northern Lincolnshire was an obvious target for early railway promoters. In March 1848, the first section of the route between Louth and Boston was opened and, although nominally owned by the East Lincolnshire Railway, it was the very first line of what was to become the Great Northern Railway's empire. At the same time, the Manchester, Sheffield & Lincolnshire Railway opened the first of its lines to Grimsby, that company later becoming the Great Central Railway.

Largely as a result of the rail connections, Grimsby Docks became increasingly busy, but the question of easing the congestion there was not tackled seriously until the early 1900s. Instead of building additional facilities at Grimsby, the Great Central Railway eventually proposed a new dock at Killingholme, near the village of Immingham six miles up-river from Grimsby. The new dock took the name of Immingham instead of Killingholme, and was formally opened on 22 July 1912. The essential matter of rail connections to Immingham was taken care of by three lines: the Humber Commercial Railway, which was a heavy duty freight line from Ulceby on the New Holland branch, the Grimsby District Light Railway (qv) and the Barton & Immingham Light Railway. Despite their titles, all three were, in effect, appendages of the Great Central Railway.

The main purpose of the Barton & Immingham Light Railway was to complete a passenger route to and from from Hull, on the other side of the River Humber. There was a ferry service between Hull and New Holland, and the new light railway connected with the existing New Holland branch, thereby providing the last link in the Hull-Immingham chain. At New Holland, the wooden pier later became very dilapidated and work started on a concrete replacement in 1923, a new station at the pier opening in March 1928.

The B&ILR ran for 8¼ miles from Western Jetty at Immingham to Goxhill station on the Grimsby-New Holland branch. The section between Immingham and Killingholme opened to goods traffic on 1 December 1910 and the Killingholme-Goxhill section was unveiled on 1 May 1911. On 2 May, passenger services between Immingham and New Holland commenced. The initial service comprised seven trains each way on weekdays with an additional one from New Holland to Immingham on Saturdays. The stopping places en route were, from the direction of Immingham, Killingholme (2 miles), East Halton halt (4¾ miles) and Goxhill (8¼ miles), the end of the journey being at New Holland (10½ miles from Immingham). A primitive halt, Killingholme Admiralty platform, was added in the late 1920s as an advertised stopping place serving the nearby Naval base. The line was single track throughout and worked by electric tablet.

The GCR's use of the Light Railways Act might have enabled the line to be built on the cheap but it had hardly been in keeping with the spirit of the legislation; there had been few attempts even to pretend that the B&ILR was an independent concern which needed the advantages of light railway status. The charade was formally ended on 31 December 1912 when the B&ILR was vested in the Humber Commercial Railway & Dock Co and was subsequently leased to the GCR. Apart from its questionable 'independent' status, the Barton & Immingham Light Railway's major anomaly was that it did not run to Barton. Early plans for the line to extend to Barton had soon been dropped, the existing branch from New Holland to Barton being deemed adequate for local requirements. The practice of working the Grimsby-New Holland and the New Holland-Barton branches as separate entities continued until 1981.

The GCR and, after the Grouping, the LNER used standard stock for the services on the B&ILR. Precise details of the locomotives used are sparse, but the popular theory that passenger services were worked by steam railmotors can be discounted. The GCR's railmotors were certainly in the area around 1910-12, but on the Barton-New Holland and, for a time, the Grimsby District Light Railway.

It appears that, by 1921, Parker-designed 4-4-0s (later LNER 'D7' class) had become established on the B&ILR line despite their 16-ton axle weights, and went on to maintain a presence throughout much of the 1930s. The 31 members of the class had been built between 1887 and 1894. By 1934, nine of the 12 survivors were based in northern Lincolnshire,

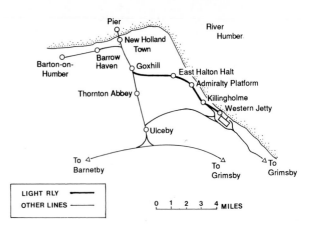

with Immingham and its sub-shed at New Holland having their fair share. It seems that ex-MS&LR (LNER 'E2' class) 2-4-0s worked on the line around the time of the Grouping, North Lincolnshire being the class's last outpost with the three survivors of 1923 all being based at New Holland, while 'A5' class 4-6-2Ts were used in later years.

By 1940, passenger services between Immingham and New Holland via the old B&ILR route consisted of four trains each way on weekdays; after the war, a 'Saturdays Only' Immingham-New Holland service was added. Predictably, the increase in car ownership during the 1950s saw a reduction in the line's passenger traffic and the first economy was made in September 1956, when Killingholme station was reduced to the status of a halt. Around that time services were often worked by a well-worn 'K2' class 2-6-0 and a three-coach set. The continuing reduction in traffic resulted in the withdrawal of passenger services between Immingham and Goxhill on 17 June 1963.

Today, some of the former B&ILR tracks in the Immingham and Killingholme areas are still used as private-owner sidings. At Barton, the community which the B&ILR never reached, a passenger service operates to and from Grimsby and Cleethorpes but the pattern is now rather different to that of GCR days. When the Humber Bridge opened in June 1981, the ferry service from New Holland Pier became redundant and was therefore discontinued. The trains were subsequently rerouted via a new platform at New Holland so that they could work through to Barton, where a connection was provided with the bus service across the Humber Bridge.

Left: **Killingholme Admiralty Platform on the Immingham-Goxhill line was hardly the most-photographed station in the land. It might, however, have appealed to modellers who had a surfeit of matchsticks. This 'carriage-window' picture of 28 September 1954 was taken from an Immingham-bound train.** H. C. Casserley

7 Basingstoke & Alton Light Railway

Despite having reached only as far as the letter 'B', it has already been seen that the London & South Western Railway was swift to take advantage of the Light Railways Acts but, in eastern Hampshire, the company got its come-uppance. The very first line to be sanctioned under the Act of 1896 was the Basingstoke & Alton Light Railway. The intention of the Act, that of encouraging the construction of railways to serve rural communities, was not exactly uppermost in the L&SWR's corporate mind when it backed the promotion of the B&ALR. The L&SWR's motive behind supporting the would-be line was, not so much to provide a means of communication for the folk who lived between Basingstoke and Alton, but more as a blocking measure against a rival scheme for a new railway between Portsmouth and Basingstoke. The perks offered by the Light Railways Act convinced the L&SWR that the B&ALR could be built on the cheap, therefore halting the plans of its rival with minimal expense.

The necessary Order was obtained and, seemingly without realising the huge irony of the situation, the President of the Board of Trade cut the first sod. The 14-mile line opened on 1 June 1901; despite being single track throughout and taking a circuitous route in order to avoid extreme earthworks, it had still required considerable engineering. Furthermore, the roundabout route meant that the three intermediate stations, Cliddesden (3 miles from Basingstoke), Her-

riard (6½ miles) and Bentworth & Lasham (9¼ miles), were anything between 1 and 2½ miles from the communities they were alleged to be benefitting, and consequently were not over-attractive propositions for the locals. The L&SWR might have foiled its rival's proposed line, but the victory had been nothing like as cheap as had been anticipated.

The maximum axle-load permissible on the line was 14 tons. A 25mph speed limit prevailed, but 10mph was the maximum on the approaches to Butts Junction, near Alton, and the line's five level crossings. The solitary passing place was at Herriard, and the only appendages were a siding to Thorneycroft's works south of Basingstoke, one to a small fuel depot, and one serving Treloar's Hospital, at the Alton end of the line. That hospital had originally been established during the Boer War, and in 1908 it was taken over by the Lord Mayor Treloar Cripple's Hospital and College. In 1918, a platform known as Alton Park was provided near the hospital but it never appeared in any public timetables. Nevertheless, the platform was to out live the railway, as it survived until 1939. One distinctive feature of the B&A line was that the three intermediate stations had their own wells and water tanks, Herriard's tanks being fed by an oil engine, the tanks at the two other stations being fed by wind-pumps.

At first the line was worked by 0-4-4Ts, 'O2' class No 203 having been in charge on opening day, while '395' class 0-6-0s looked after the freight turns. The 0-6-0s, known as 'Jumbos', were the heaviest locomotives permitted on the line until it was relaid in 1924. However, the L&SWR became painfully aware that passenger traffic on the line was sparse and so, in an attempt to minimise overheads, a pair of steam railmotors was built specially for use

Left: **If this photograph is anything to go by, staff wages on the Basingstoke & Alton Light Railway were adequate to pay for substantial dinners. This photograph of the line's first regular passenger locomotive, 'O2' class 0-4-4T No 203, is believed to date to circa 1901/02.** Bucknall Collection/Ian Allan Library

Above: **Almost-new L&SWR 'H12' class railmotor No 2 poses at Cliddesden station in July 1904. The machine remained on the Basingstoke-Alton line for only six weeks and finished life in November 1916, its final duties being local staff and parcels workings to and from Waterloo.** Bucknall Collection/Ian Allan Library

on the line. The railcars' engine units were constructed at Nine Elms Works and the coach bodies at Eastleigh, and the units entered traffic in May and June 1904. Each had seating for eight first- and 32 third-class passengers, and a small luggage compartment. In service, the steep gradients and sharp curvatures, particularly around Cliddesden, presented obstacles which the railcars sometimes found insurmountable and so they were replaced by 'O2' class 0-4-4Ts as from 12 August, after just six weeks regular service on the line.

Predictably, the 'independent' Basingstoke & Alton

Light Railway was formally taken over by the L&SWR but, of course, this made no difference whatsoever to the operation of the line. It had started life as a poorly-patronised route and continued in a similar manner, and so the L&SWR was quite relieved when, in 1917, the rails were requisitioned for the war effort. At the Grouping in 1923, the Southern Railway inherited the partly-intact track-bed but to the company's horror, proposals for formal abandonment were strongly opposed. Grudgingly, the line was relaid, and

Right: **L&SWR working timetable, 1 June to 30 September 1909.**

Below: **Despite the running-down and sparse usage of the Basingstoke-Alton line in the early 1930s, Herriard station was well maintained. This picture of 13 June 1931 shows a single track, the passing loop having been lifted during World War 1 and never reinstated.** H. C. Casserley

it reopened on 18 August 1924, albeit with the option of reviewing the situation after 10 years. It came as little surprise when the Southern did not exactly put heart and soul into reviving the line's fortunes. A hint of the company's disinterest in the line had been seen during the relaying of the tracks as the passing loop at Herriard had, conspicuously, not been reinstated. Some of the 10-year 'breathing space' had still to elapse when, on 12 September 1932, passenger services were withdrawn; the last train was the 7.30pm Alton-Basingstoke, which comprised one bogie composite coach and a four-wheeled brake van. Local enthusiasm for the line and the overwhelming sadness at its demise was illustrated by the loading of that last train. According to a local newspaper report, it carried just one passenger.

The section between Basingstoke and Bentworth & Lasham was retained for freight until 1 June 1936. That was not the end of the story, however, as part of the comedy classic, *Oh! Mr.Porter* was filmed on the line in June 1937; it starred Will Hay, Moore Marriott and Graham Moffatt, and the station at Cliddesden was transformed to become 'Buggleskelly' in the film. Adams '395' class 0-6-0 No 3509 and 'X6' class 4-4-0 No 657 were used in the film, and for their roles they were treated to more-modern looking Brighton-style chimneys. Conversely, Kent & East Sussex Light Railway 2-4-0T No 2 *Northiam*, which

took part in the film under the guise of *Gladstone*, was fitted with an even longer chimney than normal and, furthermore, had part of its cab removed. Even then, make-up departments knew no bounds.

A sequence for a lesser-known film, *The Wrecker*, had, in fact, been shot on the line in August 1928. Ex-SE&CR 'F1' class 4-4-0 No A148 and a six-coach set had been purchased by the film's makers, Gainsborough Pictures, and had been painted with the inscription of the 'United Coast Lines'. The filming had required the staging of a collision between the train and a Foden lorry at Salter's Ash level crossing, the lorry having been packed with a charge of dynamite so that it would explode on impact. The impact had been violent enough for the locomotive and carriages to perform no further part in British railway history. For the record, the film was directed by Michael Balcon and it starred Carlyle Blackwell, Benita Hume and Pauline Johnson.

After the glamour of film-making, the only sections of the Basingstoke & Alton line to survive were the sidings to Thorneycroft's near Basingstoke and to Treloar's Hospital, at the Alton end. The latter, in particular, saw a wide range of motive power, including ex-L&SWR types, Southern Railway 'Q1s', then BR Standard classes and, eventually, diesels. However, all that ceased in July 1967 when the last remnants of the line closed completely.

BASINGSTOKE AND ALTON LIGHT RAILWAY.

This is a Single Line between Basingstoke West Box and Butts Jc. and is worked under the Regulations for workin Single Lines by the Electric Train Tablet Block System.

The maximum load of Trains on the Basingstoke and Alton Line is as follows :—Goods Trains, 15 Loaded Wagons or 18 Mixed Wagons, or 25 Empty Wagons. A load of Coal, sand, or Bricks to be counted as 1½ Wagons. Passenger Trains, 5 Bogie Vehicles. (V. 19,748.)

Dist. from Basingstoke.	UP TRAINS. WEEK-DAYS.	1 Pass.		2 Goods. A		3 Pass.		4 Pass.		5 Pass.		6 Pass.		7 Cattle. Weds. when reqd. C		8 Pass. D		1		2	
M. C.		arr.	dep.	arr.	dep.	arr.	dep.	arr.	dep.	arr.	dep.	arr.	dep.	arr.	dep.	arr.	dep.	arr.	dep.	arr.	dep.
— —	Waterloo	a.m.	a.m.	a.m.	a.m.	a.m.	a.m.	p.m.	p.m.	p.m.	p.m.	p.m.	p.m.	p.m.	p.m.	p.m.	p.m.				
		...	5 50	...	...	...	7 40	...	11 15	...	12 50	...	2 50	...	...	...	5 0				
— —	Basingstoke	...	7 15	...	7 55	...	9 35	...	12 40	...	2 35	...	4 20	...	...	...	6 10	...	...	...	...
3 2	Cliddesden	7 24	7 25	8 4	8 9	9 44	9 45	12 49	12 50	2 44	2 45	4 29	4 30	...	4 45	...	...	...	...	...	...
6 46	Herriard	7 35	7 36	8 20	8 55	9 55	9 56	1 0	1 1	2 55	2 56	4 40	4 41	5 5	5 38	6 19	6 20	...	...	...	...
				Cross 1 Dn.		Cross 2 Dn.										6 30	6 31				
9 19	Bentw'h &Lasham	7 44	7 45	9 4	9 14	10 4	10 10	1 9	1 10	3 4	3 5	4 49	4 50	5 47	5 48	6 39	6 D40	...	...	...	...
														Cross 6 Dn.		Cross 7 Dn.					
13 4	Butts Junction	7 57		9 29		10 17		1 22		3 17				6 3		6 52		...	...	...	...
13 67	Brewery Siding	...	...	...	...	...	...	...	...	...	...	5 2		6 6	6 12	...	...	...	...	...	...
14 14	Alton	8 0	...	9 33	...	10 20	...	1 25	...	3 20	...	5 5	...	6 15	6 20	6 55	...	...	...	...	...
51 9	Waterloo	10 21	...	...	...	12 12	...	3 7	...	5 32	...	7 1	...	...	...	8 46	...	...	...	...	...

Sectional Distances.	DOWN TRAINS. WEEK-DAYS.	1 Pass.		2 Cattle. Weds. when required. B		3 Pass.		4 Pass.		5 Pass.		6 Pass.		7 C Goods.		8 Pass.		1		2	
M. C.		arr.	dep.	arr.	dep.	arr.	dep.	arr.	dep.	arr.	dep.	arr.	dep.	arr.	dep.	arr.	dep.	arr.	dep.	arr.	dep.
— —	Waterloo	a.m.	a.m.	a.m.	a.m.	a.m.	a.m.	p.m	a.m.	p.m.	p.m.	p.m.	p.m.	p.m.	p.m.	p.m.	p.m.				
		...	6 0	...	...	...	8 55	...	11 45	...	1 10	...	3 5	...	...	...	5 30				
1 10	Alton	...	8 7	...	9 26	...	10 39	...	1 36	...	3 27	...	5 13	...	5 30	...	7 9	...	...	...	...
	Butts Junction	8 10		9 30		10 42		1 39		3 30		5 16		5 36	5 39	7 12		...	...	...	...
				After 2 Up																	
3 65	Bentw'h &Lasham	8 22	8 23	9 45	9 46	10 54	10 55	1 51	1 52	3 42	3 43	5 28	5 29	5 54	6 18	7 24	7 25	...	...	...	...
2 53	Herriard	8 31	8 32	9 55	10 25	11 3	11 4	2 0	2 1	3 51	3 52	5 37	5 38	6 27	7 0	7 33	7 34	...	...	...	...
		Cross 2 Up.		Cross 3 Up.								Cross 7 Up.		Cross 8 Up.							
8 44	Cliddesden	8 42	8 43	10 36		11 14	11 15	2 11	2 12	4 2	4 3	5 48	5 49	7 11	7 16	7 44	7 45	...	...	...	...
3 2	Basingstoke	8 52	...	10 45	...	11 24	...	2 21	...	4 12	...	5 58	...	7 25	...	7 54	...	...	...	...	...
47 71	Waterloo	10 11	...	...	...	12 28	...	5 5	...	5 39	...	7 31	...	...	...	10 5	...	...	...	...	...

A—On Week-days when required (Mondays excepted).—Cattle Traffic, Great Western Railway to Aldershot, via Basingstoke.—When Wagons with Cattle for Aldershot are handed over at Basingstoke too late to go forward, via Woking, by the 3.20 a.m. Goods from Southampton, Mr. Prince, Basingstoke, to arrange to send the Wagons forward by the 7.55 a.m. Goods to Alton. The latter Train will be extended to Aldershot, when necessary, the Engine to return from Aldershot to Alton Pilot to the 10.5 a.m. Train from Woking. Basingstoke and Alton to arrange and advise all concerned. (S. D 2/18,964.) (T.K. 40,250.)

B—Cliddesden to call over the 10.39 a.m. Train from Alton daily and advise Basingstoke when there are Passengers for London.

C—When No. 7 Up Train runs the 5.30 p.m. Goods from Alton will start at 5.58 p.m. and arrive Bentworth at 6.18 p.m.

D—Bentworth to call over the 6.10 p.m. Train from Basingstoke daily, and advise Alton when there are Passengers for Medstead and below.

E—2 minutes earlier, commencing 12th July.

THORNEYCROFT'S SIDING BETWEEN BASINGSTOKE AND CLIDDESDEN.—Basingstoke to arrange to work Traffic to and from this Siding as may be necessary at the following Speed Table :—

Basingstoke	0 0	
Thorneycroft's Siding	0 4	0 16
Basingstoke	0 20	...

8 Bentley & Bordon Light Railway

Another thinly-veiled subsidiary of the London & South Western Railway surfaced in Hampshire in the early 1900s. It was the Bentley & Bordon Light Railway which had been promoted primarily to provide access to the military base at Longmoor Camp. The camp had been established in 1900 and, from 1908, a substantial railway network was developed there; known at first as the Woolmer Instructional Military Railway, it assumed the more familiar title of the Longmoor Military Railway in 1934.

The L&SWR had minimal trouble in obtaining its Order for the Bentley & Bordon Light Railway, due in part to the support of the War Department. The line was authorised in 1902 and the serious business of extracting money from fare-paying customers commenced on 11 December 1905. In the genteel style of the day, *Bradshaw's* charmingly described the railway as '...a line 4 miles 5 furlongs in length, commencing in the parish of Selborne and terminating in the parish of Binstead by a junction with the (L&SWR's) Farnham and Alton Railway near Bentley Station'.

The 4¾-mile Bentley & Bordon Light Railway started from a bay on the down side of Bentley station, just inside the eastern border of Hampshire on the L&SWR's Guildford-Alton main line. The branch was single throughout and was worked by the electric tablet block system; the axle-weight limit was 16 tons, and a 25mph speed limit was imposed. There were no passing places and the only intermediate stop was at Kingsley Halt (opened in 1906), 2¾ miles from Bentley; although land was purchased to provide full

station and freight facilities at Kingsley, these never materialised. At Bordon, there was a twin-faced platform, a modest goods yard and a single-road engine shed. From the station yard, the Army line to Longmoor Camp diverged and, over the years, the siding accommodation at Bordon was enlarged for the benefit of the military traffic. Until the establishment of the Woolmer Instructional Military Railway in 1908, the War Department maintained an engine shed of its own in the station yard.

From 7 March 1906, the Bordon branch was worked by Guildford-based steam railmotor No 9, one of a batch of seven which had been built in 1905/06. Later railcars of identical design, Nos 7 and 10, eventually took turns with No 9 on the branch. Costing £1,475 each and finished in a livery of salmon pink with green wheels and cylinder covers, the branch's railmotors were classified 'H13' and differed from the 'H12' class units used on the Basingstoke & Alton Light Railway in having their engines completely enclosed by their coachwork. The power units were built at Nine Elms Works and the coach bodies at Eastleigh Carriage Works. The railmotors proved very economical in operation. On the Bordon branch, they used 13.2lb of coal per mile compared with the 18.6lb of the motor-fitted tank engines and the 26.8lbs of the 'O2' class 0-4-4Ts. The corresponding running costs per mile were 3.4d (1¾p) for the railmotors, 5.7d (2½p) for motor-fitted tanks and 11.1d (10½p) for the 'O2s'. To offset those advantages, the railmotors were not always popular

with the passengers, and in the eyes of the operating department they did not offer the flexibility of loco-motive-hauled trains as, if peak-time loadings demanded, a locomotive-hauled train could always have an additional coach or two attached but the rail-motors could not. It is known that Nos 10 and 11 were each fitted with a corridor connection at the rear, but there is no record of trailer cars ever having been attached in service.

By 1909, the services usually comprised around 15 passenger trains each way on weekdays and five on Sundays. Apart from the occasional through workings to or from Farnham or Guildford, and trains which had through coaches to or from Waterloo, every advertised passenger working was a motor train which had first- and third-class accommodation. The jour-ney times between Bentley and Bordon in 1909 were 13min in the down direction and 14min up; in that same year, there were usually two freight workings each way on weekdays, one each to and from Farn-ham and Guildford. The allocation lists for May 1917 show that Guildford shed, which serviced the Bordon line, had on its lists motor-fitted 'M7' class 0-4-4Ts Nos 36/242/248/672, but it must be emphasised that the Bentley-Bordon duty was not the only motor-train working serviced by Guildford depot.

The line passed to the Southern Railway at the

Above: **Push-pull fitted 'M7' class 0-4-4T No 30110 stands in the Bordon bay at Bentley station.** Ian Allan Library

Below left: **In the best pre-Nationalisation tradition, Bentley station was impeccably maintained. On 17 May 1934, 'M7' class No 131 (later BR No 30131) waits with a Bordon train, the main line platform being used because the train has worked through from Farnham.** H. C. Casserley

Below: **On 14 September 1953, 'M7' 0-4-4T No 30028 rests at Bordon. It is clear that the station was past its heyday.** H. C. Casserley

Grouping. In the early post-Grouping period, four Adams '415' class 4-4-2Ts were shedded at Guildford for Bordon branch duties; they were all on the dupli-cate list and carried Nos 045, 0428, 0517 and 0524. Three of the four had, between 1913 and 1916, been fitted with pulley and cable apparatus for motor oper-ation but, mysteriously, there is no record of the other one, No 0428, having been similarly treated. The quartet ended their days on the line, their respec-tive withdrawal dates being December 1924, July 1925, December 1925 and November 1925.

The 'M7' 0-4-4Ts subsequently took over and, during the late 1930s, Guildford shed's stud of 'M7s' was usually around 10 or 11 but, again, the Bordon duty was not the only one for which that depot sup-plied motor-fitted locomotives. The 1940 timetables show weekday passenger services of 10 trains each way on the line and, by 1952, that number had risen to 11 plus an additional 'Saturdays only' service. The jour-ney times of 15min were the same as those of 30 years earlier. Inevitably, the branch lost an increasing amount of its trade to road transport during the 1950s, and the activities on the line grew more and more leisurely. Local folk lore has it that, adjacent to Bordon station, an allotment was kept by one of the branch's regular drivers who enthusiastically spent much of his waiting time at the station on gardening duties.

The eventual decision to withdraw passenger ser-vices came as little surprise. The last scheduled passen-ger workings took place on 16 September 1957, the final week's services being handled by 'M7' 0-4-4T No 30110 and 'Ironclad' set No 384. The line remained open for goods traffic until 4 April 1966, by which time military activities at Longmoor Camp were on the decline. Nevertheless, the total closure of the Bordon branch meant that the Army had to divert its traffic to Liss, on the Guildford-Alton line, where interchange facilities had been provided in 1933. The connection at Liss was altogether less convenient than the old one at Bordon, but that problem was to be short-lived as the Longmoor Military Railway closed completely on 31 October 1969.

9 Bere Alston & Calstock Light Railway

This delightful little line was, for almost all of its length, tucked just across the River Tamar in south-east Cornwall. Although born as a result of a Light Railway Order, the line's history dates back to the 1860s when it commenced operations as a narrow gauge industrial tramway. In south-east Cornwall, the area around Kit Hill and Callington was mined for copper, tin and arsenic, and during the mid-1800s, the local mining industry was prospering. In order to improve transportation, the Tamar, Kit Hill & Callington Railway was formed in 1863 to provide a link to a quay on the River Tamar, from where the minerals could be exported. Isolated sections of the tramway became operational in 1867 but it was 7 May 1872 before it opened throughout.

Even before the tramway had opened, its title had been changed, firstly to the Callington & Calstock Railway and then to the East Cornwall Mineral Railway. Built to a gauge of 3ft 6in, it ran for 7¾ miles from Kelly Bray, 1¼ miles north of Callington, and passed a number of mine workings on its route to a quay at Calstock. The quay was some 350ft below the level of the tramway and so a 1 in 6 incline was constructed; this was worked on the counterbalance principle but with the assistance of a stationary engine. From Kelly Bray to the top of the incline, the tramway was worked by a pair of Neilson 0-4-0STs. For a time, the mines and the tramway prospered, but after the slump of the late 1870s, the East Cornwall Mineral Railway struggled to keep its corporate head above water. It eventually decided enough was enough and, on 4 January 1894, it formally sold out to the Plymouth, Devonport & South Western Junc-

tion Railway for a price of £21,500 in cash plus £48,250 in shares.

The Plymouth, Devonport & South Western Junction Railway had been incorporated in 1883 to build a main line between Lydford, north of Tavistock, and Plymouth for use by the London & South Western Railway, that company having encountered numerous problems while sharing the GWR's single-track line from Lydford to Plymouth. The PD&SWJR was, however, rather more than just another L&SWR subsidiary as it had been formed and largely financed in Plymouth. The PD&SWJR's 22¼-mile double-track line between Lydford and Plymouth had opened on 2 June 1890 and, as intended, had been worked by the L&SWR from the outset.

After taking over the East Cornwall Mineral Railway in 1894, the PD&SWJR continued to work the narrow gauge line despite the continuing decline in the local mining industry. In 1900, the PD&SWJR was granted a Light Railway Order to divert the eastern end of the tramway's route from Calstock Quay

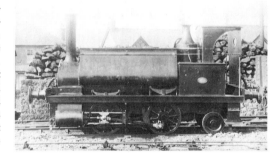

Above: **Ex-LSWR '02' class 0-4-4T No 231 rests outside Callington shed sometime during 1936.** Rail Archive Stephenson

Left: **East Cornwall Mineral Railway No 2 started life as a 3ft gauge 0-4-0ST but, on being taken into PD&SWJR stock, was converted to a standard gauge 0-4-2ST. It was retained for use on the Bere Alston & Calstock section until 1912, this picture being taken at Callington circa 1908.** Bucknall Collection/Ian Allan Library

Below left: **The PD&SWJR purchased 0-6-2T No 4 *Earl of Mount Edgcumbe* specifically for the Bere Alston & Calstock section. It stands at Callington shed in the company of its twin, No 5 *Lord St Levan*.** Bucknall Collection/Ian Allan Library

to Bere Alston, on the Lydford-Plymouth main line, the Order being in the name of the Bere Alston & Calstock Light Railway. A revised Order of 1905 confirmed the proposed diversion and also permitted conversion of the entire Bere Alston-Callington (Kelly Bray) line to the standard gauge. The engineer appointed to oversee the conversion work was none other than Holman (later Lt-Col) Stephens.

For much of its length, the standard gauge branch followed the route of the old 3ft 6in gauge tramway. At its eastern end, however, major work was required to build a completely new section across the River Tamar to join the main line at Bere Alston station. The crossing of the Tamar necessitated the construction of a viaduct which had 12 spans, each of 60ft

width, and an ingenious wagon lift. The lift was on the Cornish side of the viaduct and was installed to enable trucks to be lowered vertically to Calstock Quay, 112ft below the rail level of the viaduct; powered by a stationary engine, it could raise or lower one 20-ton truck at a time. Despite its design, the wagon lift seemed an unnecessary extravagance as the new route to Bere Alston was intended to encourage through traffic and, as per expectations, the traffic handled at Calstock Quay decreased significantly. It remains unconfirmed when the wagon lift was last used but it was not dismantled until 1934.

The new standard gauge single-track branch between Bere Alston and Callington opened for traffic on 2 March 1908. It operated as the Bere Alston & Calstock Light Railway although it was managed and worked by the PD&SWJR. The route started at Bere Alston, where branch trains used the outer face of the up platform. There were intermediate stopping places at Calstock (1¾ miles), Gunnislake (4½ miles), Chilsworthy (5½ miles), Latchley (6½ miles) and Luckett (7¾ miles) before the terminus at Callington was reached. In March 1910, an additional stopping place, Seven Stones halt, was opened between Latchley and Luckett, primarily to serve workers at the nearby Phoenix mines, but it closed in September 1917. Of the intermediate stations, the only one with passing facilities was Gunnislake which, interestingly, had an island platform. The stations at Luckett and Callington were originally entitled Stoke Climsland

35

and Callington Road respectively but, among the real locals, the latter was always referred to as Kelly Bray.

For the opening of the Bere Alston & Calstock Light Railway, the PD&SWJR could boast five locomotives, all of which lived at the twin-road shed at Callington. Nos 1 and 2 were the 3ft 6in gauge Nielson 0-4-0STs which had been inherited from the East Cornwall Mineral Railway; the former was soon sold in its original form but the latter was rebuilt as a standard gauge 0-4-2ST. It worked on pilot duties at Callington but failed to impress, and was sold in 1912 to the Selsey Tramway (later known as the West Sussex Railway), one of the 'Colonel Stephens' lines, where it survived until 1927.

The three other locomotives were purchased new from Hawthorn Leslie and over the years it has often been remarked that their general design seemed to have influenced Lt-Col Stephens on the odd occasions when he lashed out on new locomotives. One was 0-6-0T No 3 *A. S. Harris*, which was designated the freight locomotive; it had 3ft 10in diameter wheels, outside cylinders of 14in x 22in and weighed 35tons 3cwt. The other two, No 4 *Earl of Mount*

Edgcumbe and No 5 *Lord St Levan*, were 0-6-2Ts with 4ft diameter driving wheels, outside cylinders of 16in x 24in and weights of 49tons 19cwt. They were earmarked for passenger duties. All three were finished in a dark blue livery with brass trimmings but, in 1914/15, they succumbed to green plumages. The three locomotives proved very capable performers, but when GWR '850' and '2021' class 0-6-0PTs had to be hired to assist during World War 1, local crews became very impressed with the Swindon steeds. Other locomotives which had brief spells on the line during the war failed to create the same enthusiasm; they included an ex-LB&SCR 'Terrier' 0-6-0T and an L&SWR 'O2' class 0-4-4T. None of those incomers did especially well on the ferociously-graded line, which at its steepest, reached 1 in 33.

With the continuing decline of the mining industry in east Cornwall, the branch came to rely on passenger traffic. Trade was not at all bad, and by the summer of 1922 it warranted five passenger services each way on Mondays to Fridays and an additional one on Saturdays; the journey times were around 40min. The coaching stock came from that ever reliable source, the North London Railway.

At the Grouping, the Bere Alston & Calstock Light Railway and its parent, the PD&SWJR, passed to the Southern Railway, the three remaining locomotives becoming SR Nos 756 (0-6-0T No3) and 757/58

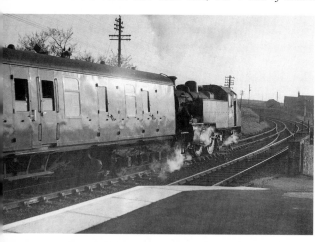

Left: **Bere Alston station was the point at which the Callington branch joined the main Okehampton-Plymouth line. In the late afternoon of 28 April 1962, ex-LMSR '2MT' No 41214 leaves Bere Alston with a Plymouth train.** Brian Haresnape

Below: **The Bere Alston-Gunnislake section of the Callington branch retained its passenger services and must now rate as one of the most scenic routes in Southern England. On 20 April 1993, DMU No 150239 crosses Calstock Viaduct with the 13.45 ex-Plymouth.** Paul Burkhalter

SECTION OF LINE.		Vehicle Limit.	MAXIMUM LOAD INCLUSIVE OF BRAKE VAN.				
From	To		E.757 and E.758.	E.029, E.083, E.0101, E.0496, E.0506, E.0509, E.0515.	E.0153, E.0154, E.0155, E.0162, E.0163, E.0167, E.0397, E.0400, E.0433, E.0436, E.0439, E.0440, E.0441, E.0442.	E.557–E.596 inc. E.657–E.666 inc.	E.050, E.054, E.0125 E.0147, E.0169, E.0298, E.0329, E.0460–E.0464 inc., E.0466–E.0478 inc., E.0486, E.0490, E.0517, E.0519– E.0520 inc., E.0522, E.177–E.187 inc., E.189, E.191–E.204 inc., E.207, E.208, E.212, E.213, E.214, E.216–E.236 inc., E.526, E.735, E.756.
					Equivalent to Loaded Goods.		
Bere Alston	Calstock	30	20	20	20	20	12
Calstock	Gunnislake	21	14	12	11	11	10
Gunnislake	Hingston Down	27	18	18	18	15	12
Hingston Down	Callington	45	30	30	30	25	18
Callington	Calstock	30	20	20	20	20	12
Calstock	Bere Alston	21	14	12	11	11	10

Table 63 — BERE ALSTON and CALLINGTON

Down — Week Days — Sundays

Miles	Down													
		50 London (W.) dep	Bere Alston...dep	Calstock	Gunnislake	Chilsworthy	Latchley	Luckett	Callington C.. arr					

Up — Week Days — Sundays

Miles	Up						
	Callington ...dep	Luckett	Latchley	Chilsworthy	Gunnislake	Calstock	Bere Alston....arr
	50 London (W.)....arr						

C Station for Stoke Climsland (1 mile) Omnibus Services, operated by the Western National Omnibus Company, run between Callington Station and Callington Village, also Callington Station and Stoke Climsland. H Saturday mornings only. Runs until 23rd August only. J Dep. 8 45 a.m. on Saturdays.
K Saturdays only. Arr. 1 37 p.m. Mondays and Fridays, commencing 25th July. L Arr. 3 53 p.m. on Saturdays SO or S Saturdays only. SX Saturdays excepted.
T Morning time. H 4 minutes later on Saturdays. Y 7 minutes later on Saturdays. Z Wednesdays, Thursdays, and Saturdays.
Z Until 7th September passengers can dep. 12 0 noon by the Devon Belle. 1st and 3rd class Pullman Cars. Limited bookings. Extra charge.
§ Fridays only. Devon Belle. 1st and 3rd class Pullman Car. Limited bookings. Extra charge

(0-6-2Ts Nos 4/5). In 1931, 0-6-0T No 756 *A.S.Harris* was sent to Eastleigh for a major overhaul but, instead of returning to home territory, went on to do the rounds of various SR sheds, never to see Devon or Cornwall again. The 0-6-2Ts remained loyal to the Callington branch where they were helped out by an 'O2' class 0-4-4T and, very occasionally, a '0395' class 0-6-0. During the 1920s and 1930s, the mineral traffic carried on the branch became negligible, but an increase in market gardening in the area resulted in a steady flow of produce from Calstock and Gunnislake stations.

After the birth of British Railways in 1948, the two ex-PD&SWJR 0-6-2Ts duly became Nos 30757/58, but in September 1952 ex-LMS '2MT' 2-6-2Ts Nos 41313/15 were transferred to the Callington branch, which in 1950 had passed from the Southern to the Western Region. Consequently, there was little left for the 0-6-2Ts to do and they spent their time in and out of storage at Friary shed in Plymouth before being dispatched to Eastleigh in 1956 for works shunting duties. They did not last long, No 30758 *Lord St Levan* being condemned in December 1956 and No 30757 *Earl of Mount Edgcumbe* being withdrawn one year later. Their one-time chum, 0-6-0T No 30756 *A. S. Harris,* had been retired in October 1951.

During the late 1950s, the passenger traffic on the line was not as sparse as that of many other country branches, and this was partly due to the lack of good roads in south-east Cornwall. In those years, the '2MT' 2-6-2Ts maintained a near monopoly of the Callington turns, although an 'O2' 0-4-4T substituted when necessary. The rolling stock of that period invariably comprised a pair of ex-Turnchapel branch push-pull sets and a former-L&SWR railmotor set.

The branch ran out of steam in 1964 when, as a part of the Western Region's scheme to dieselise everything west of Exeter, DMUs were introduced on the line. This resulted in the closure of the engine shed at Callington. On 5 November 1966 all services were withdrawn from the Gunnislake-Callington section, but happily the remainder of the branch was left untouched, and today a regular service of '150' class DMUs and, sometimes, single cars still operates between Plymouth and Gunnislake. Things might have turned out even better, as in 1980 the Plym Valley Railway, a Plymouth-based preservation group, approached British Rail to enquire about operating steam-hauled trains on the branch on Sundays. Sadly, BR was not interested.

Top: **The loading limits for the Callington branch, as detailed in the SR working timetable for July 1932.**

Above: **Southern Region public timetable, 30 June to 14 September 1952.** Author's files

10 Bideford, Westward Ho! & Appledore Railway

The BWH&AR in North Devon is one of the most unsung of all the little railways in Britain, and this must be due, at least in part, to the fact that the line operated for less than 16 years, during which time it had no physical connection to any other railway. The line's claim for inclusion in a book about light railways might be considered contentious as the original section of the BWH&AR, that between Bideford Quay and Northam, was authorised by an Act of Parliament. However, the extension from Northam to Appledore was the consequence of a Light Railway Order and, furthermore, the Order enabled the original part to be officially worked as a light railway.

The community of Westward Ho! was named after Charles Kingsley's famous novel, partly to help the area's promotion as a holiday resort. A few schemes were proposed for railways in or through the area, some of which used the London & South Western's station at East-the-Water in Bideford as a starting point, but the major obstacle they faced was crossing the River Torridge at Bideford. The scheme which eventually succeeded circumvented the problem of the river crossing by starting its railway west of the Torridge, thereby having no physical connection whatsoever with the outside world.

Construction of the BWH&AR commenced in 1898. In the best traditions of Victorian railway engineering, the contractors defaulted and the bill increased beyond even the most pessimistic estimates. Nevertheless, the section between Bideford Quay and

Above: **The opening of the Bideford, Westward Ho! & Appledore Railway took place on 24 April 1901, but it cannot be determined which of the company's three locomotives appears in this opening day picture. Points of interest include the original locomotive livery, the side-plates and central buffer, and the pair of 48ft composite coaches.** Chris Leigh Collection

Northam opened on 24 April 1901, by which time the company had become a subsidiary of the British Electric Traction Group. It has been suggested that the BET take-over was merely to defend its own plans for the Western Counties Light Railway, an electric tramway between Bideford and Hartland, but the BWH&AR did not have serious plans to extend to Hartland and, in the event, the BET tramway was never constructed. As things turned out, the BET's take-over had no outward effect on the day to day business of the BWH&AR.

The BWH&AR's standard gauge 5½-mile line started at Bideford Quay where, much to the chagrin of the town council, the rails were laid into the road in true tramway fashion. For a time, the BWH&AR and the council grudgingly learned to live with each other, but when the railway company laid a much-needed run-round loop at the Quay, the council promptly demanded its removal. With corporate sulks, the BWH&AR complied but this set the trend for an uneasy relationship between the two parties. On one occasion, the council fined the railway company 40 shillings (£2) for contravening the bye-law governing the maximum time a locomotive could remain on the Quay.

Between Bideford Quay and Northam, there were stopping places at Strand Road (also known as The Yard), Causeway Crossing, Kenwith Castle, Abbotsham Road, Cornborough Cliffs and Westward Ho!. Of these, only the last-named had any sort of facilities, the others being halts. Apart from the necesary crossing loop, Westward Ho! station had a goods shed and a siding to the gasworks; the station buildings were surprisingly substantial, and there was a small concert hall in which passengers were entertained by a troupe of blacked-up minstrels. The BWH&AR's accounts for the second half of 1906 show a payment of £17/9/7d (£17.48p) *'for services of minstrels'*.

Despite being entitled the Bideford, Westward Ho! & Appledore Railway, a few years elapsed before anything positive was done to reach the town of Appledore. However, the extension was eventually authorised under a Light Railway Order and was opened for traffic on 1 May 1908, thereby completing the 7½ -mile run from Bideford; the only intermediate halts on the extension were at Richmond Road and Lovers Lane. Under the Order the original section was also 'downgraded' to the status of a light railway, thereby enabling the removal of gates at five level crossings.

Journey times between Bideford and Appledore were usually around 30min, the normal third-class fare in 1910 being 8d (3½p) although special fares of 6d (2½p) were available on market days. Two-coach trains were operated during the summer season, but the peak season was all too brief in North Devon and so one-coach trains were the norm for most of the year. It was often remarked that the BWH&A's staff of 28-30 men invariably outnumbered the total loading of two or three off-peak trains. The passenger service, which had usually comprised some 15 trains

each way before 1908, was later reduced to a maximum of seven. Freight made a negligible contribution, as illustrated by the company's mileage figures for the second half of 1906. During that six-month period the total passenger mileage was 22,310, but the figure for mixed trains was just 85 miles. The fleet of under-used goods wagons comprised six open trucks, four vans and a brake. The passenger rolling stock consisted of six bogie carriages which had American-style open platforms at each end; the exteriors were of polished teak and the interiors of mahogany and teak.

The BWH&AR had three locomotives, all bought new from the Hunslet Engine Co of Leeds in 1900. They were 2-4-2Ts which had 3ft 3in diameter driving wheels, 12in x 18in outside cylinders and 140lb boilers; each locomotive weighed 27 tons. Their nominal tractive effort at 75% was 6,978lb, and this restricted them to loadings of 95 tons on the 1 in 47 gradient between Kenwith and Abbotsham. The locomotives carried Works Nos 713/14/15 and became, respectively, No 1 *Grenville*, No 2 *Kingsley* and No 3 *Torridge*. They were finished in a smart livery of green and black with white lining although in later years the lining was dispensed with.

Because the locomotives worked over the roadway at Bideford Quay, they were fitted with side plates to cover the wheels, and cow-catchers were later added below the front buffer beams. In common with the rolling stock, the locomotives were each fitted with a single central buffer at each end, and while this was not unknown on narrow gauge lines, it is believed that the BWH&AR was the only British standard gauge company to incorporate this feature. The com-

Below: **Mixed trains were the norm on the BWH&AR, but few such workings were ever photographed. This very early picture seems to be of locomotive No 1 *Grenville*.** Ian Allan Library

pany had no turntables, and so when the locomotives were delivered, one was placed on the tracks facing Bideford and the other two faced Westward Ho!. They were to spend the rest of their working days in North Devon facing the same respective directions.

Virtually from the start, the BWH&AR's traffic figures had been far from healthy. The line's isolation had not helped matters as, although the company later operated a bus service between Bideford Quay and the L&SWR station at East-the-Water, the L&SWR's own buses offered a service direct to Westward Ho!, thereby relieving passengers of a second change of transport. Furthermore, the BWH&AR's bus service was rather self-defeating, as it accounted for the company's second highest item of annual expenditure. Closure became inevitable, and the last trains ran on 27 March 1917. The line's final demise had been hastened by the war effort, the rails having been requisitioned by the Government. The three locomotives were removed on 29 July by means of a temporary track which was laid across Bideford Bridge to provide a connection with the L&SWR.

The subsequent adventures of the locomotives remain unconfirmed, although it is known that No 2 *Kingsley* later turned up at the Ministry of Munitions in Avonmouth, near Bristol, the site of which later became part of the National Smelting Co. The NSC's records show that *Kingsley* was used as a works shunter until being scrapped in 1937. As for Nos 1 and 3, it seems that they eventually found their way to the Min-

istry of Munitions site at Pembrey in South Wales, but further details are uncertain. There is a story that all three were dispatched by sea from Avonmouth for war duties abroad and their ship was sunk off the Cornish coast, but that version has been debunked by many, including the line's respected historian, Chris Leigh, who has conducted extensive research into the subject. The remaining assets of the BWH&AR were auctioned in 1921, and the Saxby & Farmer signalling equipment was purchased by a certain Lt-Col Stephens for use on the Weston, Clevedon & Portishead Light Railway in Somerset.

And so the Bideford, Westward Ho! & Appledore Railway, the only railway company in the land to include an exclamation mark in its title, came to an irreversible end. The original section of line, that between Bideford and Northam, had had a life-span of only 16 years, but the extension from Northam to Appledore had survived for just nine years.

Above: **This early-1900s picture shows a two-coach train waiting on the loop at Bideford Quay.**
Chris Leigh Collection

Left: **A comprehensive listing of who owned what, and how it was worked, appeared in Bradshaw's Shareholders' Guide. This extract is from the 1915 edition.**
Author's files

BIDEFORD, WESTWARD HO! AND APPLEDORE.

DIRECTORS:

Chairman—C. H. DADE, Esq., Electrical Federation Offices, Kingsway, London, W.C.

H. S. Day, Esq., Electrical Federation Offices, Kingsway, London, W.C. | H. C. Whitehead, Esq., 1, Kingsway, London, W.C.

OFFICERS.—Sec., S. M. Wright; Man., H. Sowden; Acct., H. W. Davis; Auditors, Dixon, Wilson, Tubbs. and Co.; Solicitors, S. Morse, London, and Flinch and Chanter, Barnstaple; Registrar, F. C. Cocking.

Head Offices—1, Kingsway, London, W.C.

Local Offices—20, Quay, Bideford, North Devon.

Incorporated by act of 21st May, 1896, for constructing three railways in the county of Devon—No. 1, a railway or tramway, 1 furlong 9 chains 50 links in length, in the parish of Bideford; No. 2, from termination of No. 1 to Westward Ho! length, 4 miles 3 furlongs 9 chains 50 links; No. 3, from termination of No. 2 to Appledore, length, 2 miles 3 furlongs 4·20 chains. Period for completion of works, 5 years. The line was only constructed as far as the golf links below Northam, but fresh powers to construct the remaining portion were obtained, and the line is now constructed as far as Appledore, the authorised terminus. Capital, 80,000*l*. in 10*l*. shares, with power to divide into preferred and deferred half-shares. Borrowing powers, 14,166*l*. The whole system is being worked as a Light Railway.

REVENUE.—For the year ended 31st December, 1913, the total revenue was 2,070*l*. Deficit, 776*l*. for year.

Capital expenditure to 31st December, 1913, 85,478*l*.

No. of Directors.—Maximum, 4; minimum, 2; quorum, 2. *Qualification,* 25 shares.

11 Brackenhill Light Railway

This little-known railway was promoted in 1899 by the Yorkshire District Light Railway Syndicate of Leeds, a consortium of businessmen fronted by Sebastian Meyer. Meyer was also the secretary of the then-uncompleted Dearne Valley Railway and, although it has been suggested that he was the Yorkshire equivalent of Holman Stephens, Meyer's railway activities usually concentrated on lines which served heavy industry rather than the rural passenger branches normally associated with Stephens.

After a revision of the original plans, the Order for the Brackenhill Light Railway was granted on 19 March 1901, but it was 1 July 1914 before the line was officially opened for business. The BLR consisted of a three-mile line from Brackenhill Junction, which was south of Ackworth station on the Swinton & Knottingley Joint Railway's line between Pontefract (Baghill) and Swinton, to Hemsworth colliery. There was also a ¼-mile spur to Ackworth Moor Top, where a freight depot was established primarily for the traffic from Camplin's Quarries.

The North Eastern Railway, which with the Midland Railway was the joint proprietor of the Swinton & Knottingley Railway, needed to avoid binding itself legally to a working agreement. Therefore, although the NER worked the line from the outset, the BLR retained theoretical responsibility for its own motive power despite the handicap of not possessing any locomotives. The NER serviced the BLR from Selby shed, and the line was usually included in the diagrams of the pick-up goods workings to Gascoigne Wood, some of the marshalling being undertaken at Pontefract. It is known that authorisation was granted for the operation of 'Paddy Trains' (the Yorkshire terminology for miners' trains) from Pontefract to Hemsworth Colliery via the BLR, but there are no records of such workings ever having been made. It seems, however, that 'Paddys' to Hemsworth Colliery were operated from Doncaster; a local newspaper report of 1920 announced that weekly miners' fares from Doncaster to Hemsworth were to be increased to 6s/10d (34p), but it is believed that those services ran, not via the BLR, but to Fitzwilliam station on the Doncaster-Wakefield main line.

The locomotives used on the BLR were, for many years, Selby-based 'Q5' and, later, 'Q6' 0-8-0s. At the time of the Grouping in 1923, Selby had two of the former and 14 of the latter on its allocation list. The 'Q7s', which were introduced in 1919/24, were authorised for the BLR, despite their 19 ton axle weights, but it remains unrecorded whether any members of the class ever ventured on to the line.

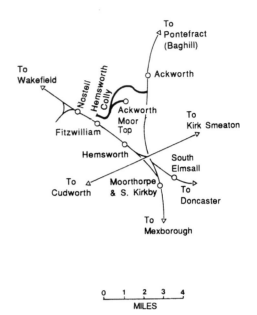

With the closure of Selby shed in 1959, York depot took over the responsibility for working the BLR, and it became not uncommon to see 'B16' 4-6-0s and 'WD' 2-8-0s handling the trains from Hemsworth Colliery.

As already stated, Brackenhill Junction was to the south of Ackworth station on the Pontefract-Swinton main line. In the early 1900s, Ackworth featured in two other light railway schemes. One was the 54-mile Ackworth & Lindsey Light Railway, promoted in 1904 to provide a line via Kirk Smeaton to Killingholme, where the new Immingham Dock was about to be constructed. That scheme soon fell by the wayside, but in 1905 a revised proposal, under the title of the Ackworth Light Railway, surfaced with plans for a line from Ackworth to Shaftholme Junction, to the north of Doncaster on the West Riding & Grimsby Railway's line. Despite being granted a Light Railway Order in 1907, the Ackworth Light Railway passed into oblivion without having cut its first sod. As for the Brackenhill Light Railway itself, it continued its low-profile existence until being officially closed from 1 January 1962, the goods depot at Ackworth Moor Top having been relegated to the status of a public delivery siding on 15 September 1958.

41

12 Burry Port & Gwendraeth Valley Railway

The forerunner of the Burry Port & Gwendraeth Valley Railway was Kymer's Canal, which opened circa 1769 with the distinction of being the first canal in Wales to have obtained the necessary Act of Parliament. It provided a connection between the quay a Kidwelly and Pwllyllgoed, near Carway, serving limestone quarries and anthracite collieries along its route. Kymer's Canal was superseded by the Kidwelly & Llanelly Canal, the first sections of which opened in 1824 although the ultimate target, Cwm Mawr, was not reached until 1837. However, the problem of extensive silting at Kidwelly had already prompted thoughts of developing a harbour at Pembrey as an alternative outlet, and the Pembrey Harbour Company (later to become the Burry Port Company) was incorporated in 1825 with powers to construct tramroads connecting with the canal system.

In the mid-1860s, a rival scheme for a railway in the Gwendraeth Valley encouraged the conversion of the Kidwelly & Llanelly Canal and its tramroads to a fully- fledged railway. Consequently, the corporate title was changed in 1866 to that of the Kidwelly & Burry Port Railway and, the following year, a further change of identity resulted in the birth of the Burry Port & Gwendraeth Valley Railway.

The BP&GVR's 'main line' followed the route of the old canal along the valley of the Gwendraeth Fawr. For most of its length, the railway was laid on the towpath, but it was necessary to use the old canal bed at points where bridges and aqueducts passed overhead. Because of the less-than-perfect drainage of the old canal bed, flooding of some sections of the line was far from uncommon. Two overbridges had 'depth of water' markers on their walls, the working instructions of the 1950s stating firmly that, when the water reached a level of 1ft 5in above the rails services were to be suspended. The section between Burry Port and Pontyberem was opened in July 1869, but Cwm Mawr was not reached until June 1886. One branch ran from Trimsaran Road to Kidwelly (opened 1873), and another from Burry Port to Llanelly (opened 1891) to connect with the Llanelly & Mynydd Mawr Railway at Sandy Gate Junction. Only freight traffic was accommodated.

Below: **Some of the pre-Grouping GWR four-wheeled coaches were still in use on the BP&GVR line until the cessation of passenger services in 1953. This picture, taken at Burry Port (ex-BP&GVR) station on 7 July 1947, shows '1901' class 0-6-0PT No 1967 resting with its assortment of carriages.** H C. Casserley

Above: **The passenger terminus of the BP&GVR at Cwm Mawr was clearly in need of some tender loving care when this picture was taken on 7 July 1947. The locomotives are '1901' class 0-6-0PTs No 1957 (left) and No 1967 (right), the latter being at the head of the 3.20pm to Burry Port. Although 13 of the 15 ex-BP&GVR locomotives were still in action when this picture was taken, standard GWR 0-6-0PTs were favoured for the infrequent passenger services.**
H. C. Casserley

The BP&GVR's first locomotives were two 0-4-0STs, built by Henry Hughes & Co of Loughborough for the contractors engaged on laying the line. One is believed to have survived until the turn of the century. The company's next locomotive was a Fairlie 0-4-4-0T which had been constructed in 1870 for a Swedish company but was sold, instead, to the BP&GVR; its original name of *Pioneer* was soon replaced by *Mountaineer*. A second Fairlie locomotive, this time an 0-6-6-0T named *Victoria*, arrived on the BP&GVR in 1873 after having seen a fair bit of the globe in its short life. It had been built in 1866 for a 3ft 6in gauge line in Australia, but had been returned to the manufacturer and regauged for resale to a company in Uruguay. The first Fairlie, 0-4-4-0T *Mountaineer*, lasted until 1891 while the second, 0-6-6-0T *Victoria*, was rebuilt in 1896 and survived for a further seven years.

A secondhand Manning Wardle 'M' class 0-6-0ST was purchased for £650 in 1886 and named *Burry Port*, a Peckett 'X' class 0-6-0ST named *Dyvatty* was purchased new in 1892, and another secondhand Manning Wardle 'M' class 0-6-0ST (subsequently named *Cwm Mawr*) was purchased in 1894. The last-named was later used on Weston, Clevedon & Portishead Light Railway (qv). In 1899, a numbering scheme was introduced despite the fact that the

BP&GVR had only six locomotives, all of which were named. Unfortunately, the sparsity of official records defies any attempt to give a definitive list of the original numbers.

The cost of £33,000 for the conversion of the canal system to a railway was an awful lot for the BP&GVR to recoup and, consequently, the company struggled. The failure in 1880 of one of the company's principal customers, the Pontyberem Colliery Co, was a major catastrophe, and in the following year the BP&GVR was placed under control of a Receiver. Nevertheless, the BP&GVR continued to operate and, furthermore, also worked its tiny neighbour, the Gwendraeth Valley Railway, under the terms of an arrangement of 1876. That working agreement, usually serviced by the GVR's own Fox Walker 0-6-0ST *Kidwelly*, was to last until 1905.

An upturn in trade, the fruits of various economies, and a restructuring of corporate finances enabled the BP&GVR to be discharged from receivership in 1898. That same year, workmen's trains were introduced for the benefit of colliery company employees, the colliery companies themselves purchasing the carriages and, furthermore, paying the BP&GVR £2/10s/0d (£2.50p) per coach per week for haulage services. It seems that the years of financial hardship had taught the BP&GVR something about having a cake and eating it. It became common, albeit highly illegal, practice for miners' families and friends to use the trains, and that was brought to the attention of the Board of Trade in 1903 when an investigation was required after a collision between a light engine and an alleged workmen's train. The BP&GVR was given a severe rap over its corporate knuckles, but the episode prompted thoughts of upgrading the line for legitimate use by the public. Consequently, an application was made for a Light Railway Order, and this was granted in June 1909.

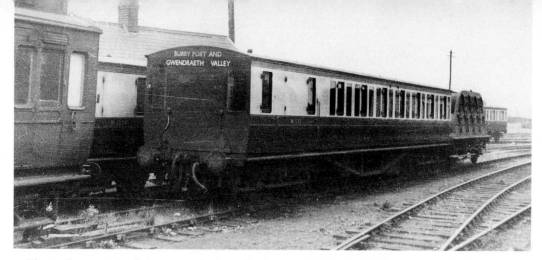

Above: **The intended use of the 'cut-down' brake third, No W1323, is clearly evident in this picture which was taken at Burry Port in May 1951. The carriage, built in 1939, is known to have survived until at least 1963, 10 years after passenger services ceased on the old BP&GVR line.** H. C. Casserley

The engineer appointed to oversee the upgrading was Holman Frederick (later Lt-Col) Stephens. The Burry Port-Pontyberem section required relaying with 75lb rails and relatively minor realignments to obviate some of the tightest curves, and was opened to public passenger traffic as early as 2 August 1909. The Pontyberem-Cwm Mawr section, however, required a completely new alignment to circumvent the 1 in 32 climb on the original route, and was not ready for opening until 29 January 1913.

The line started at Burry Port station which was just on the south side of, but unconnected to, the GWR's station on South Wales main line. From Burry Port, the stopping places were Pembrey halt (1½ miles), Pinged halt (3 miles), Trimsaran Road (5 miles), Pontnewydd halt...renamed Glyn Abbey in 1910 (6 miles), Pontyates (8 miles), Ponthenry (9 miles), Pontyberem (11 miles) and Cwm Mawr (13

miles). Craiglon Bridge Halt (2½ miles) was added after the Grouping. The standard facilities on the stations were spartan buildings clad in corrugated-iron, but most stations were lit by electricity supplied by the nearest colliery. Unadvertised stopping places for miners' trains were at Carway, Ponthenry and Glynhebog Collieries, and at Trimsaran Junction. Additional miners' platforms were later provided at Pentremawr in 1913 and Ty Coch (on the Kidwelly line) in 1927. Initially, the single-track line was devoid of

Locomotives of the Burry Port & Gwendraeth Valley Railway taken over by the GWR

(Dimensions are those shown by the GWR after the Grouping)

BPGV No	GWR No	Name	Type	Maker	Date	Wheels	Cyls	Weight	T/effort	Wdn
1	2192	Ashburnham	0-6-0ST	C/Furneaux	1900	3ft 8in	16in x 24in (o)	42ft 13c	16,620lb	4/51
2	2162		0-6-0T	H/Clarke	1914	3ft 9in	15in x 22in (o)	36t 8c	14,960lb	3/55
3	2193	Burry Port	0-6-0ST	C/Furneaux	1901	3ft 6in	15in x 22in (o)	35t 12c	14,025lb	2/52
4	2194	Kidwelly	0-6-0ST	Avonside	1903	3ft 6in	15in x 20in (o)	32t 1c	13,660lb	2/53
5	2195	Cwr Mawr*	0-6-0ST	Avonside	1905	3ft 6in	15in x 20in (o)	32t 1c	13,660lb	1/53
6	2196	Gwendraeth	0-6 0ST	Avonside	1906	3ft 6½in	15in x 22in (o)	38t 0c	16,830lb	1/56
7	2176	Pembrey*	0-6-0ST	Avonside	1907	3ft 6½in	15in x 22in (o)	38t 0c	16,830lb	3/55
8	2197	Pioneer	0-6-0T	H/Clarke	1909	3ft 9in	15in x 22in (o)	36t 8c	14,960lb	10/52
9	2163		0-6-0T	H/Clarke	1909	3ft 9in	16in x 24in (o)	42t 8c	18,570lb	4/44
10	2198		0-6-0T	H/Clarke	1910	3ft 9in	16in x 24in (o)	37t 11c	15,430lb	3/59
11	2164		0-6-0T	H/Clarke	1912	3ft 9in	16in x 24in (o)	44t 0c	18,570lb	2/29
12	2165		0-6-0T	H/Clarke	1913	3ft 9in	16in x 24in (o)	44t 0c	18,570lb	3/55
13	2166		0-6-0T	H/Clarke	1916	3ft 9in	16in x 24in (o)	44t 0c	18,570lb	5/55
14	2167		0-6-0T	H/Clarke	1919	3ft 9in	16in x 24in (o)	44t 0c	18,570lb	2/53
15	2168		0-6-0T	H/Clarke	1920	3ft 9in	16in x 24in (o)	44t 0c	18,570lb	5/56

* Names later removed.

crossing places other than those at stations, but a loop was laid at Ty Mawr, between Burry Port and Trimsaran Junction, in 1914.

By the time of the BP&GVR's upgrading to a light railway, the company's fortunes were very healthy indeed. Within just 10 years of discharge from receivership, the company was paying a dividend of around 10%, and that figure hardly varied for the rest of its independent existence. As for locomotives, seven 0-6-0STs had been purchased new between 1900 and 1907, although one of those was sold for colliery use in 1914. For the introduction of authorised passenger services in 1909, two new 0-6-0Ts were bought from Hudswell Clarke, and seven basically similar engines were purchased between 1910 and 1919.

The company's official locomotive livery was lined green, but the Avonside 0-6-0STs retained dark green liveries while at least two of the BP&GVR's locomotives were later finished in Midland-style red. The company's only engine shed was the three-road timber-built structure between the station and the dock at Burry Port. The repair shop at the shed could carry out all but the heaviest work, and also serviced machinery for local colliery companies and the adjacent dock. For the BP&GVR's own passenger services, 10 non-bogie eight-wheeled coaches were purchased from the Metropolitan Railway in 1909, 20 further coaches being bought between 1910 and 1920, some of the Metropolitan and others from the North London and the London & South Western Railways. The accommodation comprised only third class 'workmen's'.

At the Grouping, the BP&GVR became part of the GWR, the official date of absorption being 1 July 1922. At that time, freight traffic was such that trains of up to 60 wagons were operated, some colliery shunting having to be undertaken double-headed. Advertised passenger services on the line usually consisted of three or four trains each way on weekdays, there being no Sunday service. After the Grouping, the GWR drafted in some '850' class 0-6-0PTs and quickly replaced the old BP&GVR carriages with four-wheeled vehicles. The choice of elderly carriages was not intended as a slight on the old BP&GVR, but was necessitated by the restricted height of the underbridges on the line. The veteran GWR carriages conformed to the lower BP&GVR loading gauge which, for most of the line's subsequent life, prevented the use of most types of standard locomotives and rolling stock. The gauge was 11ft 6in in height at the centre of the rails, 10ft 9in at the side of the rails and 9ft in width. When, in 1939, the old four-wheeled carriages needed replacing, the GWR provided six bogie brake thirds similar to standard 'B' sets but with the obligatory lower-profile roofs. Nevertheless, four-wheeled stock was not completely dispensed with, and some clung on until the cessation of passenger services in 1953.

The dock at Burry Port had been owned by the BP&GVR and, therefore, became GWR property after the Grouping. However, much of the dock's trade soon dwindled, and after the General Strike of

Below: **One of the BP&GVR's sturdy-looking Hudswell Clarke 0-6-0Ts, formerly No 12, is seen as GWR No 2165 at Burry Port shed in April 1953.**
Rail Archive Stephenson

1926, the dock was more or less abandoned. Passenger traffic on the old BP&GVR also declined, the familiar story of motorbus competition having a similar effect on the line's receipts as that experienced by many other little railways throughout Britain.

At the time of Nationalisation, around 36,000 passengers used the line annually...a drop of almost 50,000 since 1938 alone. Nevertheless, the public timetables showed three down and five up trains on weekdays, with one additional train in the up direction and two down on Saturdays. Journey times for the 13-mile trip were around 45min. The freight traffic was, however, quite healthy, some 250,000 tons of open-cast coal being transported each year. The inevitable economy was the withdrawal of passenger services, that taking place on 21 September 1953.

During the early 1950s, inroads were made into the stud of ex-BP&GVR locomotives, all but two of the 15 inherited by the GWR at the Grouping having survived until Nationalisation. Throughout their lives, most of the former BP&GVR engines remained on, or very close to, home territory. The GWR's '16XX' class 0-6-0PTs, which had first appeared in 1949, were the obvious replacements because of their lower

heights, the problem of the low bridges on the line still not having been circumvented in BR days. After the demise of steam traction, the line was worked by pairs of Class 03 and, later, Class 08 diesels, with their roofs cut down to conform with the loading gauge.

The eternal problem of restricted clearances on the line was one of the factors behind the decision to close, on 17 September 1983, the section between Burry Port and Kidwelly Junction. However, rail access was still needed at Coed Bach Washery (almost adjacent to Kidwelly Junction), as well as Cwm Mawr, and so BR decided to relay the Kidwelly-Coed Bach section (which had been lifted in 1960) thereby giving access to the washery, and through to Cwm Mawr, from the west. This also enabled breakdown trains to gain access to the upper reaches of the line without having to worry about restricted clearances.

Today, the Cwm-Mawr-Coed Bach section is worked by three Class 08 diesels, Nos 08993 *Ashburnham*, 08994 *Gwendraeth* and 08995 *Kidwelly*, wih Class 37s hauling trains from Coed Bach washery to destinations including Swansea Docks, Immingham and Seaforth.

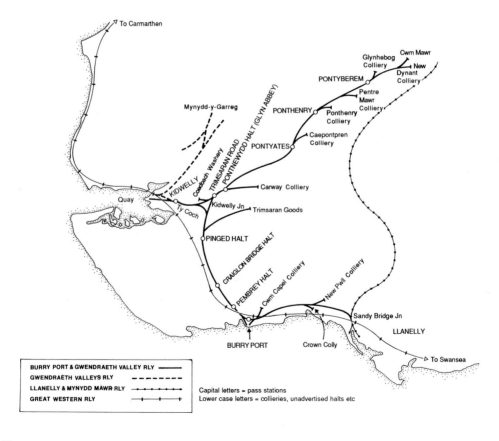

BURRY PORT & GWENDRAETH VALLEY RLY ———
GWENDRAETH VALLEYS RLY – – – – –
LLANELLY & MYNYDD MAWR RLY —•—•—•—•—
GREAT WESTERN RLY —+—+—+—

Capital letters = pass stations
Lower case letters = collieries, unadvertised halts etc

13 Cairn Valley Light Railway

Four schemes of the 1860s planned to provide the village of Moniaive, north-west of Dumfries, with a rail connection. Two of those schemes proposed a connection with the Dumfries-Glasgow line at Thornhill, another aimed to make a connection with the main line at Auldgirth, and the fourth homed in on Dumfries itself, but none of them came to fruition. With the passing of the Light Railways Act in 1896, two of the schemes were resuscitated, and that which won the day was for a line between Moniaive and Dumfries. The proposal was taken up by the Glasgow & South Western Railway which, in order to take advantage of Light Railway legislation, created the 'subsidary' of the Cairn Valley Light Railway.

The line opened to public traffic on 1 March 1905. From Dumfries, the intermediate stations were Irongray (5 miles), Newtonairds (7½ miles), Stepford (8¾ miles), Dunscore (10¾ miles), Crossford (13¾ miles) and Kirkland (15¼ miles), before the line reached Moniaive (17½ miles). There were passing loops and goods yards at Irongray, Newtonairds and Dunscore, the other intermediate stations having only basic passenger facilities, while at Moniaive there was a run-round loop, freight facilities befitting a small country branch terminus and also a small engine shed at which a Dumfries locomotive was usually out-stationed for a week at a time. One pair of enginemen was assigned to Moniaive.

The inaugural train on the Moniaive branch was hauled by 4-4-0 No 190, a locomotive which had once performed on the Carlisle-Glasgow leg of 'The Diner', the prestige St Pancras-St Enoch express, before being ousted by 4-6-0s and transferred from Corkerhill to Dumfries. After No 190 had attended to the opening duties on the branch, services were subsequently taken care of by steam railmotor No 1 and, later, classmate No 3, two of the trio which the G&SWR had built to a James Manson design in 1904/05.

Unlike the other two railmotors, No 3 had been

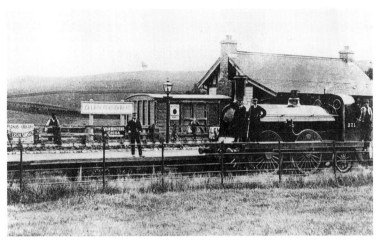

Left: **This picture of Dunscore station can be dated between March 1905 and July 1906 as the line was not opened until the former date and the locomotive, G&SWR Stirling 0-4-2 No 271, was placed on the duplicate list on the latter date.** Lens of Sutton

Below left: **The 'Rood Fair' at Dumfries attracted crowds from the surrounding area and, as can be seen, a nine-coach train was needed on the Cairn Valley line on this particular occasion. The station is Dunscore and the 0-4-4T is an unidentified member of Manson's '266' class.** Lens of Sutton

Above: **Somewhat insultingly for G&SWR traditionalists, ex-Caledonian 'Jumbo' 0-6-0s were used on the Cairn Valley line in later years, No 17452 being in charge of the 3.52pm from Moniaive to Dumfries on 21 June 1937.** H. C. Casserley

built with a separate engine and coach unit, but both sections were close-coupled without buffers between them. The power unit was in the form of a 0-4-0WT, its 'side tanks' being, in fact, coal bunkers; the coach section, which was gas-lit, was 40ft 6in long and accommodated 56 third-class passengers. Railmotor No 3 had been built as an 'articulated' unit to prevent the oscillation from the outside cylinders being transmitted to the coach section, railmotor passengers having previously complained bitterly about the excessive vibration. On the Moniaive branch, the railmotor was later replaced by 0-4-2T No 206A, a locomotive which had started life in 1871 as a tender engine but had been rebuilt to tank form in 1888. As for the railmotors, all three of the G&SWR's machines were withdrawn from service at the end of 1916.

The Moniaive branch was worked on the Sykes non-token system, and this was usually quite secure in view of the light traffic on the line. However, an accident occurred at Irongray on 6 January 1911 when a northbound freight was waiting in the loop to enable a southbound passenger train to cross. Before the passenger train arrived, the station master mistakenly set the points to enable the goods train to leave the loop, the outcome being that the passenger train entered, not the platform road, but the loop in which the freight train was standing. Although several passengers were injured, few of the casualties were serious. The locomotives involved in that accident were Stirling 0-4-2 No 261, which was at the head of the freight, and Manson 0-4-4T No 269 which was operating bunker-first on the passenger service. The 0-4-4T had to undergo repairs, and during its absence Glasgow suburban '326' class 0-4-4T No 332 was drafted to the Moniaive branch. The return of 0-4-4T No 269 to the line was fairly brief as, from about 1912, 0-4-2s took over the majority of the line's duties. Whereas the 0-4-2 involved in the Irongray accident was an unrebuilt Stirling engine, the 0-4-2s which later worked the line were Manson renewals of the Stirling machines, No 232 being one of the Moniaive regulars. In all, 30 0-4-2s had been

renewed between 1901 and 1904, and all later passed to the LMSR to become Nos 17046-75. The last pair, Nos 17066/67, were to survive until 1931.

There is an unconfirmed story that, on one particular Saturday, the crew working the 9pm train from Dumfries to Moniaive were a little 'tired and emotional' after having spent a lively afternoon at the Rood Fair in Dumfries. It seems that the locomotive was as much under the weather as the crew, and a total loss of steam was experienced one-mile short of Moniaive. The passengers were persuaded to walk the rest of the way and, after dropping the fire, the crew followed suit. The following morning, the crewmen crept back to the scene, relit the fire, and brought the engine into Moniaive shed.

The initial passenger service on the branch comprised four trains to Moniaive each weekday and five in the return direction, an additional service each way being provided on Saturdays. Throughout much of the branch's later life, however, the pasenger services comprised just two trains each way on weekdays and three on Saturdays. The majority of freight traffic consisted of livestock, timber from the Craigdarroch estate and road metals from Morrinton quarry near Stepford.

As with so many rural branch lines, passenger traffic declined during the 1920s and 1930s, and as a wartime economy, passenger services were withdrawn on 1 May 1943. Although it was originally intended that the cessation of passenger services would be only temporary, they never resumed. The line remained open for freight only until 4 July 1949, the stone from Morrinton quarry being virtually the sole source of traffic. The last passenger working had been hauled by ex-Caledonian 0-6-0 No 17405, that same engine being a regular performer during the final years of freight-only operation.

14 Campbeltown & Machrihanish Light Railway

Located almost at the very end of the Kintyre peninsula in Argyll, the Campbeltown & Machrihanish was Scotland's only truly independent light railway. It had no connection with the outside world, but that situation did not exist simply out of corporate pride as the nearest mainland railway to the C&MLR was the Caledonian line to Oban which, even at its closest point, was some 90 miles from Campbeltown. There was, admittedly, another railway within 25 crow-miles of the C&MLR, and a narrow gauge one to boot, but that was the Ballycastle section of the Northern Counties Committee, across the North Channel in Ireland.

Even today, the remoteness of the Campbeltown area raises doubts about how it ever supported a railway, and that 'out-of-the-way' atmosphere can be emphasised by a personal note. The author's wife took her driving test in Campbeltown in the 1960s, and even then local tests did not involve all the obstacles they might have done. The nearest traffic lights and pedestrian crossing were in Glasgow...some 140 road miles away.

The reason a railway was needed in such an isolated location was coal. The only workable coal deposits in western Scotland were near Machrihanish, and the nearest useable port was at Campbeltown; coal had been extracted in the area since the late 1400s and, in 1794, a three-mile canal was opened to link the collieries to Campbeltown. The logical successor to the canal was a freight railway and, on 23 May 1877, a 2ft 3in gauge line opened between Campbeltown and the collieries; it was extended to Drumlemble in 1881. The

4¾-mile line was worked by an Andrew Barclay 0-4-0T named *Pioneer*, a second Barclay locomotive, outside-framed 0-4-0ST *Chevalier*, being purchased in 1885; both were later fitted with trailing axles to become 0-4-2STs. A Kerr Stuart 0-4-2T, *Princess,* was acquired in 1900.

In 1901, a consortium of interested parties formed the Argyll Railway Co which took over the Campbeltown Coal Co (which had previously taken over the collieries) and its mineral railway. One of the new concern's plans was to apply for a Light Railway Order for the upgrading and extending of the railway, and the Order was obtained in May 1905. Under its new banner of the Campbeltown & Machrihanish Light Railway, the line reopened, this time for public traffic, on 17 August 1906.

The new line retained the old gauge of 2ft 3in and was single throughout; for most of its length, it was laid with flat-bottomed rails of 50lb/yd. Stretching for just over 6 miles into Machrihanish, it started on the quayside at Hall Street in Campbeltown and then curved inland to pass Limecraigs, where there was a spur leading to a coal depot. The triangle formed by the junction of the spur was used for locomotive turning, and in the triangle were the company's engine and carriage sheds. On the outskirts of Campbeltown, the line

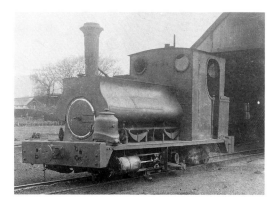

Right: **Despite the absence of a nameplate, the C&MLR's former colliery engine in this picture was officially christened *Chevalier*. It shows off its home-made cab outside Limecraigs shed on 12 May 1925.**
Real Photographs/Ian Allan Library

Below: **A train of Pickering-built coaches is coupled to Barclay 0-6-2T *Argyll* in this undated photograph. The location appears to be Machrihanish.**
Real Photographs/Ian Allan Library

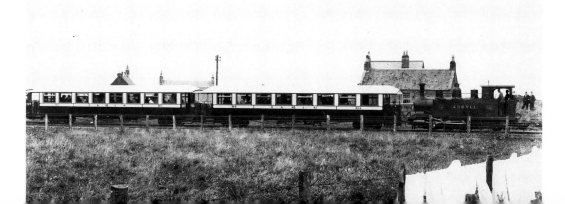

Left: **This, believe it or not, is Machrihanish station soon after the opening of the line to passenger traffic. The locomotive is Barclay 0-6-2T *Argyll*.**
Real Photographs/Ian Allan Library

crossed a ridge by climbing a 1 in 33 gradient, peak season loadings on the trains occasionally being such that the assistance of a banking engine was necessary.

When over the ridge, it was almost level running to Machrihanish. 'Halts' were eventually advertised at Plantation (1¾ miles), Moss Road (2½ miles), Lintmill (2¾ miles), Drumlemble (4½ miles), Machrihanish Farm (5 miles) and Trodigal (5¼ miles), but these were merely points where the line crossed public roads and offered no platforms, let alone facilities. Furthermore, if none of those 'halts' suited the passengers, the trains would usually stop at any other road crossings as required. Along the line, there was a passing loop at Lintmill, which warranted the only signals between the two terminii, and a spur from Machrihanish Farm halt to the Argyll colliery.

The terminus at Machrihanish was, at first, devoid of any creature comforts, but a small waiting room was later provided; the 'station' had a run-round loop, coal stage and water tower. There were 10 level crossings along the route, none of which were gated but, in true light railway fashion, were protected by cattle grids. Apart from minor cuttings and embankments, the only engineering work on the entire line was an over-bridge, the span of which was all of 20ft.

When the railway reopened in 1906, two of the three original locomotives were still in action, the casualty being the oldest of the trio, *Pioneer*, which had been retired in 1900. An additional locomotive was considered essential for the anticipated passenger traffic, and so a vacuum-braked 0-6-2T was ordered from Andrew Barclays. It took the name *Argyll*, and was joined in 1907 by a similar machine which was christened *Atlantic*. The two older engines, *Chevalier* and *Princess*,

were painted in a lined black livery, but the new 0-6-2Ts were finished in the much-debated North British Railway plumage of 'gamboge yellow'. However, it seems that locomotive cleaning was not high on the list of the C&MLR's priorities, and accumulated layers of coal dust later resulted in reports of 'olive green' locomotives. The 0-6-2Ts went on to monopolise the company's passenger duties but, towards the end of the railway's days, the non-vacuum fitted *Chevalier* was occasionally put to use on one-coach trains. In 1926/7, it was extensively rebuilt at Campbeltown shed using parts from the recently-withdrawn *Princess*.

Passenger rolling stock comprised six bogie coaches, all in liveries of olive green and cream. Freight stock consisted of 4-ton coal trucks plus some veteran 2-ton ones inherited from the Campbeltown Coal Co, a milk wagon and a brake van. The locomotives, coaches and wagons were each fitted with a single central buffer.

In the early years of the line, services comprised three trains each way on Mondays to Fridays and six on Saturdays; in that kirk-going part of the world, Sunday services were not even considered. The journey times were usually 30min. Over the years, the services altered and a proliferation of 'Saturdays only' and 'Mondays, Wednesdays and Fridays only' clauses appeared in the timetables. During the 1920s, the services still included a plethora of conditional workings but, on average, there were eight trains each way on most weekdays.

The area was popular among tourists and so there was a marked increase in traffic during the summer months, many of the visitors arriving at Campbeltown by steamer. The sea journey across Kilbrannan Sound was quite often a rough one, and there are countless stories of trippers who arrived at Campbeltown in a similar olive green livery to that of the railway's rolling stock. At Machrihanish, the open coastline was promoted as a tourist attraction and, for the benefit of golf-loving Scots, special tickets were available for visits to the course at Machrihanish. The peak year for the company was 1920, when combined receipts from passenger and freight traffic just exceeded £5,000.

By the mid-1920s, however, motor buses had

Locomotives of the Campbeltown & Machrihanish Light Railway

Name	Type	Maker	Works/No	Built	Wheels	Cylinders	Wdn
Pioneer	0-4-0T*	Barclay		1876	2ft 0in		1900
Chevalier	0-4-0ST*	Barclay	269	1885	2ft 0in	7in x 15in(o)	1931
Princess	0-4-2T	Kerr Stuart	717	1900	2ft 2in	6in x 9in(o)	1926
Argyll	0-6-2T	Barclay	1049	1906	2ft 9in	11½in x 18in(o)	1931
Atlantic	0-6-2T	Barclay	1098	1907	2ft 9in	11½in x 18in(o)	1931

*Converted to 0-4-2T/ST.

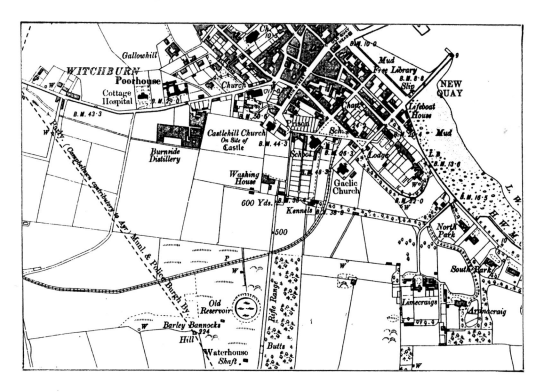

Crown Copyright

		CAMPBELTOWN and MACHRIHANISH LIGHT.													NOTES.
		Week Days only.													
Miles.			c mrn	d	aft	aft		aft	Sats.	aft					
	Campbeltown ¶....dep.	6 0	10 20	1 10	3 0	4 20	....	6 30		9 45	....	....	....	....	¶ "Halts" at Plantation, Moss Road, Lintmill, Drumlemble, Machrihanish Farm, and Trodigal if required.
6	Machrihanish......arr.	6 30	10 50	1 40	3 30	4 50	....	7 0		10 15	....	....	....	....	
Miles.		Week Days only.													
		h mrn	d	aft	aft		aft								
	Machrihanish ¶...dep.	8 10	11 0	2 15	3 45	5 45	....	7 30	....	....	....	....	....	....	
6	Campbeltown .....arr.	8 40	11 30	2 45	4 15	6 15	....	8 0	....	....	....	....	....	....	
		c Does not run when Colliery is idle.			d Does not call at Halts.				h Runs on School Days only.							

started to offer stiff competition for the railway. The railway's crews frequently responded to the competition by racing the buses, and train speeds of up to 40mph (double the legal limit) were far from unknown. Because of the speeds of well-loaded trains, run-throughs happened on several occasions at Campbeltown, more than one stopping precariously close to the wall of the Royal Hotel. Despite the local penchant for treating the rule-book as a work of fiction, serious accidents were mercifully rare.

In the late 1920s, the national recession affected even the Kintyre peninsula. In 1929, Argyll colliery closed and so the railway lost the source of virtually all of its freight traffic. Passenger figures declined as well and, for the first six months of 1931, the C&MLR operated its passenger services with two secondhand buses; trains were reinstated in June of that year, but lasted only until November. Surprisingly, the precise date of the last revenue-earning train seems to be unrecorded but it is known that, after November 1931, nothing stirred on the line.

Top: **This 6in Ordnance Survey map of Campbeltown map dates to 1898 and, therefore, the railway shown is the old colliery line before the upgrading to Light Railway status. The terminus of the colliery line in Campbeltown was, however, retained by the C&MLR as a coal depot.**
Crown Copyright

Above: **Public timetable, July 1922.**

The locomotives and goods wagons were sold for scrap, but the passenger carriages were bought privately for use as grandiose beach huts; some of the carriage bodies were to finish up being used at the Naval Stores Depot in Campbeltown, and were known to have remained in situ long after the depot closed in the late 1940s.

CARMYLLIE LIGHT RAILWAY
see (23) ELLIOT JUNCTION & CARMYLLIE LIGHT RAILWAY

15 Cawood, Wistow & Selby Light Railway

The town of Cawood is situated nine miles south of York and just over four miles north-west of Selby. The idea of a railway to bring the agricultural produce of the Cawood area to the market town of Selby first surfaced in 1879 but the plans came to nothing, and it took a further proposal of 1894 to start the ball rolling. That later scheme was for a tramway, but the advent of the Light Railways Act in 1896 quickly prompted a change of tack and, consequently, the Cawood, Wistow & Selby Light Railway was born.

The railway was officially opened to the public on 16 February 1898, although it is known that farm produce had been transported over the line for several months previously. Originally, the line started from a wooden platform near Brook Street in Selby, the point at which the branch joined the

NER's Leeds-Hull main line about one mile west of the main station. In the public timetables, the platform was referred to as Brayton Gates Junction. The NER was not keen to admit the light railway into its own station, partly because extensive alterations to the site were on the cards, and the NER's ploy of quoting a high charge for use of its station

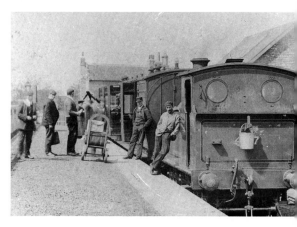

Right: **Worsdell 'H2' (later LNER 'J79') class 0-6-0T stands at Cawood circa 1905.** Lens of Sutton

Below : **The LNER's petrol-driven Leyland railbus spent around four years on the Cawood branch. It was also exhibited at the Stockton & Darlington Centenary celebrations in July 1925.** Rail Archive Stephenson

was enough to deter the CW&SLR from further argument. Along the line, the only intermediate station was at Wistow, 2¾ miles from Brayton Gates Junction, and its passing loop was situated beyond the end of the platform. The terminus at Cawood (4¼ miles from Brayton Gates) was a single-platform affair which had goods sidings and facilities for watering the locomotives. The line was single-track and was of flat-bottomed rails; untypically for a light railway, its three level crossings over public roads were all gated.

The CW&SLR's locomotive was a green-liveried Manning Wardle 'L' class 0-6-0ST (Works No 1360) named *Cawood* which had 3ft 6in diameter wheels and inside cylinders of 12in x 18in. It was hired for the sum of £205/5s (£205.25p) per annum from the Yorkshire Railway Waggon Co, the same firm which provided the railway company with its two passenger carriages for an annual rental of £69/19s (£69.95p). For opening day, the two coaches had to be augmented by five NER carriages.

Almost from the start, the NER showed great interest in the CW&SLR and, on 1 January 1900, the latter sold out for £32,000, some £7,000 more than it had cost to construct the line. Despite the NER's ownership of the line, it was 1 July 1904 before Cawood branch trains started to use the main line station at Selby. The branch continued to do well, with farm produce providing the mainstay of the traffic and, on occasions, necessitating trains of

20 or more wagons. Passenger services had originally comprised five trains each way on weekdays, with additional specials on market day.

The NER looked towards providing more substantial motive power for the Cawood branch and, in 1901, Worsdell 0-6-0T No 407, one of a pair built at Gateshead Works in March 1897, was fitted with larger tanks for duties on the line. The locomotive had 3ft 5¼ in wheels, cylinders of 14in x 20in, and the new tanks increased its weight from 25 to 27 tons. It was later classified by the LNER as 'J79' and was sold in June 1937 to the Whitwood Chemical Co; it was to finish its life with the NCB and was scrapped in 1954. The light railway company's Manning Wardle locomotive *Cawood* was returned to the leasing company and was used by assorted contractors and industrial concerns before being scrapped in the 1930s. Until the NER takeover, the branch locomotive had been housed in a sturdy brick-built shed at Brayton Gates Junction in Selby. The building survived until 1963 but it appears that, after 1900, it was not used by the NER.

For much of the Cawood branch's existence the usual motive power was less conventional. On

Below: **'J72' class 0-6-0T No 68686 crosses the road at Wistow with a freight working on 22 April 1960.**
Hugh Davies

Miles	Down.		Week Days only.					Miles	Up.			Week Days only.				
			mrn|mrn	aft	aft	aft				mrn|aft	aft	aft	aft	
—	Selby.........dep	8 51|140	3 31	7 20				—	Cawood ......dep	8 30|12 5	4 0	7 45		
3¼	Wistow............	8 16|151	3 42	7 31				1¾	Wistow ..|768, 770	8 35|1210	4 5	7 50		
5¼	Cawood ......arr	8 22|157	3 49	7 37				5¼	Selby358,761,ar.	8 47|1222	4 17	8 2		

Top: **Bradshaw's, summer 1922.**

Left: **This extract is from the order authorising construction of the Cawood, Wistow & Selby Light Railway.** Author's files

32. Subject to the provisions in the Railways Clauses Consolidation Act 1845 and in Part. I (relating to the construction of a railway) of the Railways Clauses Act 1863 contained in reference to the crossing of roads on the level the Company may in the construction of the railway carry the same with a single line only whilst the railway shall consist of a single line and afterwards with a double line only across and on the level of the roads next herein-after mentioned (that is to say) :—.

Power to cross roads on the level.

Railway.	Number on Deposited Plan.	Parish.	Description of Road.
No. 1 -	12	Wistow - - - -	Public carriage road.
No. 1 -	11	Selby - - - -	Public carriage road.
No. 1 -	16	Selby - - - -	Public carriage road.
No. 1 -	43 / 3	Selby - - - · / Brayton - - · -	Public carriage road.

1 July 1908, the NER's two petrol-electric autocars, Nos 3170/71 were transferred to Selby for Cawood duties, the autocars being basically similar in design to the standard Tyneside electric stock, but powered by 85hp Wolseley 4-cylinder engines. When the cars had been built in May 1903 they had used Napier engines, but those had proved troublesome and the Wolseley engines had been quickly substituted. Each car was 53ft 6in long and seated 52 passengers; in 1909/10, they each had four of their seats removed in order to create a proper luggage compartment. With a full load of 70gal of petrol, the weight of each car was 35tons 15cwt.

Of the two cars, No 3171 remained at Selby until being withdrawn in April 1931. Its companion, No 3170, spent the summer of 1923 at Harrogate, but apart from that interlude it also saw out its days at Selby, withdrawal coming in May 1930. At Selby depot, the cars were provided in 1913 with a lean-to shed at the rear of the coal stage and, remarkably, that structure was to remain until the abandoned depot was demolished in 1964. Nominally, the cars' stay at Selby was for Cawood branch duties, but during the early 1920s they were seldom used on those services or, for that matter, any other.

By 1922, weekday passenger services on the Cawood branch had been reduced to four trains each way on Mondays, but only two on other days. All advertised journey times were 17min and, in keeping with the NER's railcar services, were clearly marked 'one class only'. The working timetables for 1926 showed that the first train of the day from Cawood ran through to York, but the longevity of that service cannot be confirmed.

In 1923, the autocars were joined at Selby by the unique ex-NER Leyland rail motorbus, a petrol-driven 26-seat machine which was to remain there until being withdrawn. Its official withdrawal date was April 1927 but, ever since somebody at Selby shed had decided in November 1926 to check the contents of its tank under the illumination of a paraffin lamp, the bus had consisted of little more than a charred chassis.

After the demise of the rail-bus, the autocars were reinstated on passenger duties, but in March 1928 Selby shed received two new 59-seat Sentinel-Cammell vertical-boilered steam railcars. Selby's first Sentinels were 100hp two-cylinder chain-driven machines, *Waterwitch* and *True Blue*, but the former had to be put down in June 1929 after an accident at Doncaster. Its replacement at Selby was six-cylinder gear-driven *Cleveland*, and the new pairing's duties included, for a brief period, the Cawood line. Freight turns on the branch were handled by ex-NER 'J71' class 0-6-0Ts but, until the arrival of the Sentinel cars, Westinghouse-fitted 'J71s' had occasionally helped out on passenger duties.

During the 1920s the passenger traffic on the branch dwindled, and it came as little surprise when passenger services were withdrawn on 31 December 1929. In contrast, freight figures were still healthy, with sugar beet and potatoes providing enough traffic to dispel any immediate fears of total closure but, inevitably, things gradually changed as road transport slowly took over. By the 1950s, only an 'as required' service was deemed necessary, and even then loadings often comprised no more than a couple of trucks. In September 1959, Selby shed closed and the Cawood line's most usual freight locomotive, 'J77' No 68406, was replaced by a lightweight 204hp Drewry diesel, but the newcomer had little time to familiarise itself with its new duties as, on 2 May 1960, the Cawood branch closed completely.

16 Cleobury Mortimer & Ditton Priors Light Railway

The Clee Hills in southern Shropshire were a long-established and prolific source of iron, copper, limestone and basalt, but while the southern slopes of Titterstone Clee were connected to the main railway line near Ludlow in 1864, Brown Clee was left without even a reasonable cart track. Admittedly, plans for a railway to Brown Clee were proposed on several occasions, but it took the advantages of the Light Railways Act to prompt more serious thoughts. The outcome was the formation of the Cleobury Mortimer & Ditton Priors Light Railway.

The necessary Order for the CM&DPLR was gained in 1901, but the company's directors insisted that any contractor who wished to tender for the job of constructing the line would have to guarantee that a new quarry at Abdon would be operational as as soon as the railway opened. From the directors' point of view, that condition was a sensible one as it would ensure a steady source of mineral traffic from the outset but, for the next five years, no contractor proved plucky enough to accept such a condition. In 1906, however, Messrs Bott & Stennett stepped forth and secured the contract without the contentious condition, the CM&DPLR's change of heart having something to do with the fact

that, by then, a certain Mr Stennett had been appointed as a director of that railway company.

Construction of the line started in January 1907 and proceeded at a cracking pace. The first freight train ran on 21 July 1908, and the passenger service was inaugurated on 19 November. Apart from passing loops, the line was single throughout and, being devoid of signals, was worked on the 'one engine in steam' principle; the rails were 72lb/yd. There was no turntable on the line but, as the use of only tank engines had been envisaged, that was no problem. The usual practice throughout the line's life was for locomotives to work chimney-first towards Ditton Priors.

The CM&DPLR was connected to the GWR's Bewdley-Tenbury Wells line at Cleobury Mortimer station. In the years following the formation of the CM&DPLR, relations with the GWR had not been particularly friendly, and so the former had planned to build its own platform alongside that of the latter at Cleobury Mortimer. However, the two factions had eventually buried the hatchet, and the CM&DPLR had been offered use of the existing facilities by the GWR. Along the light railway, the first intermediate station at Cleobury Town was far better sited for the locals than the GWR station. The CM&DPLR's headquarters were at Cleobury Town, the offices being adjacent to the station; the station buildings, in common with the single-road engine shed, were constructed from timber but were replaced by new concrete buildings in 1918.

Below: **The CM&DPLR's two locomotives were identical Manning Wardle 0-6-0STs, *Cleobury* and *Burwarton*. They were absorbed by the GWR at the Grouping, renumbered 28/29 and fitted with pannier tanks.**
Bucknall Collection/Ian Allan Library

The first proper stations after Cleobury Town were Stottesdon (6¾ miles) and Burwarton (9½ miles). The land on which Burwarton station stood was part of the estate of Viscount Boyne, one of the railway's main promoters, and his Lordship had preferred the idea of a private siding rather than a public station which, he had felt, might attract working-class riff-raff. His magnanimous compromise had been that all scheduled passenger trains should call, instead, at every other stopping place on his estate. Viscount Boyne had, however, passed away less than a year before the railway opened; his son had looked on the idea of a public station far more favourably and, consequently, had given permission for its construction. The next station along the line was Cleobury North Crossing (10½ miles) which, during the period when Viscount Boyne had had difficulty accepting the general travelling public, had been designated Burwarton. However, when the late Viscount's decision had been reversed by his son, a shuffling of names had resulted.

The terminus of the line, for passengers at least, was at Ditton Priors (12½ miles), and it was equipped with the usual run-round loop and cattle dock; in common with the other stations on the line, the platforms were only 12ins high. Beyond the station, a spur extended to Oakwood, from where a rope-worked incline provided the connection with the all-important Abdon stone quarry. The quarry, which was over a mile away from the station, had its own locomotive-worked sid-

ings at the top of the incline and a 2ft gauge tramway between the quarry faces and the crushing plant.

Apart from the stations already mentioned, there were three 'request stops' between Cleobury Town and Stottesdon. These were at Chilton Siding, Detton Ford Siding and Prestcott Siding, which had originally been designated Neen Savage, Detton Mill and Oreton respectively. In 1909, a seven-mile aerial ropeway was opened westwards from Detton Ford to Magpie Quarries on Titterstone Clee.

Before the CM&DPLR opened, the GWR offered a working agreement but the little company decided to go it alone. An order for two 0-6-0STs was placed with Manning Wardle but neither engine arrived until a month after freight traffic commenced, and so the CM&DPLR had to borrow one of the contractor's locomotives, a Hudswell Clarke 0-6-0ST of 1888 named *Fleetwood*, as a stop-gap measure. The Manning Wardle locomotives, Works Nos 1734/35, had 16in x 22in outside cylinders, 3ft 6in diameter wheels and were named *Burwarton* and *Cleobury*. At first, passenger rolling stock comprised a quartet of vacuum-fitted four-wheeled carriages purchased from

Right: **After its 'Swindonisation', ex-CM&DPLR locomotive *Cleobury* was hardly recognisable. As GWR No 28, it hauls a typical mixed train on the Ditton Priors branch.** Lens of Sutton

Below: **Former GWR 0-6-0PT No 2144, at the head of an ammunition train for Ditton Priors, attacks the 1 in 66 gradient through Burwarton station on 23 February 1954. The spark arrester was an essential safeguard for such workings.** Geoffery F. Bannister

Above: **An MoD Ruston & Hornsby diesel shunter passes through Cleobury Town station on 26 March 1965, less than two months before the old CM&DPLR closed completely.** Andrew Muckley

the North London Railway. The freight stock consisted of ten 10-ton opens and two goods brake vans, much of the line's mineral traffic being conveyed in private-owner wagons.

The initial passenger service comprised three mixed trains each way on weekdays with average journey times of 70-80min, the reasons for the journeys taking so long being threefold. Firstly, there were gradients in excess of 1 in 60 and an abundance of sharp curves, secondly there were speed checks for 13 level crossings, only two of which were gated and, thirdly, the locomotives had to undertake their own shunting en route. The CM&DPLR's penchant for mixed trains is emphasised by the fact that, of the 17,240 train miles which were operated in 1909, just 286 were accounted for by passenger-only workings. Passenger fares during that period were 1/6d (7½ p) for a single first class ticket between Cleobury Mortimer and Ditton Priors, or 1/- (5p) third class. Despite the slowness of the journeys, passenger traffic was healthy; freight figures did not disappoint either and, gradually, the emphasis shifted more towards freight. During World War 1, stone was transported from the Clee Hill quarries in such quantities that GWR '850' class 0-6-0PT No 2001 had to be hired to assist.

At the Grouping the CM&DPLR was absorbed by the GWR and the two 0-6-0STs became GWR Nos 28/29. In 1924 No 29 was dispatched to Swindon where it was rebuilt with pannier tanks, and No 28 followed suit in 1931; during their respective rebuildings, both lost their nameplates. During the 1920s and 1930s freight traffic increased but passenger figures showed a marked decline, and the announcement that passenger sevices would be withdrawn from 24 September 1938 was greeted with little surprise. The shock to the locals,

however, was the sheer number of enthusiasts who descended on the line for 'last-day' rites and, in order to cope with the demand, two carriages had to be taken out of storage to supplement the usual pair.

Later in 1938, the Admiralty established a sizeable ammunition store at Ditton Priors and, when that was pressed into use after the outbreak of war, the two regular locomotives and the usual 'standby', 0-6-0PT No 2001, were, from necessity, fitted with spark arresters. Shunting inside the Admiralty complex was given over to a 'Planet' diesel. After the war, the line's fortunes were very different, as the quarries and their associated industries at Ditton Priors had closed.

Because of the lack of work on the line, one the original CM&DPLR locomotives, No 28, was transferred away from the area in the early 1950s. Since the closure of Cleobury Town shed in 1938, Kidderminster shed had been responsible for the line's motive power. In November 1953 No 28 was withdrawn and No 29, which had largely remained on home territory, suffered the same fate in February 1954. By then, there was usually just one weekly freight working on the line, the regular locomotive being '2021' class 0-6-0PT No 2034 which, for Ditton Priors duties, was fitted with the spark-arrester from the late No 29. Between 1955 and 1957, '16XX' class 0-6-0PT No 1661 took over as the regular steed.

On 30 September 1957, the Ministry of Defence took over the line completely and, until its total closure on 16 April 1965, the MoD's own Ruston & Hornsby diesel shunters were used. Although the last years of the line's life were spent in Government ownership, the old CM&DPLR line claimed the distinction of being one of the last of Britain's light railways to survive intact. The last recorded passenger working over the line had been on 21 May 1955, when 0-6-0PT No 2144 had hauled a four-coach enthusiasts special from Cleobury Mortimer to Cleobury North Crossing and back. That train had seen the only known use of bogie coaches on the line.

17 Corringham Light Railway

This obscure line in the south of Essex was constructed primarily as a means of staff and freight transportation for one specific company and, throughout the line's life, its source of traffic rarely varied. The company behind the line's birth was Messrs Kynoch Ltd, the Birmingham-based explosives manufacturer.

In the late 1890s Kynoch's established a sizeable factory near Thames Haven and developed a residential area for its employees. In typical Victorian pseudo-grandeur, the community was named Kynochtown. Additional housing had to be provided in the small villages of Stanford-le-Hope, Fobbing and Corringham, none of which were exactly within walking distance of the factory, and so Kynochs provided a railway for the staff who lived in those two villages, the line having a freight spur connecting with the London, Tilbury & Southend Railway at Thames Haven. At one time, the LT&SR had entertained great hopes of turning Thames Haven into a major port, but the dreams had failed to become reality and, by the time Kynoch's arrived in the area, the LT&SR had withdrawn its Thames Haven passenger services.

The Corringham Light Railway, a nominally independent concern, was opened to freight traffic on 1 January 1901 and to passengers on 29 June. It was a standard gauge line built with 56lb/yd flat-bottomed rails and, even including the spur to the LT&SR, was only around 2¾ miles in length. The land which the line crossed was so flat that any undulations could usually be explained by buried sofas or the work of moles with gout and so, with the need for minimal earthworks, the bill for constructing the line was just £7,530.

The simple but extremely attractive station at Corringham was, in fact, situated mid-way between the village of its name and Fobbing. From Corringham, the line struck out south-eastwards, and for passengers the other end of the journey was at Kynoch Town station (later amended to Kynochtown), adjacent to Kynoch's fatory gates. Beyond the station, the line continued into the factory but, of course, that was a freight-only section. There were three main sidings on the factory site, and these were supplemented by a network of horse-worked narrow gauge sidings. Between Corringham and Kynochtown stations the spur to the LT&SR diverged. It was connected to the CLR's 'main line' by means of a triangular junction, but the Corringham-Thames Haven side of the triangle was little used and subsequently lifted.

The CLR's first locomotive was a Kitson 0-4-0WT, purchased from the Barry Dock Co in South Wales. Named *Cordite* (later rechristened *Cordite Major* by the CLR), it was considered of inad-

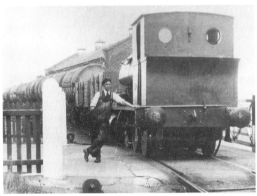

Top: **The Corringham Light Railway's Kerr Stuart 0-4-2T** *Kynite* **is seen at Corringham on 16 June 1909 with the 1.15pm to Kynochtown. The carriage appears to be the part-enclosed, part-'toast-rack' one built by Kerr Stuart in 1901.** LCGB/Ken Nunn Collection

Above: **One of the Corringham's Avonside 0-6-0STs waits to cross the road between Kynoch's factory and Kynochtown station.** Lens of Sutton

Right: **This 25in Ordnance Survey map of 1922 shows Corringham station and the Brick Works spur.** Crown Copyright

equate power, and so in 1901 a brand-new Kerr Stuart 0-4-2T was purchased and named *Kynite*. A further Kerr Stuart locomotive, a 0-4-0ST, was obtained in 1915 and two Avonside 'B3' class 0-6-0STs were bought, one in 1917 and the other in 1923, the first being obtained new and the other second-hand from the Royal Engineers Garrison Railway at Shoeburyness. The Avonsides were usually referred to as the '1914' and the '1917' engines after their construction dates. The CLR's locomotives were housed in a shed

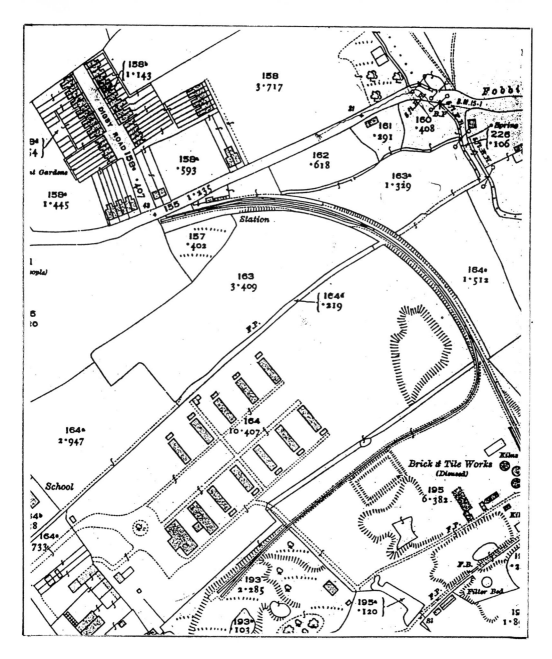

near Kynoch's factory gates and, for heavy repairs, were sent to Messrs Samuel Williams of Dagenham.

At first, the CLR's entire stud of passenger rolling stock comprised two bogie coaches. One was completely open-sided but, in deference to the first class status of Kynoch's management, half of the other coach was enclosed and, luxury of luxuries, lit by oil lamps. Before long, however, a trio of four-wheeled coaches was purchased from the LT&SR and, during World War 1, additional coaches were bought from

the Midland Railway. Records of freight stock seem sketchy, but it has been suggested that much of the traffic from Kynoch's factory was conveyed in LT&SR gunpowder vans.

The initial passenger service on the line comprised seven trains each way on weekdays and four on Sundays, the trains being scheduled to fit in with shift times at Kynoch's factory. The third-class single fare between Corringham and Kynochtown was 1½d (⅔p). The company's figures for 1910 showed that the conveyance

Steam locomotives of the Corringham Light Railway

Name/No	Builder	Works No	Type	Built	Bought	Wheels	Cyls	Weight	Wdn
Cordite[†]	Kitson	T260	0-4-0WT	1893	1901	3ft 0in	8in x 12in(i)	10t 2c	1930
Kynite	Kerr Stuart	692	0-4-2T	1901	1901	2ft 3in	9½in x 15in(o)	16t 0c	1930
No 3	Kerr Stuart	1283	0-4-0ST	1915	1915	2ft 9in	16in x 11in(o)	14t 3c	1920*
—	Avonside	1771	0-6-0ST	1917	1917	3ft 3in	20in x 14in(o)	30t 0c	1957
—	Avonside	1672	0-6-0ST	1914	1923	3ft 3in	20inx 14in(o)	30t 0c	1957

*Locomotive sold.

[†]Later renamed *Cordite Major*

of 1,311 tons of freight and 2,236 passengers generated gross receipts of £2,210, while expenditure for that year was just £866. Services eventually stabilised at five each way on weekdays but, predictably, the outbreak of war in 1914 resulted in a phoenomenal increase in production at Kynoch's works, and train services for staff were consequently increased. During World War 1, over 6,000 staff were employed at Kynoch's; a number of them came from London each day in through trains from Fenchurch Street, the CLR's locomotives often having to work double-headed after taking over at Thames Haven. Because of the lengths of most trains, the platforms at Corringham and Kynochtown had to be extended, the latter being treated to a passing loop and headshunt at the same time.

In 1921, the Kynoch company beame part of Cory Brothers Ltd, the Cardiff-based oil refiners, and Kynochtown was subsequently renamed Coryton. There was nothing like emphasising the corporate empire, it seems. The site of the old explosives factory was redeveloped in 1923 as an oil storage depot and refinery, and the railway was retained by the new local landlords who, in anticipation of future traffic, rebuilt Coryton station (as it had by then become). In 1925, the railway carried 6,172 passengers and 15,554 tons of freight, but those heady heights were not to last. When a new road was laid between the village of Fobbing, near Corringham, and the Coryton complex in the 1930s, the passenger traffic on the line started to dwindle.

During World War 2, the official policy of the CLR was that all passenger services were to be operated by a 15-seat motorbus, but it is known that trains still ran, albeit sporadically. For official purposes, railway activities were concentrated on transporting oil from Coryton to Thames Haven. When peace was restored, the passenger service was formally reinstated, but by then most local workers had become accustomed to using the buses. The outlook for the railway looked grim and at Nationalisation in 1948 the line was ignored by the British Railways Executive.

The last passenger services between Corringham

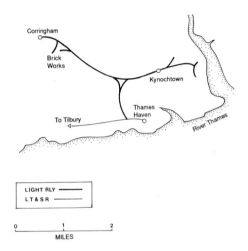

and Coryton ran on 1 March 1952, and the obligatory enthusiasts' specials found their way on to the little-known, but still independent, line to perform the last rites. By then, only the two Avonside 0-6-0STs remained in action. The section of line between Coryton and Thames Haven was retained for oil traffic, and two small Ruston & Hornsby diesels were bought to replace the 0-6-0STs.

The Corringham Light Railway continued to exist as an independent concern until 6 September 1971 when the oil depot's current owners, the Mobil Oil Co, formally took it over. Mobil later relaid the tracks to Thames Haven in order to facilitate movement from the bulk terminal adjacent to Coryton refinery and, during the 1980s, the terminal dispatched some 70 trains each week although the current figure is usually eight, regular destinations including Cambridge, Norwich, Banbury and Didcot. The trains are hauled from the terminal to Thames Haven by Mobil's own locomotives, one of which is a Vanguard and the other a Hunslet Barclay while, from Thames Haven, the usual form of main line motive power is a Class 37.

18 Derwent Valley Light Railway

The forerunner of the Derwent Valley Light Railway was promoted by a group of local councils in the Vale of York in order to provide a line through a highly fertile agricultural area. The necessary Order was obtained in 1902, but when the projected cost of £100,000 became apparent, a bout of cold feet swiftly ensued. A reconstituted company, the DVLR itself, surfaced in 1907 and this time things got underway, albeit rather slowly.

The DVLR was a standard gauge line. The Cliff Common-Wheldrake section opened to goods traffic on 29 October 1912 and, on 21 July 1913, public passenger services commenced over the entire line. Its starting point in York was at Layerthorpe station which was equipped with a single platform, a modest goods yard and a single-road engine shed. Layerthorpe was 1¼ miles from the North Eastern Railway's main line station and was reached via the NER's Foss Islands freight branch. The DVLR's 16-mile line terminated at the rear of Cliff Common station on the NER's Selby-Market Weighton line, the DVLR enjoying its own facilities at that station.

For a comparatively short railway, it had a positive proliferation of intermediate stopping places. From York, these were Osbaldwick (1 mile) which closed

Below: **The Derwent Valley's Sentinel locomotive poses at Layerthorpe station in York in 1925.**
Rail Archive Stephenson

as early as 1 March 1915, Murton Lane (2½ miles), Dunnington halt (3¾ miles), Dunnington for Kexby (4¼ miles), Elvington (6½ miles), Wheldrake (9 miles), Cottingwith (10½ miles), Thorganby (11½ miles) and Skipwith (13 miles). The stations were uniformly finished with attractive wooden plaster-panelled buildings and, apart from Dunnington halt and Cottingwith, all had siding accommodation.

The route of the DVLR passed over almost level land, and consequently earthworks were minimal. The line was laid using ex-Midland Railway bull-head rails of 80lb/yd, and the route was subject to a 25mph speed limit. It has often been remarked that, by light railway standards, the line had few ungated level crossings. There was just one signal on the line, that being at Wheldrake where a sharp bend obscured the drivers' view of a level crossing. The axle-weight limit over the DVLR was, at first, 14 tons although strengthening work in later years raised the limit to 17 tons.

Before the line had opened, an agreement had been made whereby locomotives, crew and stores would be hired from the NER, and the engine which officiated on opening day was Worsdell 2-2-4T No 1679. That locomotive was officially designated by the NER as an 'Officers Special Tank Engine', and had been rebuilt in its guise in 1894. It had, in fact, started life as a three-cylinder 4-2-0 in 1846, and been rebuilt in 1853 as a 2-2-2 before being renewed as a two-cylinder 2-2-2 in 1860. It remains unconfirmed whether the

Above: **A regular visitor to the DVLR in the 1950s was ex-NER 'J25' class 0-6-0 No 65700, seen here taking on water at Wheldrake.** Ian Allan Library

2-2-4T performed regularly on the DVLR after the line's official opening, but it is known that the locomotive remained allocated to the NER (later LNER) shed at York until its withdrawal in 1931.

When the line opened, the DVLR's coaching stock comprised two ex-NER carriages. The initial service consisted of three through trains ex-York and four ex-Cliff Common on weekdays, with additional conditional workings between York and Wheldrake. In 1915 almost 50,000 passengers were carried, and the following year, the DVLR tried to increase its revenue by repainting the third class compartments as second class and, of course, increasing its charges accordingly. It was not the most popular marketing ploy.

By the early 1920s, the passenger timetables for the DVLR bristled with conditional workings. Apart from one early morning train in each direction every weekday, the services ran only on certain days of the week; one of those was a lunchtime Saturdays only service from York to Wheldrake which, in the public timetables, was annotated: '*For parties of 10 or more, arrangements will be made to run beyond Wheldrake*'. It seemed a little uncertain whether the DVLR was trying to provide services which fitted in with local requirements, or whether the company was trying to bludgeon the locals to adapt to its own ideals.

Despite its close links with the NER, the DVLR was excluded from the plans for the Grouping. When

the motive power agreement with the newly-formed LNER expired in 1923, the DVLR tried out a four-cylinder 36hp road lorry which was capable of travelling on rails or roads. It had been claimed by the manufacturers that the contraption would haul 160 tons on the level, but the DVLR found the reality rather different and so the experiments were not pursued. In 1925, a 100hp vertical-boilered Sentinel locomotive (Works No 6076) was given a trial but, although extremely economical, it suffered from teething troubles. The LNER seemed more impressed than the DVLR with the Sentinel's potential and, over the years, the former was to purchase 49 Sentinel locomotives for light shunting duties. The DVLR example, however, spent much of its time under repair before being dispensed with in 1927.

For passenger services the DVLR bought a Ford-powered twin-unit railbus which had road-type wheels fitted with flanges, and when the railway company took to using the units singly, light turntables were installed at Layerthorpe and Skipwith. When combined, the buses' seating accommodation was 36. However, that brave foray into the field of unconventional motive power was to be short lived. By the mid-1920s, the familiar story of serious competition in the form of road transport had reared its head, and in 1925 the DVLR had carried only 18,430 passengers who provided gross receipts of just £664. The railbus might have been economical to operate but the passengers simply weren't there, and so it was announced that passenger services would be withdrawn on 31 August 1926. There was, however, no

Above: **After the demise of the 'J25s' in 1962, a Drewry 204hp diesel was the usual form of motive power on the DVLR. In this mid-1960s picture, No D2269 is seen at Elvington hauling a train which includes the DVLR's vintage ex-SE&CR six-wheeled brake coach.**
Michael P. Jacobs

suggestion that goods services should be discontinued as the 1925 freight figure was a healthy 37,244 tons. Despite the cessation of scheduled passenger services, several excursions were run either during the holiday season or in connection with specific events, and it is known that these continued until at least 1932. As for the railbuses, they were sold in 1927 to the County Donegal Railways in Ireland, where they were rebuilt for narrow gauge operation.

To the surprise, not to mention relief, of the DVLR's management, freight traffic remained steady throughout the late 1920s and the 1930s, and increased considerably during World War 2. Farm produce provided the mainstay of the traffic, but general Government traffic including the products of the mustard gas factory at Cottingwith provided welcome, if sometimes controversial, revenue. It was remarked that the weed-ridden state of the tracks provided excellent camouflage in case of enemy air raids. The locomotives hired from the LNER during the 1930s and 1940s included an ex-NER 0-4-4T, at least one former-Hull & Barnsley Railway 'N12' class 0-6-2T and various lightweight 0-6-0s.

After the war, a number of new light industrial and agricultural concerns were established along the route of the DVLR, and most became steady users of the railway. At Nationalisation, the line remained in private ownership although, to outward appearances, the use of standard locomotives made it seem like just another of British Railways' rural branches. The strengthening of the permanent way had enabled 'J21', 'J24' and 'J25' class 0-6-0s to work the line, the

'J25s' being the most common visitors with No 65700 and, later, No 65714 being regular performers during much of the 1950s. When away for repair, the replacement was usually an ex-LMSR Ivatt 2-6-0.

As late as 1960, there was one pick-up goods service to collect the local farm produce each weekday and, after the last of the 'J25s' was retired in June 1962, duties usually fell to a York-based 204hp Drewry diesel shunter, quite often No D2269. The diesel was stabled overnight at the officially-closed shed at Layerthorpe. Remarkably, a visit to the still-independent line in 1964 revealed well-kept and smartly-painted stations all along the route, despite the fact that none had been used by passengers for almost 30 years. Even more astonishing was that the company had a staff of 23. In true light railway fashion, however, the tracks were, in places, hardly distinguishable among the weeds. Furthermore, a vintage ex-South Eastern & Chatham Railway six-wheel brake coach, complete with birdcage-style centre lookout, was still in daily use; it was painted in the DVLR livery of green and proudly carried the company's initials.

Being an independent concern, the DVLR was not affected directly by the Beeching Report, but BR's closure of the main line between Selby and Market

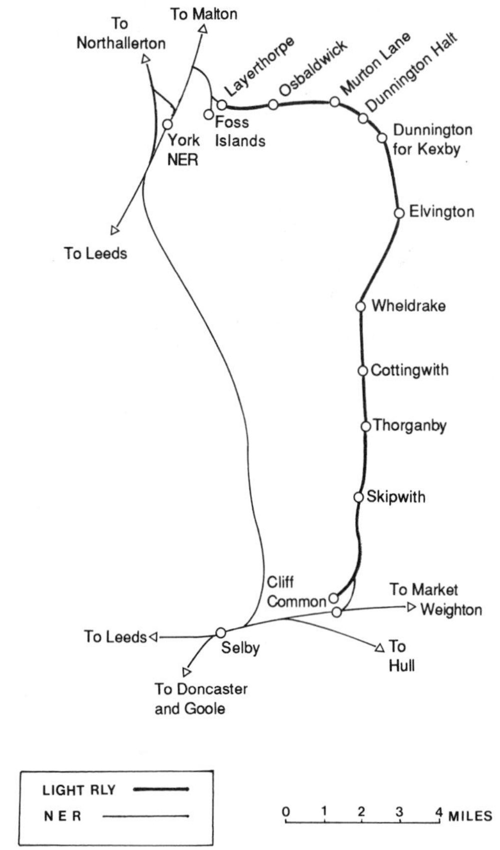
To Northallerton
To Malton
Layerthorpe
Osbaldwick
Murton Lane
Dunnington Halt
Foss Islands
York NER
Dunnington for Kexby
Elvington
To Leeds
Wheldrake
Cottingwith
Thorganby
Skipwith
Cliff Common
To Market Weighton
To Leeds
Selby
To Hull
To Doncaster and Goole
LIGHT RLY
N E R
0 1 2 3 4 MILES

Weighton rendered the southern part of the line superfluous. Consequently, the section between Wheldrake and Cliff Common was closed in February 1965 but, predictably, an enthusiasts' special was laid on before the tracks were lifted.

During the 1960s, the coal yard at Layerthorpe was mechanised and this helped to secure the DVLR's immediate future; the light industries which had sprung up along the line over the years also played their part. Around 10,000 tons of freight were still being transported over the DVLR during that period but, despite the line's healthy usage, the Wheldrake-Elvington section was closed from 17 May 1968. Nevertheless, in spring 1969 the still-independent DVLR purchased surplus Drewry 204hp 0-6-0 diesel locomotives Nos D2245/98 from British Railways, although it is believed that the former was acquired merely for cannibalisation in order to provide spares for the latter.

Despite owning its own motive power, the DVLR started to lose some of its traffic in the 1970s. The Elvington-Dunnington section was closed in December 1972 thereby leaving just 4¼ miles of line from Layerthorpe to the grain-drying plant at Dunnington still open. That final section was closed from 28 September 1981, the station at Layerthorpe having been officially closed on 3 September 1979 although the railway had continued to serve various tenants in the yard. The Derwent Valley Railway (the word 'Light' had been formally dropped in 1973) had seen its last flurry of passenger activity during the summers of 1977-79 when steam-hauled specials had operated between Layerthorpe and Dunnington. Those specials had been an indirect consequence of the opening of the National Railway Museum in York in 1975, and most of the workings had been entrusted to preserved 'J72' class 0-6-0T No 69023.

Below: **Bradshaw's, summer 1922.**

YORK, ELVINGTON, and CLIFF COMMON.—Derwent Valley Light.
Gen. Man., W. T. D. Grundy, York.

Miles	Up. — Week Days only.	mrn	b aft (Except Saturdays.)	aft (Saturdays only.)	aft (Saturdays only.)	aft (Except Saturdays.)	aft (Saturdays only.)
—	**York** (Layerthorpe)..dep.	9 20	1230	1 20	4 20	6 0	6 0
2¼	Murton Lane ¶	9 26	1236	1 26	4 26	6 6	6 6
4¼	Dunnington, for Kexby..	9 32	1242	1 32	4 32	6 12	6 12
6½	Elvington, for Sutton...	9 38	1248	1 45	4 38	6 18	6 18
9	Wheldrake	9 45	1255	1 57	4 45	6 25	6 25
10½	Cottingwith	9 48		2 0	4 48	6 28	
11½	Thorganby	9 52		2 4	4 52	6 32	
13	Skipwith and N. Duffield	9 56		2 8	4 56	6 36	
16	**Cliff Common 761**..arr.	10a6		2 18			

Miles	Down. — Week Days only.	mrn	mrn (Except Mondays and Saturdays.)	mrn (Mondays and Saturdays.)	aft (Saturdays only.)	aft (Mondays only.)	aft (Saturdays only.)	aft (Saturdays only.)	aft (Except Saturdays.)
—	**Cliff Common**.......dep.			1050	3 0	4 15			
3	Skipwith and N. Duffield	7 50	1020	11 0	n	4 20	5 5		6 45
4¼	Thorganby	7 54	1024	11 4	n	4 24	5 9		6 49
5½	Cottingwith	7 58	1028	11 8	n	4 28	5 13		6 53
7	Wheldrake	8 1	1031	1111	n	4 34	5 16	6 45	6 56
9½	Elvington, for Sutton...	8 8	1038	1118	n	4 41	5 23	6 52	7 3
11¾	Dunnington, for Kexby ¶	8 14	1044	1124	n	4 47	5 29	6 58	7 9
13¾	Murton Lane	8 20	1050	1130	n	4 53	5 35	7 4	7 15
16	**York ‡ 728**.........arr.	8 26	1056	1140	3 45	5 0	5 41	7 10	7 20

a Mondays and Saturdays.

b For parties of 10 or more, arrangements will be made to run beyond Wheldrake.

n Stops when required to take up for York or to set down from Cliff Common.

‡ York (Layerthorpe); 1¼ miles to York, North Eastern Station.

¶ "Halt" at Dunnington between Murton Lane and Dunnington (for Kexby).

19 Dornoch Light Railway

Throughout Britain, many rural light railways offered views of glorious countryside, but one of the most striking standard gauge routes of all was that of the Dornoch Light Railway. The line started on the Highland Railway's Inverness-Wick line at The Mound, which took its name from Thomas Telford's road embankment of 1817, and finished at Dornoch, the county town of Sutherland. As a snippet of total irrelevance, Dornoch was the place where, in 1722, Scotland's last execution for withcraft took place, the miscreant having been accused of having turned her daughter into a pony.

On to more pertinent matters the Dornoch Light Railway opened on 2 June 1902 and, although it was worked from the outset by the Highland Railway, it retained its nominal independence until passing to the LMSR at the Grouping in 1923. As if to emphasise its presence, the Highland opened its own hotel at Dornoch in 1904, the premises being taken over during World War 1, firstly by the Gordon Highlanders and, later, by the Canadian Forestry Corps.

The line closely followed the old coach road to Dornoch. At The Mound, branch trains had their own platform. On leaving the station, the line fell away at 1 in 50 to the shore of Loch Fleet which it crossed, in company with the road, on a long causeway. Beyond the half-way point of Skelbo, there were climbs of around 1 in 50, which had at the time of the line's construction been considered preferable to expensive earthworks. Despite the savings on earthworks, the line had been more costly to construct than most light railways because the Board of Trade had insisted on the provision of gates at all level crossings and fencing for the entire length of the line. It remains unclear whether the Board of Trades stipulations were because the line was, in effect, little more than a branch of the Highland Railway. If that were the case, it could be

Left: **Highland Railway 0-4-4T No 46 was one of four locomotives built in 1905/06 for branch work. It spent a considerable time on the Dornoch line, this picture being taken at the branch terminus.**
Bucknall Collection/Ian Allan Library

Below: **Former Highland Railway 0-4-4T No 40 became LMSR No 15052 after the Grouping. This classic shot shows the locomotive waiting to leave Dornoch with the 9am train for The Mound.** H. C. Casserley

Above: **Ex-Highland 0-4-4T No 55051 approaches The Mound on 23 April 1952.** H. C. Casserley

asked why similar conditions could not have been imposed on the London & South Western Railway which blatantly used the Light Railways Act to facilitate construction on the cheap.

The inaugural train on the line was hauled by Stroudley 0-6-0T No 56 which, in deference to its new sphere of activity, had its original name of *Balnain* replaced by that of *Dornoch*. Having an axle weight of 10 tons, the locomotive was ideal for the line, and it was the regular steed until 1919. Occasionally, Jones 0-4-4T No 53 *Lybster* was seconded to the line from its usual duties on the Wick & Lybster Light Railway but, after the 0-6-0T's departure, the more usual performers on the Dornoch line were Drummond 0-4-4Ts. The intermediate stopping places on the branch were at Cambusavie platform (1¼ miles from The Mound), Skelbo (3¾ miles) and Embo (5½miles). The terminus at Dornoch (7¾ miles) was a single–platform affair with a run–round loop, and had a modest goods yard and single–road engine shed.

The timetables for the 1920s through to the mid–1940s usually showed a service of three trains each way on weekdays with journey times of around 25min; Cambusavie platform was invariably listed as a 'request stop'. For a short period a through sleeping car from London to Dornoch was advertised, but it failed to attract the necessary passengers. By the early 1950s, branch services usually consisted of just two trains each way on weekdays, but because the train crews were by then required to operate the gates at all six level crossings themselves, the schedules gave pas-sengers 45min in which to enjoy the scenery. By then, trains on the line normally consisted of just one corridor composite brake coach behind which a handful of assorted freight wagons was usually attached.

After Nationalisation, the motive power usually comprised a pair of the Drummond 0-4-4Ts, Nos 55051/53, each of which did a week about on the branch. They went on to become the last two ex-Highland locomotives to remain in active service on British Railways. The former was retired in June 1956 but the latter was treated to a major overhaul and an immaculate lined black livery, the only ex-Highland locomotive ever to receive the full BR passenger tank plumage. With its gleaming paintwork, No 55053 must have seemed set for at least a few more years service but, sadly, that was not to be as in November 1956 its front driving axle broke while it was hauling a mixed train. Despite one of the wheels parting company with the fractured axle and causing the locomotive to lurch violently, the train was not derailed and, fortunately, nobody was hurt. Predictably, No 55053 was withdrawn immediately, and by then the list of alternative candidates for working the branch long-term was a little thin on the ground. The solution to the line's motive power problem came from a most unexpected source.

In February 1957, six year-old Western Region '16XX' class 0-6-0PT No 1646 was transferred to Helmsdale shed, the parent of the small shed at Dornoch, for duties on the branch; in July 1958, classmate No 1649 was sent along to join in. They remained the regular locomotives until the branch closed to all traffic on 13 June 1960, and were then put to use as station pilots at Dingwall until their withdrawal in December 1962.

Above: **The use of WR 0-6-0PTs on the Dornoch line provided an unexpected bonus for local enthusiasts. On a thoroughly dismal day in April 1959, No 1649 crosses the road at Cambusmore, at the southern end of The Mound causeway, with the 1pm mixed train from Dornoch.** Rev R. T. Hughes

Right: **Advertisement for the Station Hotel, Dornoch.**

Below: **LMSR Public timetable, 7 October 1946 to 4 May 1947.** Author's files

DORNOCH, Sutherlandshire.

STATION HOTEL.

OVERLOOKS FIRST GREEN.
MOST FASCINATING GOLF LINKS IN THE KINGDOM.
Highland Railway Company.
H. H. WARD, Hotels Manager.

Table 358	THE MOUND JUNCTION and DORNOCH	

Miles		Week Days only							Miles		Week Days only						
		a.m			p.m						a.m			p.m				
	The Mound Junc.... dep	1150	..	..	2 0	..	..	..		Dornoch............. dep	1040	..	..	1 10	..	..	..	..
1¼	Cambusavie Platform...	Aa	..	..	Aa	..	..		2¼	Embo..................	1047	..	..	1 17	..	..	..	
3¼	Skelbo.................	12 3	..	..	2 13	..	..		4	Skelbo...............	1059	..	..	1 24	..	..	..	
5¼	Embo..................	12 9	..	..	2 19	..	..		6¼	Cambusavie Platform...	Aa	..	..	Aa	..	..		
7¼	Dornoch...........arr	1219	..	..	2 28	..	..		7¼	The Mound Junc.... arr	1111	..	..	1 37	..	..	..	

Aa Calls to set down on notice at previous *stopping* station or when there are passengers on platform to be taken up

20 Easingwold Railway

The Easingwold Railway had been operational for 37 years before it applied for authorisation to be worked as a light railway. In its time, it had been a remarkably charismatic little line, but when it obtained its Light Railway Order, over half its working life was over.

The railway opened on 27 July 1891 and ran from Alne, on the North Eastern Railway's York-Northallerton main line, to the elegant market town of Easingwold. The route was only 2½ miles long, but the total cost of the line's construction, including Parliamentary expenses, was an astonishing £17,000. The Easingwold Railway was built to the standard gauge and its first locomotive was a lightweight Hudswell Clarke 0-4-0ST which set the company back the princely sum of £720. That machine was ordered more for its modest price tag than its potential capabilities and, before long, was found to struggle even when hauling the pair of antique ex-NER four-wheel carriages which represented the Easingwold's entire coaching stock.

Consequently, a 0-6-0ST was hurriedly ordered from Hudswell Clarke and it was delivered at the end of August. Named *Easingwold*, it was replaced in 1903 by a larger and more-powerful Hudswell Clarke 0-6-0ST which was designated 'No 2'. When additional motive power was required, locomotives were hired from Hudswell Clarke, the North Eastern Rail-

way or, in later years, the LNER. The line's resident locomotive lived at the small engine shed at Easingwold station.

It has often been suggested that the Easingwold's choice of locomotive livery was lined maroon, but as that colour scheme was the very one used by Hudswell Clarke, it seems likely that the livery was dictated by the manufacturer and not the railway company. Over the years, the Easingwold acquired a variety of secondhand four- and six-wheel carriages from the North Eastern, North London and Great Central Railways. Freight wagons used on the line were always supplied by the NER (later the LNER) and, most usually, were tacked on to the rear of passenger trains. Until 1948, a freight-only working was a rarity.

The line's traffic figures were steady and, from 1910, the company paid annual dividends of three or four per cent to its shareholders; although modest, this was more than many larger and more-famous companies achieved with any regularity. The Easingwold was not affected by the Grouping and so, as a totally independent concern, it had to watch the pennies very carefully. In 1928, the company was granted a Light Railway Order which enabled it to make further operational savings and, ultimately, stake a claim for inclusion in this book. The economies made as a result of the Order are unclear, but it is known that the level crossings near Alne and at Crankley retained their gates which, presumably, could have been dispensed with under the terms of the Order.

The Easingwold Railway continued to operate its own passenger services which, until 1939, usually comprised seven trains each way on weekdays. World

Below: **The Easingwold Railway purchased its Hudswell Clarke 0-6-0ST, No 2, in 1903 and the engine soldiered on until 1947. It stands at the head of three ex-North London Railway coaches.** Real Photographs/Ian Allan Library

EASINGWOLD and ALNE.—Easingwold.

Miles	Down.	Week Days only.									Miles	Up.	Week Days only.							
		mrn	mrn	mrn	mrn	aft	aft	aft	aft				mrn	mrn	mrn	aft	aft	aft	aft	aft
	Easingwold...dep.	7 36	8 34	1015	1115	1 20	3 15	5 0	6 45	....		Alne.........dep	8 10	9 6	1040	1227	1 38	3 37	5 45	7 18	....
2¼	Alne 728, 762 arr.	7 44	8 42	1023	1123	1 28	3 23	5 8	6 53	....	2¼	Easingwold.. arr.	8 18	9 14	1048	1235	1 46	3 45	5 53	7 26	....

Top: **By 1949, passenger services had ceased on the Easingwold Railway and, it seems, so had much of the pride in the cosmetic appearance of the line. Folorn-looking 'J71' class 0-6-0T No 68246 sits alongside the equally folorn shed building at Easingwold**
Real Photographs/Ian Allan Library

Above: **Public timetable, Summer 1922.**

War 2 brought a significant quantity of additional freight traffic to the line, but the scheduled passenger services were reduced to just three each way. During the war, the locals turned to road transport and, when peace was restored, the line's passenger figures failed to return to their pre-war standards. The Easingwold Railway's accounts for 1947 revealed that just £18/0/8d (£18.03½p) was earned from passenger traffic, the odd 8d (3½p) being accounted for by the one first-class passenger who had used the line that year. On the subject of class differentials, through bookings from York to Easingwold could be made for either first- or third-class, but the accommodation on the Easingwold branch train was strictly first- or second-class only.

The inevitable withdrawal of passenger services took place on 29 November 1948. Nevertheless, the line remained open for freight and, after the Easingwold's own locomotive, 'No 2', was deemed unrepairable in 1947, the motive power usually took the form of 'J71' or 'J72' class 0-6-0Ts. The last engine to work the line was 'J72' No 68698, which hauled a train of sugar beet from Easingwold on 27 December 1957.

21 East Kent Light Railway

The Kent coalfield covers some 80 square miles, and the first proper railway which was planned to tap the coalfield's potential traffic was the East Kent (Mineral) Light Railway, a partially French-backed concern which was promoted in 1910. The original plans for the railway incorporated a route of over 30 miles in length, but a shortening was required before a Light Railway Order was granted. The truncated scheme was presented by a reconstituted form of the original company, the 'new' one operating under the banner of the East Kent Light Railway.

The construction of the EKLR was placed under the guidance of Holman (later Lt-Col) Stephens who had, by then, gained considerable experience in the engineering of light railways. Work on the line was delayed by the outbreak of war in 1914, and although some coal traffic had used the unfinished line as early as November 1912, it was 16 October 1916 before the EKLR opened to public passenger and goods traffic. Despite having been built with economy in mind, the eventual cost of constructing the line was a whopping £25,262 per mile, almost double that of any other light railway in Britain.

When unveiled to the public in 1916, the route of the EKLR started from a platform at Shepherd's Well, close to the South Eastern & Chatham Railway's Dover-Canterbury main line, and terminated 10¼ miles away at Wingham Colliery station. At first, the only operational collieries in the line's catchment area were those at Guilford (near Eythorne), Tilmanstone, Woodnesborough and Wingham. Tilmanstone was, by then, producing almost 2,000 tons of coal weekly, but the other three waited for the railway to arrive before commencing serious commercial production.

For its passenger traffic, the EKLR provided intermediate stopping places at Eythorne (1¾ miles from Shepherd's Well), Elvington (2½ miles), Knowlton (3½ miles), Eastry (5¾ miles), Woodnesborough Colliery (6½ miles), Ash Town (8 miles) and Staple (8¾

Below: **East Kent 0-6-0ST No 7 takes on water at Woodnesborough. The wooden water tower, the cattle grid, the ageing ex-'main line' locomotive and its one-coach train were typical, not only of the East Kent, but also many other light railways.**
Bucknall Collection/Ian Allan Library

Left: **Hudswell Clarke 0-6-0ST No 4** *Walton Park* **had performed on other 'Col Stephens' railways before arriving on the East Kent. This undated picture shows the locomotive and one six-wheeled coach at Wingham Town station.** Lens of Sutton

miles). Eastry South halt (5¼ miles) was added in 1925. By the early 1920s, the passenger service between Shepherd's Well and Wingham usually comprised just two or three trains each way on weekdays, but additional services were provided between Shepherds Well and Tilmanstone for the benefit of colliery staff. Journey times for the 10¼ -mile trip to Wingham were around 50min.

The line was laid mainly with 80lb/yd flat-bottomed rails, 90lb/yd rails being used on gradients. The major engineering feature was the 477yd-long Golgotha tunnel near Shepherd's Well which, along with most of the bridge abutments along the route, was constructed so that a double track line could later be laid, but the second track was never required. The maximum gradients were 1 in 50 and the sharpest curves 9 chains; legal limits enforced a speed limit of 25mph and a maximum axle weight of 14tons. Originally, there were aspirations that the EKLR would be worked by electric traction with Tilmanstone coal providing the necessary fuel, but that plan was one of many which fell by the wayside.

Three locomotives were on hand for opening day. One was a Fox Walker 0-6-0ST which had started life in 1875 on the Whitland & Cardigan Railway; when, in 1890, the GWR had taken over the W&CR, the locomotive had become GWR No 1386. On its arrival in Kent in 1911, the locomotive was put to work on constructing its future line and, later, became EKLR No 1. The two other original EKLR locomotives were both transferred from outposts of the 'Colonel Stephens' empire. The first of those, EKLR No 2, was a Hudswell Clarke 0-6-0ST which, in its life-span of just eight years, had seen service on the Weston, Clevedon & Portishead Light Railway (where it had been named *Walton Park*) and then on the Shropshire & Montgomeryshire Light Railway. The other was a 46¾-ton Hawthorn Leslie 0-8-0T which had been built for the Kent & East

Sussex Light Railway in 1904; named *Hecate*, it was not considered a permanent fixture on the EKLR and, therefore, was not regarded as company stock.

During its loan period on the EKLR, *Hecate* assisted in the construction of the Sandwich Road branch and also that of the marshalling yard at Tilmanstone colliery; it then worked the transfer trains between Tilmanstone and Shepherd's Well until being returned to the K&ESLR for repair in 1919. Another K&ESLR locomotive, 2-4-0T No 2 *Northiam*, was loaned to the EKLR between 1923 and 1930.

Over the years, further locomotives were required and, in typical fashion, Lt-Col Stephens was less concerned with their pedigrees than their price tags. In 1918, an ex-L&SWR 'Ilfracombe Goods' 0-6-0 of 1880 became EKLR No 3, and a standard Kerr Stuart 0-6-0T was purchased in 1919 from the War Surplus Disposals Board to become EKLR No 4. In 1921, another ex-L&SWR locomotive was acquired, this time one of the celebrated Adams 4-4-2Ts, and became EKLR No 5 while, in 1923, the Southern Railway was the source of EKLR No 6, built in 1891 as one of the numerous 'O' class 0-6-0s for the SE&CR. EKLR No 7, purchased in 1925, was an ex-L&SWR '330' class 0-6-0ST of 1882. Two other locomotives were purchased by the EKLR and became No 8 and, illogically, No 100; both were ex-SE&CR 0-6-0s, the former being purchased in 1928 and the latter, after having been rebuilt to 'O1' class specifications, in 1935. A further ex-SE&CR 'O' class 0-6-0 was acquired in 1944 and retained its Southern Railway livery and the number 1371. The EKLR's locomotives were housed at Shepherd's Well shed and were repaired and overhauled on-site.

In the motive power stakes, the EKLR's enigma was a locomotive named *Gabrielle*. It was built by Hawthorn Leslie in 1914 to specifications laid down by Holman Stephens although, over the years, it has often been wrongly described as having been designed by Stephens himself. The locomotive, which was an outside-cylindered 0-6-0T, was intended to be used in the construction of the EKLR before entering revenue-earning service, but the outbreak of World War 1 put paid to those plans. Despite being fitted with its nameplates and being inscribed with 'East Kent Railway' on its tanks, it was commandeered by the Government for war duties without ever having turned a wheel on the EKLR.

Before the opening of the line, a bogie vestibule coach had been acquired from the K&ESLR, but this

Above: **Shepherd's Well shed and yard on the East Kent Light Railway were not exactly in the same league as Ashford. The locomotives in the foreground are No 6 (an ex-SE&CR 0-6-0) and 0-6-0T No 4.**
Real Photographs/Ian Allan Library

Right: **The East Kent's platform at Shepherd's Well was separate from the SE&CR station. The trailing spur which disappears behind the bank on the left of the frame connected with the main line, part of which is seen on the embankment in the distance.**
Real Photographs/Ian Allan Library

did not set a precedent as the carriage was later supplemented by a motely assortment of four- and six-wheel antiquities from such sources as the North London Railway, the SE&CR and the L&SWR. Freight stock ultimately comprised 36 open wagons, two box vans, three timber wagons and a brake van, but their condition can be gauged by the fact that, after the Grouping, the Southern Railway would not permit any EKLR wagons on to its lines.

The original dreams of the EKLR had encompassed much more that just a 10¼ -mile line to Wingham colliery. There had once been plans to tap Snowdown Colliery in the west and Chislet Colliery in the north, also to extend to Richborough in the east and Canterbury in the west. At one stage, there had even been mutterings about reaching London. But, apart from spurs to Guilford and Woodnesborough Collieries, only a small part of the route to Canterbury and the extension to Richborough were ever constructed. The extension towards Canterbury only ever reached Canterbury Road station, one-mile beyond Wingham colliery and in the middle of nowhere, but despite the shortness of the completed section, there was an intermediate station named Wingham Town. The short extension was officially opened in 1925, but it is known that it was used by passenger trains well before then.

The Richborough extension had been planned to develop a major coal port, but Richborough never became the Kentish equivalent of Cardiff. The first section of the Richborough 'branch' was opened to freight traffic by 1916 but it was 1925 before the line was completed and passenger services commenced. Even then, the terminus for passengers was at Sandwich Road as the bridge which carried the railway over the river at Richborough did not gain Board of Trade approval for anything other than goods traffic. The authorisation for the bridge had contained the proviso that it should be able to be opened in order to let shipping pass through, but a fixed-span bridge had been illegally constructed instead. Furthermore, there were doubts whether the track-bed on the bridge was, in fact, above the level of the highest tides.

The reference to 'passenger services' to Sandwich Road makes things seem somewhat grander than they actually were, as the twice-daily trains to Richborough comprised merely a single carriage in front of the freight wagons, this being detached at Sandwich Road before the wagons were taken on to Richborough. The Richborough branch left the 'main' line north of Eastry, and had stopping places at Poison Cross halt (6 miles from Shepherd's Well) and Roman Road (7¼ miles) before arriving at Sandwich Road (8 miles). The 'station' at Richborough Port was never to handle public passenger traffic, and even the services to Sandwich Road did not last very long as they were officially withdrawn on 1 November 1928. In 1925, the firm of Pearson & Dorman Long had leased the sidings at Richborough from the War Department, and Ordnance Survey maps of the 1930s reveal just how extensive the siding accommodation actually was.

The EKLR's returns for 1925 reveal that 25,124 passengers were carried, the figure for freight being 237,481 tons of which 228,595 tons (96%) were coal.

Below: **East Kent 0-6-0 No 6, a Stirling-designed former-SE&CR locomotive, stands at Eastry not long before the cessation of the EKR's passenger services in 1948.** Ian Allan Library

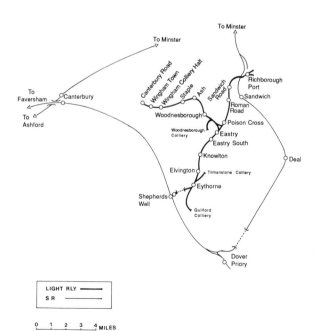

Interestingly for statisticians, the expenditure for that year (£9,296) accounted for just 72% of gross receipts (£12,120), and that was one of the healthiest percentages of any of the country's light railways. Nevertheless, the coal traffic which had been the reason for the EKLR's creation failed to reach the levels which had been anticipated, only four collieries in the railway's catchment area ever being regarded as commercial successes. The alternative sources of revenue, agricultural and passenger traffic, never materialised in sufficient quantities and, although the EKLR's returns were good when compared with those of other light railways, they were insufficient to keep the corporate kitty sufficiently topped up.

The EKLR had been excluded from the Grouping in 1923, and in 1927 the Southern Railway recieved authorisation to invest £300,000 in the still-independent company. That came a little too late in the day as, by the time the SR worked out how best to channel the money, the national depression had had a significant effect on the coal traffic. A further potential blow to the EKLR's traffic came in 1930 when an aerial cableway was constructed from Tilmanstone Colliery to Dover harbour but, as things turned out, the depression resulted in little coal being conveyed by the cableway and, by 1939, it was reported to be out of use. Predictably, a significant proportion of the EKLR's passengers were miners, many of whom travelled from Dover or Canterbury, and the increased competition of motor-bus transport in the 1930s saw the line's passenger traffic dwindle. The closure of Wingham Colliery was a major catastrophe for the EKLR and, in 1935, only 838 passengers used the railway. From then on, the line's precarious future depended almost totally on Tilmanstone Colliery.

At Nationalisation in 1948, the EKLR passed to the tender, loving care of British Railways and provided four locomotives, 0-6-0T No 4 and three 0-6-0s, for the BR stock list. Of the 0-6-0s, No 2 had originally been No 100 and had, somewhat extravagantly, assumed the number of the old 0-6-0ST after the latter's withdrawal in 1947; there was also No 1371 which had been purchased from the Southern Railway in 1944 but had retained its SR livery and number. The 0-6-0T (EKLR No 4) was designated BR No 30948, and the 0-6-0s were allocated Nos 31371 (ex-No 1371), 31372 (EKLR No 6) and 31383 (EKLR No 2) in the same block as the other surviving 'O1' class locomotives. Of the ex-EKLR 0-6-0s, No 31383 survived until 1951 and appears to be the only one

Locomotives of the East Kent Light Railway

No	Type	Built	Builder	Bought	Formerly	Wheels	Cyls	Weight	Disposal
1	0-6-0ST	1875	Fox Walker	1911	GWR No 1386	3ft 5in	13in x 20in(o)	24t 13c	Scr 1934
2	0-6-0ST	1908	H/Clarke	1916	WC&PR/S&MLR	3ft 7in	14in x 20in(o)	29t 10c	Sold 1940
3	0-6-0	1880	B/Peacock	1918	L&SWR No 0394	4ft 7½in	16in x 20in(i)	25t 16c*	Scr 1932
4	0-6-0T	1917	Kerr Stuart	1919	Government	4ft 0in	17in x 24in(o)	48t 0c	Wdn 1949
5	4-4-2T	1885	Stephenson	1921	L&SWR No 0488	5ft 7in	18in x 24in(o)	54t 2c	Sold 1946†
6	0-6-0	1891	S/Stewart	1923	SE&CR No 372	5ft 2in	18in x 26in(i)	36t 15c*	Wdn 1949
7	0-6-0ST	1882	B/Peacock	1925	L&SWR No 127	4ft 3in	17in x 24in(i)	34t 19c	Scr 1946
8	0-6-0	1891	S/Stewart	1928	SE&CR No 376	5ft 2in	18in x 26in(i)	36t 15c*	Scr 1935
100	0-6-0	1893	S/Stewart	1935	SE&CR No 383	5ft 2in	18in x 26in(i)	41t 1c*	Wdn 1951
1371	0-6-0	1891	S/Stewart	1944	SE&CR No 371	5ft 2in	18in x 26in(i)	41t 1c*	Wdn 1949

* Engine only.
† Purchased by Southern Railway. Withdrawn 1961.
NB: 0-8-0T *Hecate* not listed as it was never officially EKR stock.

Above: **Bradshaw's, March 1940.** Author's files

of the four to have actually carried its BR number. The longest surviving ex-EKLR locomotive was, in fact, 4-4-2T No 5 which had been sold to the Southern Railway in 1946 for use on the Lyme Regis branch. As BR No 30583, it was withdrawn from service in July 1961 and was subsequently acquired for preservation by the Bluebell Railway.

The Southern Region of British Railways wasted little time in announcing the cessation of passenger services on the EKLR. It was to be the first 'cut' of the Nationalisation era. The final day of passenger services was 30 October 1948 and, apart from the section between Shepherd's Well and Tilmanstone colliery, the line closed to all traffic on 1 March 1951. The branch from Eastry to Richborough, which had not been used for several years, had been officially closed as from 1 January 1950. During the 1950s, the coal trains from Tilmanstone were usually hauled by 'O1' class 0-6-0s, Nos 31258 and 31425/30/34 being based at Dover shed for EKLR duties.

With the demise of steam, a diesel shunter was used to bring the coal from Tilmanstone to Shepherd's Well. In the early 1980s, the line was upgraded so that it could accommodate loaded wagons with 25½-ton axle weights but, as the run-round loop at Tilmanstone was only some 250ft long, three trips had to be made from the colliery in order to provide enough wagons to form a block train at Shepherd's Well. The usual forms of motive power from Shepherd's Well were, by then, Class 33 or Class 73 diesels.

After 1983, rail traffic from Tilmanstone became sporadic. During January and February 1984, just eight coal trains left Shepherd's Well, their total complement of 192 wagons providing BR with gross revenue of £42,473. The final day's workings were on 1 March 1984, seven loaded HTVs leaving Tilmanstone for Shepherd's Well at 12.55 to join the 16 others which had been brought down earlier that day. At 13.58 the 23-wagon train left Shepherd's Well for Cricklewood sidings, the final destination of its load being Lambton coke ovens. At Shepherds Well, the sidings were retained for storing wagons until late 1992, but the connection with the old EKLR was severed.

Happily, it now looks as if the name of the East Kent Light Railway will live on. A preservation society of the same name was eventually formed and, on 31 August 1993, a Light Railway Order was obtained for the reopening of the Shepherd's Well-Tilmanstone section. A pair of two-car DMUs has been purchased from BR, and fund-raising activities are now in hand so that land can be purchased at Tilmanstone and an eastern terminus constructed. Repair and maintenance facilities will be established at Tilmanstone terminus, as the provision of those facilities at Shepher's Well is banned.

A small number of Britain's light railways regarded their passenger services as secondary to the freight services, but there were only three companies which obtained Light Railway Orders solely for the transportation of public goods. One of the trio was the Edge Hill Light Railway in southeast Warwickshire.

The EHLR was conceived to provide a means of transporting iron ore from the quarries on Edge Hill to Burton Dassett, on the Stratford-upon-Avon & Midland Junction Railway's line. Quarrying had commenced on Edge Hill in 1868 and a 2ft gauge horse-worked tramway had been installed at the site. In 1871, an aerial ropeway had been constructed from the quarries to Burton Dassett where the East & West Junction Railway's first section of line had just opened. The E&WJR had quickly achieved the unenviable distinction of being one of the two British railway companies which had earned the lowest revenue per mile, and the company's financial demise had come as no surprise. Having lurched from one financial crisis to another, the E&WJR had been incorporated in the newly-formed Stratford-upon-Avon & Midland Junction Railway in 1909,

thereby providing its creditors with a new target for their derision.

During World War 1, a branch line from Burton Dassett to the quarries at Edge Hill was proposed by the SoA&MJR in anticipation of an increased demand for iron ore, but that came to nothing. Undeterred, the SoA&MJR set up a subsidiary company, the Edge Hill Light Railway, to construct a standard gauge line to the quarries and, in the best traditions of light railways, the engineer appointed to oversee the line's construction was Lt-Col Holman Stephens.

The EHLR did not open until 1920, but the SoA&MJR still anticipated adequate mineral traffic in peace-time to justify the line's construction. The quarries were some 700ft up on the hills and, in order to negotiate the steep slopes, a rope-worked incline was necessary; on the 2¼-mile section between the foot of the incline and the SoA&MJR line at Burton

Below: **The rusting remains of Edge Hill No 1 (ex-LB&SCR 'Terrier' No 673) were photographed in 1935.**
Rail Archive Stephenson

Dassett, conventional locomotive haulage was used. At Burton Dassett, a passenger platform had opened in 1898 to replace Warwick Road platform, and the EHLR diverged from the line just to the west of the platform.

The EHLR acquired three locomotives, two being ex-London, Brighton & South Coast Railway 'Terrier' 0-6-0Ts, No 673 *Deptford* and No 674 *Shadwell*. The former had been been modified to 'A1X' class specifications in 1912 and, with 989,623 miles on the clock, cost the EHLR £1,300; it is known to have been purchased by the EHLR in April 1919 and, therefore, it must be assumed that it assisted in the construction of the line. The second 'Terrier' was purchased by the EHLR for £1,750. Somewhat ostentatiously, the EHLR christened the locomotives Nos 1 and 2 respectively.

The third EHLR locomotive was a Manning Wardle 0-4-0ST of 1888, and its designated sphere of activity was between the top of the incline and the quarries. Little is known about the locomotive except that it was named *Sankey* and carried Works No 1088, but that works number indicates that it had probably been built to 'E' class specifications and, therefore, had 2ft 9in wheels and 9in x 14in outside cylinders.

The health of the three locomotives was placed in the hands of Russell Willmott, the SoA&MJR's locomotive superintendent, and repairs were usually carried out at the company's Stratford-upon-Avon depot. On the SoA&MJR, locomotive failures were a part of everyday life and, when the need arose, the EHLR 'Terriers' were drafted in as temporary replacements on the passenger services between Stratford and Broome Junction.

The EHLR's life was brief and the last load of iron ore was transported on 27 January 1925, less than five years after the railway had opened. The locomotives, rolling stock and equipment were left to rust in peace until 1935 when the rails were finally lifted. The idle locomotives had received scant protection from tatty LMSR tarpaulins but it is known that No 1, at least, was not cut up until 1946. As for the SoA&MJR, the line closed to public traffic in 1965 but the section between Fenny Compton and Burton Dassett was taken over by the Army in 1971.

Below: **This picture of the rope-worked incline on the Edge Hill Light Railway was taken in 1935, 10 years after closure.** Rail Archive Stephenson

23 Elliot Junction & Carmyllie Light Railway

Above: **This fine study shows NBR 0-4-0 No 811 as originally built. The locomotive worked on the Carmyllie line before the status of a public light railway was gained.** Rail Archive Stephenson

Quarrying was a long-established industry in the Carmyllie area, to the northwest of Arbroath, and in the early 1800s tenant farmers were permitted to quarry their own farms. The main commodity extracted was slate, much of which was dispatched to Dundee or Edinburgh for building purposes. The principal local landowner was the Earl of Dalhousie who had a mineral railway constructed between Carmyllie quarries and Elliot Junction, on the route of the Dundee & Arbroath Railway. The mineral line opened in May 1854.

The Scottish North Eastern Railway (which had taken over the Dundee & Arbroath Railway in 1862) worked the Carmyllie line from February 1864 and purchased it outright the following year. The SNER was absorbed by the Caledonian Railway in 1866 and, in 1880, the D&AR lines became part of a joint agreement between the Caley and the North British Railway; the arrangement was that the Carmyllie mineral branch should be worked by the Caley and the NBR in alternate years. As if all that didn't create enough confusion, the old quarry line was reincorporated in 1898 as the Elliot Junction & Carmyllie Light Railway, the change of identity being for the purpose of carrying passengers.

The line opened to passenger traffic on 1 February 1900, a morning and evening train to and from Arbroath being advertised with average journey times of around 35min; by June of that year, four trains plied each way on weekdays. The line between Elliot Junction and Carmyllie was five miles long and had intermediate stopping places at Arbilot (1¼ miles), Cuthlie

(2 miles) and Denhead (3½ miles). However, services started and terminated at Arbroath, which was 1½ miles east of Elliot Junction, and so the public timetables always referred to the distances from the former and not the latter. The line presented an unremitting climb towards Carmyllie and, between Cuthlie and Denhead, the ruling gradient of 1 in 35¼ was the steepest in Scotland to be worked by passenger trains. At Carmyllie, the lack of a proper run-round loop meant that locomotives had to use the neck of the quarry sidings which extended beyond the station.

Before the days of passenger traffic on the Carmyllie branch, the locomotives supplied by the NBR included Wheatley-designed 0-4-0s Nos 357/58. Those two had been built at Cowlairs in 1868 for short distance freight work and were paired with small four-wheeled tenders. Both were rebuilt by Matthew Holmes in 1902 and again by William Reid in 1911, by which time they carried Nos 1010/11 in the duplicate list. Although No 1010 was withdrawn in 1921, No 1011 survived until December 1925 thereby claiming the distinction of being the last 0-4-0 tender locomotive to belong to a British main line railway company. By then, however, the 0-4-0s association with the Carmyllie branch was very much a thing of the past. After the introduction of passenger services,

Above: **On 16 June 1960, an enthusiasts' special worked through to Carmyllie, one of the locomotives in charge being '2F' No 46464 of Dundee (Tay Bridge) shed.** H. C. Casserley

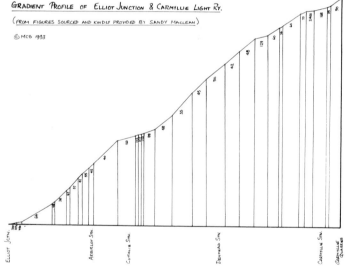

GRADIENT PROFILE OF ELLIOT JUNCTION & CARMYLLIE LIGHT RY.

(FROM FIGURES SOURCED AND KINDLY PROVIDED BY SANDY MACLEAN)

© MCS 1993

the Caley usually used its small '171' class 0-4-4Ts while the NBR found its 'R' (later LNER 'D51') class 4-4-0Ts suitable. Coincidentally, both types had been designed by Dugald Drummond.

As from 31 December 1916, passenger services were suspended as a wartime economy and were not reinstated until 1 February 1919. At the Grouping in 1923 the line's nominal operator, the Dundee & Arbroath Railway, retained its joint status but, as the Caledonian and the North British Railways were parcelled up into different groups, the new joint operators were the LMSR and the LNER. By then, the passenger service comprised just two trains each way on weekdays.

The passenger trains on the Carmyllie branch became less-heavily patronised and were subsequently withdrawn on 2 December 1929. The line nevertheless remained open for goods, principally stone traffic from Carmyllie quarries, and occasional workings continued until total closure on 24 May 1965

although the last revenue-earning train had, in fact, traversed the line on 19 May. In the branch's freight-only days, an ex-NBR 'J31' class 0-6-0 and, later, former-NER 'J24' 0-6-0s including Nos 1852, 1895 and, until its withdrawal in 1944, No 1949 were the usual locomotives. From 1950, however, '2MT' 2-6-0s Nos 46463/64, nominally of Dundee (Tay Bridge) shed but out-stationed at Arbroath, combined trips on the Carmyllie branch with duties on Dundee-Arbroath local workings. Of the '2MTs', No 46464, which became nicknamed the 'Carmyllie Pilot', is now preserved on the Strathspey Railway.

24 Elsenham & Thaxted Light Railway

One of the intentions of the Light Railways Act of 1896 was to encourage the construction of lines to agricultural areas, thereby providing a much-needed boost to local economies. In northwest Essex, the area around Thaxted provided a prime example of the type of community meant to benefit from light railways. In the mid-19th century, Thaxted's population had been over 2,500 but, by the end of the century, the severe agricultural depression had resulted in a drop to a little over 1,600. These days, Thaxted is usually described in the guide books as having an abundance of picturesque timber-framed houses and a delightful parish church but, understandably, the scenic delights were not uppermost in the locals' minds during the hard times of the late 19th century.

With a view to reversing the decline in the area's fortunes, the Elsenham, Thaxted & Bardfield Light Railway was conceived in 1896. The master plan was for a line of 2ft 6in gauge, but when the Great Eastern Railway was approached with a view to working the line, the matter of the proposed gauge presented obvious problems. Consequently, negotiations were extremely protracted and, in 1906, the original plans were superseded by those for a standard gauge line from Elsenham to Thaxted, the idea of the extension to Great Bardfield being abandoned.

Under the revised title of the Elsenham & Thaxted Light Railway, the line opened to the public on 1 April 1913, the customary ceremonies having taken place the previous day. From the outset, the branch was worked by the Great Eastern Railway and it went down in the annals as the last new 'GER' line to open. The line started at Elsenham, 35½ miles from Liverpool Street on the GER's main line between Bishop's Stortford and Cambridge. Elsenham station had the unusual arrangement of staggered platforms, the down one being on the opposite side of a level crossing to the up one. The Thaxted branch trains used the rear face of the up platform but, at that

point, there was no physical connection between the branch and the main line. The connection was made in the goods yard opposite the down platform. The other end of the line was 5½ miles away at Thaxted, where the terminus comprised a single platform, modest freight facilities and a brick-built engine shed. The intermediate stopping places on the branch were Henham halt (1¾ miles from Elsenham), Sibley's (3 miles) which was suffixed 'for Chickney & Broxted' and Cutler's Green halt (4½ miles). Mill Road halt, near Henham, was added on 18 December 1922.

The line was single-track and the ruling gradient of 1 in 50 was met at several places along the route. At first, a 14-ton axle-weight limit was imposed although, in later years, that was raised to 16 tons. The weight restriction meant that, at the outset, the motive power had to be James Holden's popular 'R24' 0-6-0Ts, usually known as 'Jubilees'. In 1902, before the opening of the Thaxted line, the GER had instigated a programme for rebuilding many of its 'R24s'

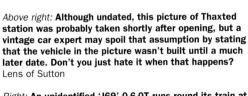

Above right: **Although undated, this picture of Thaxted station was probably taken shortly after opening, but a vintage car expert may spoil that assumption by stating that the vehicle in the picture wasn't built until a much later date. Don't you just hate it when that happens?**
Lens of Sutton

Right: **An unidentified 'J69' 0-6-0T runs round its train at Thaxted on 30 June 1951.**
H.C.Casserley

with larger boilers and tanks, primarily to help them cope with the increasingly heavy London suburban trains, and eventually, a number of the class were transferred to rural duties including the Thaxted line. In LNER days, the rebuilt 'R24s' were designated 'J69s' while the unrebuilt members became 'J67s'; the majority lasted well into the British Railways era and the last survived until 1962. For the ceremonial opening of the Thaxted branch, 'R24s' Nos 168 and 196 worked back-to-back, and the latter remained to work the scheduled services on the following day.

Although there was an engine shed at Thaxed, the parent depot was Cambridge and the usual practice was for one 'R24' to be out-stationed at Thaxted for two or three weeks at a time, returning to Cambridge on Sundays for a boiler wash-out and tube cleaning. Later, on rare occasions, other Cambridge-based locomotive types ventured on to the Thaxted branch, 'T18' (LNER 'J66') and 'C72' (LNER 'J68') class 0-6-0Ts, and 'Y14' (LNER 'J15') 0-6-0 tender engines being among the infrequent visitors. For coaching stock, the GER dispatched five six-wheel carriages to the branch but, because of the 12in height of the branch's platforms, steps and smaller diameter wheels were fitted, and the drawgear was modified accordingly. On branch duties, the carriages were perfectly acceptable but, when trips to the workshops were necessary, the steps had to be removed as they fouled the main line loading gauges.

The branch generated a reasonable amount of traffic, particularly during World War 1 when most of Britain's farms stepped up production in order to offset the loss of imported produce. During the war, weekday services on the line usually comprised five trains to Elsenham and six to Thaxted, with at least one in each direction being mixed. By 1922, there was an additional train in each direction. At the Grouping in 1923, the E&TLR logically passed to the LNER. During the 1920s and 1930s, the Thaxted branch bucked the national trend by maintaining satisfactory passenger receipts and, at Bank Holidays in particular, the line was well patronised by tourists and ramblers. Freight revenue during that period was unimpressive with sugar beet from Sibley's and Thaxted providing the mainstay but, with the outbreak of World War 2, local agriculture once again boomed and much of the produce had to go by rail.

After the war, the freight traffic reverted to its former unspectacular level but, in the years of austerity, the passenger traffic dwindled. Around the time of Nationalisation in 1948, the average number of passengers using the line daily was just 50. Predictably, British Railways took a close look at the situation and, after a conspicuous absence of a fight by Dunmow Rural District Council, the last passenger services were scheduled for 13 September 1952. The last working was given a respectable send-off, and 'J69' class 0-6-0T No 68579 looked very dignified at the head of three ex-GER bogie coaches. Remarkably, bogie coaches had first appeared on the line only in 1948. After the cessation of passenger services, a freight working was retained on Mondays, Wednesdays and Fridays only, but it was in such little demand that the service was soon reduced to Wednesdays only. The usual locomotive on those services was No 68579 which was based at Bishop's Stortford shed. Inevitably, the freight services did not last for long, the total closure of the Thaxted branch officially coming on 1 June 1953.

Right: **On 29 August 1952, the 11.50am mixed train from Thaxted to Elsenham was hauled by 'J68' class 0-6-0T No 68645. On arriving at Elsenham, the goods portion was left at the shunters' cabin for eventual marshalling while the passenger portion proceeded into the station.** R. E. Vincent

Below: **Eastern Region timetable, 18 June to 23 September 1951.** Author's files

Table 40   ELSENHAM and THAXTED (Light Railway)

Miles		Week Days only						Miles		Week Days only						
		a.m	p.m S	p.m	p.m E	p.m	p.m			a.m	a.m.	a.m	p.m	p.m E	p.m S	p.m E
	4 London (Liverpool St.) dep	6 56	1227	1255	3P36	5 18	6 36	—	Thaxted........dep	7 36	9 55	1150	4 0	5 45	6 0	7 23
—	Elsenham........dep	8 55	1 43	2 28	5 0	6 24	7 55	1	Cutler's Green Halt	7 40	9 59	1154	4 4	5 49	6 4	7 27
1	Mill Road Halt	8 59	1 47	2 32	5 4	6 28	7 59	2½	Sibley's for Chickney { arr	7 46	10 5	12 0	4 10	5 55	6 10	7 33
1½	Henham Halt	9 3	1 51	2 36	5 8	6 32	8 3		and Broxted { dep	7 47	10 6	12 5	4 11	6 0	6 15	7 34
3	Sibley's for Chickney { arr	9 8	1 56	2 41	5 13	6 37	8 8	3½	Henham Halt	7 52	10 11	1210	4 16	6 5	6 20	7 39
	and Broxted { dep	9 14	1 57	2 42	5 14	6 38	9	4½	Mill Road Halt	7 56	10 15	1214	4 20	6 9	6 24	7 43
4½	Cutler's Green Halt	9 20	2 3	2 48	5 20	6 44	8 15	5½	Elsenham........arr	8 0	10 19	1218	4 24	6 14	6 29	7 48
5½	Thaxted........arr	9 23	2 6	2 51	5 23	6 47	8 18	41	4 London (Liverpool St.) arr	9 16	11 30.	1U58	5Y58	8 3	8 3	1117

E Except Saturdays   **P** Dep. 3 42 p.m. on Saturdays   **U** Arr. 1 55 p.m. on Saturdays

Y Arr. 6 2 p.m. on Saturdays   **S** or **S** Saturdays only

One class only between Elsenham and Thaxted.   **Tickets (single only) issued on train**

25 Festiniog Railway

As has already been seen, a few railway companies such as the Bideford, Westward Ho! & Appledore and the Easingwold were originally authorised by Acts of Parliament, but obtained Light Railway Orders at later dates in order to economise in certain aspects of their operations. Another example of this pattern is the Festiniog Railway, the world-famous narrow gauge line in North Wales, which obtained its Order 87 years after opening for public traffic. In true North Wales fashion, the Festiniog had first been created to facilitate the transportation of slate.

The first slate quarry in the area had been opened at Diphwys in 1755 by Methusalem Jones. The problem of exporting the slate was eventually solved by the opening in 1824 of a new harbour at Portmadoc, and an Act of Parliament was obtained in 1832 for the construction of a railway to the harbour. The 13¼-mile line ran between Portmadoc and Duffws, near Blaenau Festiniog; it was built to a gauge of 1ft 11¼ in (later adjusted to 1ft 11½ in) and opened to freight traffic on 20 April 1836. For many years, the only form of motive power on the line was the four-legged variety, the idea of converting from horse to locomotive power not even surfacing until 1860, when the company was transporting over 50,000 tons of slate annually.

The FR's permanent way needed a degree of upgrading before locomotives could be used. The company's real problem, however, was that of the narrowness of its gauge as, in those days, most engineers considered it impossible to construct usable locomotives to such small dimensions; nevertheless, Messrs George England & Co of Hatcham Ironworks in Kent took up the challenge. The first two locomotives were delivered by England's on 18 July 1863, No 1 being named *Mountaineer* and No 2 *The Princess*. Costing £1,000 each, they were 0-4-0STs which had small four-wheeled tenders. The locomotives were transported by rail from the manufacturer by means of standard trucks, but as the only standard gauge line in the area at the time was at Caernarvon, the locomotives had to be

Below: **A short goods train is seen near the south end of Tan-y-Bwlch station. Apparently, the round-topped wagon is a gunpowder van.** Bucknall Collection/Ian Allan Library

Above: **One of the Festiniog's Fairlies, possibly No 10 *Merddin Emrys*, stands alongside the goods shed at Duffws in this late 1880s picture.** Bucknall Collection/Ian Allan Library

hauled by horse-drawn cart from there to Portmadoc. According to contemporary records, the FR paid a total of £59/11s (£59.55p) for 'delivery charges'.

The first locomotive-hauled train ran on 23 October 1863. Thoughts had already turned to operating passenger services and, after close scrutiny by the Board of Trade, the first public passenger trains between Portmadoc and Dinas were operated on 6 January 1865. Dinas was on a spur which left the main line just before Blaenau Festiniog, passenger services to Duffws via Blaenau not being introduced until January 1866. By then, two additional locomotives, No 3 *Lord Palmerston* and No 4 *The Prince* had been delivered by George England, both being basically similar to the original pair. The FR's original stud of coaching stock was described as: *'squat four-wheel 'boxes', rather wide and scarcely clearing the ground'*, Fourteen carriages of this nature were delivered between 1864 and 1867. Bogie coaches first appeared in 1871, eight being delivered between then and 1896. As for freight stock, the FR went on to amass, at its peak, a total of 1,219 slate wagons, 120 vans and some 80 other vehicles. The company livery was red with black lining, although the shade of red and the colours of the lining changed over the years. It was 1925 before the significant change to 'Swindon' green was made.

At Portmadoc, the passenger station was situated beyond the northern end of the 'Cob', a 1,600yd stone embankment across the estuary of the Afon Glaslyn. The harbour, which was slightly to the north of the station, was reached by means of a track across Britannia Bridge, while the company's locomotive department was at Boston Lodge, at the southern end of the Cob. Regarding local names, it is generally accepted that 'Port Madoc' derives from William

Madocks, a prominent local businessman who was instrumental in the formation of the Festiniog Railway. Sadly, Madocks passed away four years before the FR obtained its Act of Parliament. As for the name of Boston Lodge, Madocks sat as Member of Parliament for Boston, Lincolnshire, between 1802 and 1820.

From Portmadoc, the line was uphill all the way with a ruling gradient of 1 in 80; until 1871, the locomotives were required to work only in the direction of Dinas and Duffws, the return journeys being worked by gravity. At first, there were intermediate stations at Penrhyn (3¼ miles) which was renamed Penrhyndeudraeth in 1912 after the village which it served, and Hafod-y-Llyn (7 miles) which was replaced in July 1872 by Tan-y-Bwlch station, almost half a mile to the north. The original passenger terminus at Dinas disappeared from the public timetables after August 1870, by which time through running to Duffws (13¼ miles from Portmadoc) had become the norm. Additional stopping places were later provided at Boston Lodge halt (¾ mile) in July 1928, Minffordd Junction (2 miles) in August 1872, Dduallt (9¾ miles) in 1880, Moelwyn halt (11 miles) in August 1917 (closed by 1924), Tan-y-Grisiau (11¾ miles) in March 1866, Blaenau Festiniog Junction (12¾ miles) in June 1881 and Blaenau Festiniog (GWR) in September 1883. Of those additions, the word 'Junction' was later dropped from the titles of the stations at Minffordd and Blaenau Festiniog, the latter being suffixed, instead, 'LNW' to denote its proximity to the London & North Western Railway's station in the town.

The initial passenger service comprised five trains in each direction on weekdays, a sixth being added by 1868. Weekly quarrymens' trains were introduced in April 1872, daily services commencing in February 1881, but the 'carriages' were little more than open trucks. The railway was successful, with some 315,000 passengers being carried in its first three years of operation and over 126,000 tons of slate being carried in 1868 alone, and so additional locomotives were considered necessary. Two more 0-4-0STs, No 5 *Welsh Pony* and No 6 *Little Giant*, were delivered by England's in 1867, their wheelbases being slightly longer and their tanks larger than those of the older locomotives.

The volume of traffic on the FR started to cause problems, and so plans were made to double the line throughout. However, that became unnecessary when the FR acquired a double-boiler Fairlie locomotive in August 1869, as the engine had twice the power of the existing 0-4-0STs. Robert Fairlie was the son-in-law of George England, and the former had completed his first 'double engine' for the Neath & Brecon Railway in 1865. The FR's Fairlie 0-4-4-0T became No 7 *Little Wonder* and, on a demonstration run, proved quite at ease when in charge of a 114-ton train from Portmadoc to Hafod-y-Llyn.

The Festiniog Railway became something of a celebrity in railway circles. For an initial construction cost of just £2,000 per mile, it was operating at a profit greater than that of almost any other railway company in the land. Furthermore, its Fairlie locomotive generated considerable interest in engineering circles throughout the world and, predictably, a second such engine was soon acquired. Built by the Avonside Engine Co of Bristol to Fairlie's patent, it was delivered in December 1872 and became No 8 *James Spooner*. Further locomotives delivered during the 1870s were single Fairlie 0-4-4T No 9 *Taliesin* and double Fairlie 0-4-4-0T No 10 *Merddin Emrys,* the latter being built at Boston Lodge Works. In 1879, 0-4-0ST No 3 *Mountaineer* and the original

Below: **Avonside-built Fairlie 0-4-4-0T No 8 *James Spooner* poses at Portmadoc.** Bucknall Collection/Ian Allan Library

Fairlie, No 7 *Little Wonder* were considered worn out and were subsequently laid up. A minor flurry of renumbering resulted. The only other locomotive to join the Festiniog fleet before the end of the century was to be *Livingston Thompson,* another double Fairlie 0-4-4-0T which was completed in 1885. Originally carrying No 11, it was soon allotted No 3.

During the 1880s, the slate trade in North Wales entered a period of decline. This obviously affected traffic on the FR, and matters were not helped by the LNWR's construction of a wharf at Deganwy, near Llandudno, which soon handled a significant proportion of the slate from Blaenau Festiniog. The harbour authorities at Portmadoc chose not to reduce their charges in order to counter the competition. A further blow to the FR was the death of its dedicated director Charles Spooner, the son of James Spooner who had done so much to promote the railway in the first place. The slate traffic continued a steady decline throughout the 1890s, but an increase in tourist traffic provided a little consolation. Despite the company's unpromising financial situation, works were undertaken on the approach to Dinas in order to construct a new deviating line to serve the quarries beyond the old station. An engine shed was provided at Dinas Junction, and the old turntable from Duffws was installed alongside.

At the outbreak of World War 1 in 1914, the FR came under Government control. Although the FR's 'compensation' for loss of income was, in fact, greater that the actual receipts for the years preceding the war, the austerity of the war years presented other problems. One was the shortage of coal which dictated that the double-boiler Fairlie locomotives could be used only when absolutely essential. After the war,

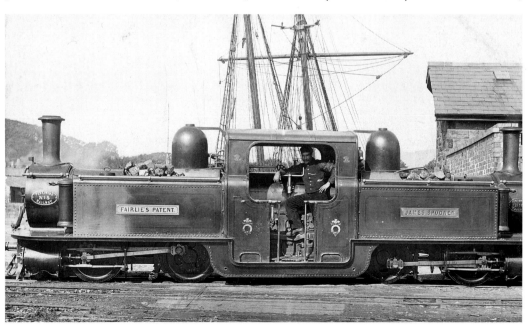

the Chairman of the FR was the suspiciously acquisitive Henry Jack, who was also the Managing Director of the North Wales Power & Traction Co with its significant interest in three other narrow gauge lines in the area: the ancient horse-worked Croesor Tramway, the North Wales Narrow Gauge Railway and the fledgling Portmadoc, Beddgelert & South Snowdon Railways. The NWNGR and PB&SSR subsequently merged and were reconstituted in March 1922 as the Welsh Highland Railway (Light Railway) Co (qv) with the benefit of a Light Railway Order, permission being granted for completion of a line from Dinas Junction, on the LNWR's line south of Caernarvon to Portmadoc.

At the Grouping, the FR had narrowly escaped the clutches of, first, the LMSR and, then, the GWR. Instead, it had elected to fend for itself as an independent concern. When the neighbouring WHR obtained its Light Railway Order, the FR not only appreciated, but also needed, the economies which such an Order offered, and it obtained its own LRO on 30 January 1923. By then, one economy had been made with the closure of Duffws station to passenger traffic from 1 January 1923, the timetables for the previous summer having showed seven trains each way on weekdays with an additional one in each direction on Wednesdays. The journey times for the 13¼ miles between Portmadoc and Duffws had usually been around one hour.

In April 1923, Lt-Col Holman Stephens was appointed as the Civil Engineer and Locomotive Superintendent of both the Festiniog and the Welsh Highland Railways. By 1925, he had become Chairman and Managing Director of both concerns, but Stephens and the Celtic race did not always see eye to eye. The fiercely-proud railwaymen of Portmadoc did not take too kindly to the intrusion of a mere Englishman who, when given the chance, retreated to his home in Tonbridge and administered his Welsh charges by a form of remote control. Most usually, visits to North Wales were delegated to Stephens's assistant, W. H. Austen, and a wealth of correspondence shuttled back and forth between the two men. Some of Stephens' letters survive today, and they reveal much about his questionable attitude to the railwaymen of North Wales. In one missive, Stephens wrote to Austen: *'The people on the Festiniog are quite different to our people…They can't help it, it's their nature'.* Another letter to Austen opined: *'you seem to have some perfectly stupid people to deal with'.*

At Portmadoc, a physical connection was made between the FR and the WHR in 1923 and a new station was opened in the town for use by both companies. For a time, it was hoped that the combined management of the two companies would reverse the downward trend in their finances, and through running from Blaenau Festiniog to Dinas Junction, the WHR's northern terminus, was eventually undertaken. The FR's 0-4-0STs were the usual locomotives on through workings, the Fairlie 0-4-4-0Ts soon being deemed uneconomical for such duties. The WHR's locomotive, 0-6-4T *Moel Tryfan,* and seven WHR carriages were cut down so that they could undertake the through run.

Despite the joint operation of the two neighbouring companies and the 'Colonel Stephens' style of economies, which included the acquisition of various internal combustion rail-tractors, finances failed to improve. During the mid and late 1920s, the FR's passenger figures rarely exceeded 150,000 per annum while the slate traffic hovered between 52,000 and 67,000 tons annually. The economic slump of the early 1930s provided yet another headache for the company and that, combined with the competition of

Above left: **The Festiniog's Fairlie No 3** *Livingstone Thompson* **produces a fine head of steam with an up working in Tan-y-Bwlch cutting. It is believed that the picture was taken in the early 1900s.**
Bucknall Collection/Ian Allan Library

Left: **Preserved No 2** *Prince* **leaves Portmadoc with the 2pm train to Penrhyndeudraeth on 8 August 1957.**
R. E. Vincent

Steam Locomotives of the Festiniog Railway

(Dimensions as originally built)

1st No	Later No	Name	Type	Maker	Built	Wheels	Cyls	Tons	T.E.	Wdn
1	3	*Mountaineer*	0-4-0ST	England	1863	2ft 0in	8in x 12in	7½t	3,177lb	1879
2	1	*The Princess**	0-4-0ST	England	1863	2ft 0in	8in x 12in	7½t	4,624lb	1946 P
3	4	*Lord Palmerston**	0-4-0ST	England	1864	2ft 0in	8in x 12in	7½t	4,489lb	1932 C
4	2	*The Prince**	0-4-0ST	England	1864	2ft 0in	8in x 12in	7½t	4,489lb	1946 P
5	5	*Welsh Pony*	0-4-0ST	England	1867	2ft 2in	8⅛in x 12in	10t	3,312lb	1938 P
6	6	*Little Giant*	0-4-0ST	England	1867	2ft 2in	8⅛in x 12in	10t	3,312lb	1932 C
7	7	*Little Wonder*	0-4-4-0T	England	1869	2ft 4in	8¼in x 13in	19½t	5,357lb	1879
8	8	*James Spooner*	0-4-4-0T	Avonside	1872	2ft 8in	8½in x 14in	22t	5,410lb	1933
9	9	*Taliesin*	0-4-4T	Vulcan	1876	2ft 8in	9in x 14in	17t	3,029lb	1932
10	10	*Merddin Emrys*	0-4-4-0T	FR	1879	2ft 9¼in	9in x 14in	24t	6,059lb	1946 P
11	3	*Livingstone Thompson**	0-4-4-0T	FR	1885	2ft 9¼in	9in x 14in	24t	6,059lb	1946
11	11**	*Moel Tryfan*	0-6-4T	Vulcan	1877	2ft 6in	8½in x 12in	14t	3,855lb	1937
12	12**	*Russell*	2-6-2T	Hunslet	1906	2ft 4in	10¾in x 15in	19¼t	7,425lb	1946 P
13	13**	-	4-6-0PT	Baldwin	1917	1ft 11½in	9in x12in	14½t		1936

* Locomotives later renamed: *The Princess* became *Princess*; *Lord Palmerston* became *Palmerston*; *The Prince* became *Prince*; *Livingstone Thompson* became *Taliesin*.
** Nos 11/12/13 acquired from North Wales Narrow Gauge Ry in 1923.
P Locomotive preserved (No 12 *Russell* on Welsh Highland Ry).
C After withdrawal, parts used in reconstruction of other FR locomotives.

road transport, caused Stephens to toy with the idea of withdrawing the passenger services completely. Indeed winter services had ceased in October 1930. The 1930s saw the continuing decline in the slate trade, although passenger traffic during the summer months actually increased as a result of fierce promotion of the area's scenic attractions. The FR took a 42-year lease of the WHR in 1934, despite the latter having withdrawn its services three years earlier, but the anticipated revival was shortlived and the last services on the WHR operated on 19 June 1937. On the FR itself, the outbreak of war in 1939 brought about a sudden cessation of passenger and workmens' services on 16 September. No further public passenger workings were to be made over FR metals until the preservation era in 1955.

The slate trains continued operating until 1 August 1946. In 1950, powers for a formal abandonment were refused but this proved fortuitous as, in 1954, a preservation society obtained the remnants of the old company. On 23 July 1955, passenger services were resumed between Portmadoc and Boston Lodge, the line being extended to Tan-y-Bwlch by 1958. The ultimate target, Blaenau Festiniog, was reached in 1982, a deviation having been necessary to circumvent Tanygrisau Reservoir which had swallowed up a sizeable part of the northern section of the original route. The Festiniog Railway Society was the forerunner of many preservation organisations, and today it still sets standards for others to follow. A full passenger service is operated from mid-July to late September, and among the impressive stud of working locomotives are four of the original Festiniog Railway machines.

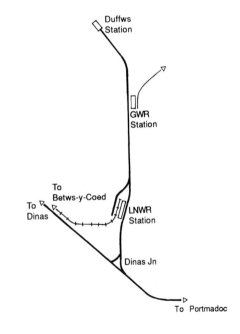

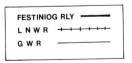

Above: **Diagramatic layout of Blaenau Festiniog.**

26 Firbeck Light Railway

By the late 1800s, the railway map of the South Yorkshire coalfield was akin to an abstract knitting pattern, but the expansion of the coalfield and its railways continued into the present century. One 20th century development was that of Firbeck Main Colliery, situated between Doncaster and Worksop, which was deemed at the outset to require a rail connection. The colliery company was formed in 1913, two years after the Great Central Railway had surveyed for a possible line between Worksop and Bawtry passing close to Firbeck Main. In view of the GCR's decision not to proceed with the line, the col-

liery's proprietors promoted a similar railway themselves but, remarkably, the GCR joined in with the opposition to the line. Although the scheme looked set to win the day, it was nevertheless dropped.

The proposal was abandoned because the colliery owners had agreed with the various railway companies in the area to join forces and promote a line which ran from Harworth Junction to Firbeck Main, but no further south. Under the banner of the Firbeck Light Railway, the necessary Order was obtained in February 1916, but the Board of Trade refused permission for construction work to start immediately because of the need to concentrate national resources for the war effort. Construction of Firbeck Main Colliery finally commenced in 1923, the temporary track of the light railway being opened on 7 April 1924. A permanent track was completed and opened on 1 October 1926. The 5¼ -mile line started at Firbeck Junction on the South Yorkshire Joint Railway's Doncaster-Worksop line which had opened throughout in 1910. From a point about 1½ miles south of Firbeck Junction, a LNER branch to Harworth Colliery was opened on 22 April 1929 and, in the colliery yard, an end-on junction was made with a branch from Scrooby.

For a light railway, the line accommodated some hefty locomotives. At the smaller end of the scale were ex-Midland '4F' and GCR 0-6-0s while, at the other end, assorted eight-coupled machines were commonplace. Former GCR, NER and GNR 0-8-0s were used regularly, with various types of 2-8-0s taking over in later years. No scheduled public passenger services ever ran on the line, but regular excursion workings for the benefit of the miners and their families seem to have been operated from Firbeck Colliery as early as 1929. At Harworth Colliery, it is known that summer excursion trains for staff operated until at least 1967. At both

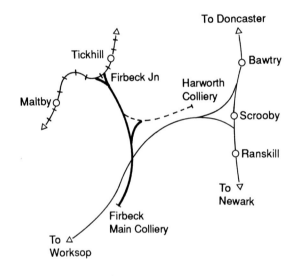

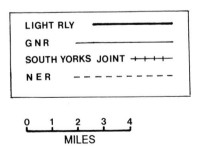

Above: **Ex-LNER '02' class 2-8-0 No 63937 approaches Firbeck Junction with a coal train on 23 July 1963.**
M.Mitchell

collieries, the internal shunting was undertaken by colliery company (later NCB) locomotives. During the late 1960s, the two NCB locomotives used at Firbeck were Avonside 0-6-0ST *Daisy* and Hudswell Clarke 0-6-0 diesel *Firbeck*, while a Peckett 0-4-0ST and a Thomas Hill diesel worked at Harworth.

In October 1968, a DMU appeared at Firbeck on an enthusiasts' special, the RCTS taking the opportunity of using the line while it was still open. The closure of Firbeck Main colliery and the line south of Harworth Junction had already been announced, and took effect on 31 December 1968. The section between Firbeck Junction, on the Doncaster-Worksop line, and Harworth remained open to serve Har-

worth colliery and Messrs Glass Bulbs Ltd, the latter concern having had, in the 1960s, two small Ruston Hornsby diesel shunters for use on its standard gauge sidings. Today, Harworth colliery remains open, its immediate future being secure because it has the largest coal reserves of any pit in British Coal's Nottinghamshire Group, and most of the coal is transported from the colliery by rail with Class 56 or 60 diesels in charge.

27 Fraserburgh & St Combs Light Railway

The hamlet of Faithlie in the Buchan area of Aberdeenshire was founded in the 1500s but, by the time of the railway era, the community had grown and adopted the more familiar name of Fraserburgh. As if to confuse incomers, however, locals referred to the town as 'The Broch'. For the benefit of mere Englishmen, it should be explained that 'broch' is not a Scottish name for a badger, but an ancient name applied to settlements and the types of castles developed by the Picts during the first century BC. Leaving the subject of Scottish military architecture to one side, the first railway to reach Fraserburgh was the Formartine & Buchan Railway which opened its line from Maud Junction, on the Aberdeen–Peterhead route, on 24 April 1865. Today that railway company might sound unfamiliar but it was, in effect, a subsidiary of the Great North of Scotland Railway.

Fraserburgh grew steadily over the next 30-odd years, and the nearby villages of St. Combs, Cairnbulg

and Inverallochie started to clamour for a branch line. With the passing of the Light Railways Act, local businessmen were encouraged to promote such a branch, but the scheme was subsequently adopted by the GNoSR which, in 1899, obtained the necessary Order.

The St Combs branch opened on 1 May 1903. It started at Fraserburgh station which had had to be extended to accommodate the branch, although the official opening of the 'new' station did not take place until 1 July. From platform three of Fraserburgh station, a separate branch track ran parallel to the main line for virtually one mile and, in a most un-Scottish manner, the branch bisected the Fraserburgh golf course. The branch, which was devoid of signals, had intermediate stopping places at Kirkton Bridge halt (1-mile) which was adjacent to the golf club, Philorth Bridge halt (2½ miles) and Cairnbulg (3½ miles); the two halts were treated as 'request stops' and, consequently, did not appear in the public timetables for many years. Cairnbulg station served, not only the village of its name, but also Inverallochy. There was considerable rivalry between the two adjacent villages

Left: **Manson-designed GNoSR 'O' (later LNER 'D42') class 4-4-0 No 17 stands in the main line section of Fraserburgh station while an unidentified 'E' (later LNER 'J91') class 0-6-0T waits at the St Combs platform on the far side.** Lens of Sutton

Below: **Ex-GER 'F4' class 2-4-2T No 7164 prepares to depart from St Combs on 17 June 1949. A six-wheeled coach is evident.** H. C. Casserley

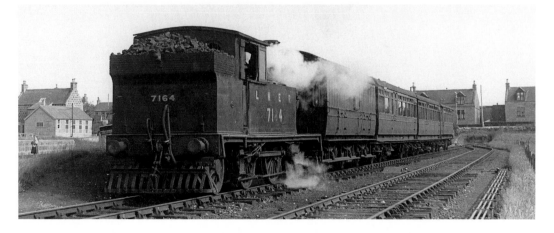

as to which should provide the name of the station, but when the Laird of Cairnbulg donated the necessary land, the Inverallochy lobby was left with little ammunition. The terminus of the branch at St Combs (5¼ miles from Fraserburgh) comprised a basic range of facilities and, in keeping with many stations elsewhere on the GNoSR, the buildings were simple ones made from timber.

It may seem mundane to state that the locomotives selected to work the line at first were 0-6-0Ts but, remarkably, the GNoSR only ever had nine six-coupled tank locomotives on its books. Those used on the St Combs branch were 'E' (later LNER 'J91') class engines which had been built by Kitsons of Leeds to a design of the GNoSR's superintendent, James Manson. Numbered 37/38/41, the three 'E' class 0-6-0Ts had originally been intended for shunting and banking duties, but had later been used on the suburban passenger services around Aberdeen, those workings being known to all and sundry as the 'subbies'. For those duties, they had been fitted with Westinghouse gear, but the 'Es' were ousted from the 'subbies' by 'R' (later LNER 'G10') class 0-4-4Ts and at least two were subsequently drafted to the St Combs branch. Because much of the line was unfenced, cowcatchers had to be fitted to the front and rear buffer beams of the locomotives, but cynics said that the slowness of the branch services was such that there was more likelihood of the cattle overtaking the trains. Another oft-repeated comment about the speed of the branch trains was that, if flower seeds were scattered from the carriage window on a down journey, they would be in bloom for the return trip.

In 1905, the GNoSR caught on to the national fad for steam railmotors and, in November that year, two such machines were delivered. Costing £1,045 each, their power units were supplied by Andrew Barclays of Kilmarnock, the bodies being built in the GNoSR's workshops at Inverurie. The railmotors' coach sections had a central passage with reversible slat seats on either side, the capacity of each car being 46 third-class pas-

sengers. The power units had vertical boilers which were made by Cochran & Co of Annan and, although such boilers had been used in other fields, they were new to the world of locomotive engineering. Before entering service, the two railmotors were subjected to trials during which they proved capable of accelerating to 30mph in 20sec and reaching speeds of 60mph. The GNoSR dispatched one of the pair to the St Combs branch and the other to the Lossiemouth branch but, unfortunately, it was soon found that their boilers steamed poorly and, overall, they failed to fulfil the expectations which had arisen during their trials. Neither lasted on its respective branch line for very long. In 1906, the coach bodies were converted to saloons which, in their last years, found their way back to the St Combs branch, while the power units were later put to use as stationary boilers. After the departure of the railmotors, the 'E' class 0-6-0Ts were hastily reinstated on the St Combs line.

The branch became part of the LNER at the Grouping, and the new proprietors seemed unimpressed by the 0-6-0Ts. Between June 1926 and July 1932, four ex-NBR 'D51' class 4-4-0Ts were transferred to Kittybrewster, the parent shed of Fraserburgh, principally for duties on the St Combs line and, for their new activities, were fitted with the obligatory cow-catchers. The 'D51s' were, by then, in the very last years of their lives, and the St Combs contingent of LNER Nos 10456/58/61/62 were to see no further action after their spells on the branch. The very last survivor of the class was, in fact, No 10462 which was withdrawn in August 1933.

By the time of the demise of the 'D15s' three ex-GER 'F4' class 2-4-2Ts had been transferred to Scotland for other branch duties, and two were viewed as suitable replacements for the 'D51s' on the St Combs line. They were LNER Nos 7176/7236 and, of course, they were fitted with cow-catchers before being let loose on the branch. In 1941, the two 'F4s' were equipped for auto-working but that principle was discontinued on the St Combs branch after just three years. Sister locomotive No 7222, which had been the other member of the trio transferred to Scotland, was dispatched to the branch in 1943 after the withdrawal of No 7176, and an additional 'F4', designated BR No 67157, was allocated to St Combs duties in 1948. The 'F4s' were displaced, in the early 1950s, by ex-LMSR '2MT' 2-6-0s and, by then, the last of the line's vintage six-wheeled coaches had just been withdrawn and so the spectacle of a modern 2-6-0 hauling veteran non-bogie stock was only narrowly avoided. Among the '2MTs' which worked the line regularly during the 1950s were Nos

Left: **This picture of 10 July 1957 looks towards St Combs; it seems that the flower displays at the base of the station nameboard have received more attention than the station buildings.** H. C. Casserley

WEEKDAYS ONLY

Miles			a.m	a.m	a.m	p.m	p.m	Sats only Ex Sats	Sats only					
			a.m	a.m	a.m	p.m	p.m	p.m p.m	p.m	p.m	p.m	p.m	p.m	
	Fraserburgh .. .. .. lev.		6 25	7 55	10 30	12 10	1 0	..	1 5	4 10	5 15	6 15	9 15	..
1	Kirkton Bridge Halt ..		D	D	D	D	D	..	D	D	D	D	D	..
1	Philorth Bridge Halt ..		D	D	D	D	D	..	D	D	D	D	D	..
2¼	Cairnbulg		6 39	8 9	10 47	12 24	1 14	..	1 19	4 24	5 29	6 29	9 29	..
5	St. Combs .. .. .. arr.		6 45	8 15	10 53	12 30	1 20	..	1 25	4 30	5 35	6 35	9 35	..

		a.m	a.m	a.m	p.m	p.m	Sats only Ex Sats	Sats only					
		a.m	a.m	a.m	p.m	p.m	p.m p.m	p.m	p.m	p.m	p.m	p.m	
St. Combs .. .. .. lev.		6 55	8 25	11 15	12 35	1 40	..	1 45	4 38	5 45	6 45	9 45	..
Cairnbulg		7 2	8 32	11 27	12 42	1 47	..	1 52	4 45	5 52	6 52	9 52	..
Philorth Bridge Halt ..		D	D	D	D	D	..	D	D	D	D	D	..
Kirkton Bridge Halt ..		D	D	D	D	D	..	D	D	D	D	D	..
Fraserburgh .. .. .. arr.		7 15	8 45	11 40	12 55	2 0	..	2 5	4 58	6 5	7 5	10 5	..

Above: **Scottish Region timetable, 14 June to 19 September 1954.** Author's files

46460/61/64, BR Standard '2MT' 2-6-0 No 78045 being a regular deputy. As for the 'F4s', the last of the class to remain in use on the branch was No 67157, and here the story of the 'D51s' was repeated as, when that 'F4' was withdrawn in June 1956, the class became extinct. For ageing LNER classes, the motto seemed to be 'see St Combs and die'.

During the steam era, the only recorded departures from 'regular' motive power on the branch were those involving 'D40' class 4-4-0s No 62270/9 in the early 1950s, neither of which was fitted with cowcatchers. In June 1959, twin-car Craven DMUs took over the passenger workings, Metro-Cammell units appearing in subsequent years, and the improved visibility from cabs of the DMUs meant that the distinctive cowcatchers were no longer necessary. With the dieselisation of the branch and the withdrawal in November 1960 of freight facilities, the sidings and loop at St Combs were removed and the station building was replaced by the body of a withdrawn van. Cairnbulg station was reduced to the status of an unstaffed halt.

As for services, the first timetable showed four passenger and two mixed trains from Fraserburgh to St Combs, with two passenger and four mixed workings in the return direction. The summer 1922 passenger timetable for the line, which was clearly marked 'One Class Only', showed six trains each way on weekdays plus an additional Saturdays-only evening train. Journey times were 20min, three minutes slower than the times advertised in 1903. By 1940, the frequency of

services was the same but at least the two halts had been treated to proper listing in the timetables, even if their entries were marked *'Stops when required. Passengers wishing to alight must inform the Guard'*. Over the years, there were many fluctuations in the frequency of services, additional Wednesday and Saturday passenger trains being commonplace in order to accommodate the local fish workers. In the early 1950s, eight trains plied each way on weekdays and nine on Saturdays.

The branch services were known as 'Bulger trainies', the term 'Bulger' being that applied to a resident of Cairnbulg. However, the Saturday night workings from Fraserburgh to St Combs became referred to as the 'Boozer Bulger trainies'. Mixed trains were the norm throughout much of the branch's life, with fish providing the mainstay of the freight traffic for many years. In later years, however, the freight traffic declined drastically and, by the 1950s, coal, agricultural produce and the occasional box of partans accounted for most of the little that remained.

The eventual withdrawal of passenger services on the branch was a highly controversial affair. That renowned railway economist, Dr Richard Beeching, proclaimed that the line did not pay its way, but that argument was scoffed at by those who could find only standing room on the early morning trains to Fraserburgh and the late afternoon trains to St Combs. The truth of the matter was that British Railways wanted to close the Aberdeen-Fraserburgh line and, as that would have left the St Combs branch totally isolated from the rest of the BR system, the branch had to be sacrificed. Predictably, officialdom had its way and the passenger services between Fraserburgh and St.Combs were withdrawn on 3 May 1965. During the last years, the 'pay-train' services on the branch had benefited from the lack of scheduled bus service between Fraserburgh and St Combs, the very first regular daily services commencing only after the closure of the railway.

Left: **Ivatt '2MT' shows off its cowcather at St Combs in the 1950s. The 'SC' (self-cleaning) legend on the smokebox clearly does not refer to the locomotive itself; possibly, though, the grubby state of the machine and the liberation of its shedplate suggest that dieselisation was only just around the corner.** R. Hamilton

28 Gifford & Garvald Railway

In and around the attractive little town of Gifford, 17 miles east of Edinburgh, there are several fine historic buildings, one of which is Yester Castle, 1½ miles southeast of Gifford. The castle has a vaulted underground chamber which, according to local legend, was built in the 13th century by a local magician named Hugo the Wizard.

As for railway matters, in 1891, authorisation was obtained for a 12-mile railway from Ormiston, on the North British Railway's MacMerry branch, to Garvald and Barra but, even after a revision of powers the following year for a shorter line, nothing was done before the coming of the Light Railways Act in 1896. Mindful of the advantages of the new legislation, a further review of the company's plans was undertaken and, in 1898, a Light Railway Order was granted for a 9¼ -mile line from Ormiston to Gifford. Although the name of Garvald was to be retained in the corporate title, the railway was never to reach that town, let alone Barra. The line opened on 14 October 1901

and, from the outset, was maintained and worked by the North British Railway. Nevertheless, the light railway company remained nominally independent until the Grouping in 1923, when it became part of the LNER empire.

The line started at Ormiston and had intermediate stations at Pencaitland (2 miles), Saltoun (3½ miles) and Humbie (5½ miles) before terminating at Gifford (9¼ miles). At first, the line was worked by lightweight Drummond 0-6-0Ts but 'R' (later LNER 'D51') class 4-4-0Ts eventually took over. The 'Rs', which had axle weights of just 12ton 12cwt, were widely used on lightly-laid branches throughout most of the NBR system, but looked

Below: **Ormiston station was the point at which the Gifford and MacMerry branches diverged, the former branch veering right beyond the bridge and the latter, which also served Winton colliery, veering left.**
Lens of Sutton

equally at home on the through workings between Gifford and Edinburgh. By the early 1920s, two of the five services each way on the Gifford branch worked through to or from Edinburgh, the times for the 21-mile journeys being around 60min. The 'D51s' were superseded in 1931 by ex-Great Eastern 'F4' class 2-4-2Ts, but the incomers had little time to become accustomed to their new home. Buses had already taken much of the trade away from the railway, and the inevitable withdrawal of passenger services took place on 3 April 1933.

Despite the loss of its passenger services, the Gifford branch remained open for freight traffic, the regular engines for the daily train being ex-NBR 'J33' class 0-6-0 No 9169 and, later, ex-NER 'J24' class 0-6-0s. During World War 2, the usual pattern was for three goods trips and one cattle train on the line each week. In the early post-Nationalisation years, 'J24' No 65617 was the usual branch locomotive and was stationed at Seafield depot in Leith, a sub-shed of St Margaret's in Edinburgh.

During the appalling floods of 1948, the bridge at Humbie was washed away; it was not replaced, and the truncated line subsequently became known to crews as the Humbie branch. The section beyond Saltoun was closed on 2 May 1960, but a daily pick-up freight working continued operating to Saltoun, the regular inwards traffic being coal and malt to

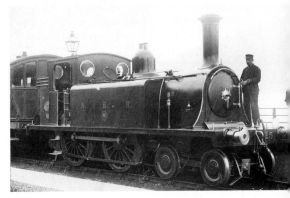

Top: **The North British Railway's Drummond 'R' (later LNER 'D51') class 4-4-0Ts were well-suited to lightly-laid branch lines. The locomotive in the picture, No 225, was built in 1882 and originally named** *Milngavie;* **it was withdrawn in 1926 without carrying its newly-allotted LNER number of 10460.** Bucknall Collection/ Ian Allan Library

Above: **LNER 'D51' class 4-4-0T No 10429 approaches Gifford. Although the picture is undated, the period can be narrowed down as the locomotive received its new number in March 1925 and was withdrawn in August 1931.** Ian Allan Library

Left: ***Bradshaw's Shareholders' Guide,* 1915.** Author's files

GIFFORD AND GARVALD.

DIRECTORS:

Chairman—WILLIAM FULTON JACKSON, Esq., 29, Royal Terrace, Edinburgh.

Deputy-Chairman—WALTER WINGATE GRAY, Esq., of Nunraw, Prestonkirk.

The Most Hon. the Marquis of Tweeddale, Yester, Gifford, and 6, Hill Street, W. Alexander Bruce Gibson Esq., Tay Works, Dundee.

Harry G. Younger, Esq., 21, Grosvenor Crescent, Edinburgh.

OFFICERS.—Sec., Alexander Guild, W.S., Edinburgh; Auditors, Robertson and Carphin, C.A., Edinburgh; Solicitors, Guild and Guild, W.S., 5, Rutland Square, Edinburgh.

Offices—5, Rutland Square, Edinburgh.

Incorporated by act of 3rd July, 1891, to construct a railway from Ormiston, by a junction with the Macmerry Branch of the North British, to Garvald and Bara. Length, about 12 miles. Agreements with North British. Capital, 110,000*l.* in 10*l.* shares, with power to divide into preferred and deferred half-shares. Loans, 30,000*l.*

By act of 24th August, 1893, powers were obtained to construct a deviation line, about 7 miles in length, in lieu of the existing authorised railway, which reduces the authorised capital from 110,000*l.* to 100,000*l.*

In 1898 an order under the Light Railways Act was obtained, and the line has been constructed as a light railway. Constructed, 9 miles 10 chains.

The whole of the shares (10,000, of 10*l.* each) have been issued and received Capital expended, 100,000*l.*

REVENUE.—The credit balance for the half-year to 19th April, 1912, was 1,858*l.* for the half-year to 19th October, 1912, 1,983*l.* The revenue for the br ken period to 31st December, 1912, was 1,205*l.* The balance available for dividend for the year 1913, was 3,569*l.*

The line is maintained and worked by the North British.

Accounts made up annually.

No. of Directors.—Maximum, 8; minimum, 3; quorum, 3. *Qualification,* 30 shares.

No. 5.—MONKTONHALL JUNCTION TO MACMERRY AND GIFFORD.

MONKTONHALL JUNCTION TO SMEATON JUNCTION.—Worked by Block Telegraph.

Carberry Colliery Branch.—Worked from Smeaton Junction under following instructions :—

(1) The Smeaton and Carberry Train Staff Section terminates at a point about 100 yards east from the Public Road crossing where a board lettered as follows has been erected on the Driver's right hand.

On the West Side—End of Train Staff Section, beginning of Yard Working Section.

On the East Side—Beginning of Train Staff Section.

The Sidings on the east side of the board are worked as a yard, and Drivers must therefore keep a sharp lookout and be prepared to stop clear of any obstruction which may be in front of them.

(2) A Brake Van must invariably be at the rear, of wagons when drawing them to and from Carberry Colliery Sidings.

(3) **Bell Communication between Smeaton Junction and Smeaton Shaw Level Crossing.**—All Trains and Engines must be signalled to the Crossing, as follows :—

When leaving Smeaton Junction, 1 ring. | When leaving Dalkeith Colliery, 2 rings.

SMEATON JUNCTION TO ORMISTON JUNCTION.—Worked by Tablet No. 6.

ORMISTON JUNCTION TO MACMERRY.—Worked by Tyer's Single Line Block Staff (No. 1) and Ticket (colour Yellow).

(S) **Dalkeith Colliery—Trains from Dalkeith Colliery to Smeaton.**—In the case of trains going from Dalkeith Colliery to any point in the direction of Smeaton, the Signalman must not reverse the Points for the Main Line until he has received a Whistle from the Driver, which must be taken as an indication that sufficient Wagon, &c., Brake Power has been applied, and that the Train is ready to proceed downhill towards Smeaton.

(4) **Cousland Sidings.—Worked by Tablet Lock.**—Owing to the steepness of the gradient, these Sidings are worked by Up Trains only ; and during the shunting operations the Engine must be at the Ormiston end of the Wagons.

Billyford Siding.—Worked by Tablet Lock.

(5) **Oxenford Siding.—Worked by Tablet Lock.**—Down Trains working the Sidings must always be drawn clear of the trap points, placed 200 yards east from the Up facing connection, and the Engine or wagons must not be uncoupled until these trap points are opened to prevent any part of the Train running away in the direction of Bog.

Limeylands Sidings.—Worked from Bog Signal-box.

(G) **Bog Siding.**

(6a) **Bog Train Refuge Sidings (West End).**—Worked by Tablet Lock—Engines of Up Trains when shunting at Bog Sidings and Junction must be at the Ormiston end of the Wagons owing to steepness of the gradient.

(b) Before any shunting operations are commenced at Bog Siding with a Down Train, the entire Train, including, of course, the Guard's Van, must be shunted off the Main Line into the Siding, so as to admit of the shunting operations being performed safely, and in such a way as will ensure against the possibility of any portion of the Train or any other Vehicle running away on the Main Line down the incline.

(c) Wagons from other Sidings must not be inter-marshalled in Bog Sidings with Wagons uplifted there.

(d) The Sidings at Bog are worked as a Yard. Drivers must keep a sharp lookout and be prepared to stop clear of any obstruction which may be in front of them.

(7) **Fleets Colliery.—Worked from Bog Signal-box.**—The Fleets Branch is worked by the Edinburgh Collieries' Pug Engine.

(P) **Ormiston Junction.**—(From the direction of Macmerry and Gifford.)

(G) **Ormiston Junction.**—(From Smeaton Junction direction.)

(8) **Winton Station.**—Guards of Up Trains working Winton Station must be careful not to uncouple their Engines from the Train until the rear brake van is drawn clear of the Public Level Crossing.

ORMISTON JUNCTION TO GIFFORD.—Worked by Electric Train Staff.

(9) **Meadow Pit Siding.—Worked by Electric Train Staff.**—This Siding is on the Gifford Line, about 100 yards out from the Junction with the Macmerry Branch. The points, which are facing to Up Trains, are worked from a Ground Frame and secured by an Annett Lock, the key of which is affixed to the Electric Staff for the Saltoun Section. It is worked from Ormiston and Guards must, in every case, have the points open for the Siding before bringing the Train or lift of wagons over the Junction.

(10a) **Woodhall Colliery Sidings—Pencaitland.—Worked by Electric Train Staff.**—Trains working these Sidings must be brought to a stand on the level part of the Line between the Up and Down Facing Points, so that the Engine will always be at the lower end of the Wagons when lifting or leaving Traffic.

(b) Not more than twenty Wagons must be propelled at one time into these Sidings.

(11) **SIDINGS WORKED BY ELECTRIC TRAIN STAFF.—**

| Pencaitland Station Sidings. | Highlee Siding (Lord Polwarth's). |
| Lempockwells Siding | Humbie Station Sidings. |

(P) **Saltoun.**

Above: **NBR working instructions for the Gifford branch.** Courtesy Charles Meader

Glenkinchie Distillery and the outwards largely comprising the distillery's bottled produce. The branch also saw some seasonal traffic in the form of farm produce and livestock. At Pencaitland, a large maltings was built in 1964 with the intention of using the branch for some of the traffic, but it proved to be a case of bad timing as the line was closed completely on 24 May 1965. During the last years, the regular locomotives were ex-LMSR '2MT' 2-6-0s Nos 46461/62 of St Margaret's shed, although Hunslet 0-6-0 diesel No D2585 underwent trials on the line in 1963. British Railways' logic in trying out the diesel engine seemed somewhat odd as it would have been necessary to train 25 sets of crews to operate the solitary machine but, as things turned out, the diesel's stay lasted for only one week.

29 Goole & Marshland Light Railway and Isle of Axholme Light Railways

In British railway history, the joint railway was not exactly a rare beast, but a joint *light* railway was a very different creature indeed. Only two organisations fitted the bill, one being the Axholme Joint Railway which crossed the flat agricultural land between south Yorkshire and north Lincolnshire. The AJR was formed by two major railway companies jointly taking over two light railway companies, the minnows being the Goole & Marshland Light Railway and the Isle of Axholme Light Railway.

The G&MLR, which had been backed by the Yorkshire District Light Railway Syndicate, opened its first section between Marshland Junction and Reedness for freight traffic on 8 January 1900. By then, the Isle of Axholme Light Railway was making good progress with its line from Haxey, on the joint Great Northern/Great Eastern Lincoln-Doncaster line, to Reedness where a connection with the G&MLR was to be made. It might seem odd that two different concerns constructed light railways in

Below: **Crowle station, Axholme Joint Railway; picture undated.** Lens of Sutton

the same sparsely-populated locality almost simultaneously, but the Isle of Axholme area was viewed, not only as a possible source of agricultural traffic, but also as a potential through route from the Yorkshire collieries to ports in northern Lincolnshire.

The light railways' potential as a through route for coal traffic had not gone unnoticed by the North Eastern and the Lancashire & Yorkshire Railways. On 2 October 1902, the NER and L&YR jointly purchased the G&MLR for £73,500 and, on 14 June 1902, the uncompleted IoALR was bought for £27,500. The new venture was called the Axholme Joint Railway.

Under the joint proprietorship, the ex-G&MLR line was completed through to Fockerby and public passenger services commenced on 11 August 1903. On that same date, the former-IoALR section from Reedness to Crowle was opened to passenger and freight traffic, the remaining section between Crowle and Haxey Junction being opened to freight traffic on 14 November 1904 and to passengers on 2 January 1905. Along the 'main line' the stations were Reedness Junction (5¾ miles from Goole), Crowle (8¾ miles), Belton (13 miles), Epworth (14¾ miles),

Haxey Town (17¾ miles) and Haxey Junction (19½ miles) where the single-platform station was adjacent to the joint GNR/GER premises. On the 'branch' from Reedness Junction, there were intermediate stations at Eastoft (3 miles) and Luddington (4¼ miles) before the terminus at Fockerby (5½ miles). The most significant engineering features on the AJR were the 104ft-span swing bridge over the canal near Crowle, and the nearby viaduct and 52ft-span girder bridge over the Great Central Railway's Doncaster-Cleethorpes line.

At one time, plans for the AJR included an extension to link up with the North Lindsey Light Railway (qv) at Winteringham, but ferocious opposition resulted in that scheme being dropped. As things turned out, the only subsequent extension to the AJR system was a 4¾-mile freight branch from Epworth to the Peat Moss Litter Works at Hatfield Moor, the line opening on 5 January 1909. A proposed extension from Hatfield Moor to Black Carr never materialised.

Although it has generally been assumed that the NER provided the motive power for the G&MLR at first, it seems that contractors locomotives were used at least until the joint NER/L&YR takeover. Evidence exists of a Manning Wardle 0-6-0ST working a two-coach train on the line, and the locomotive's name of *Halkon* cannot be coincidental; one member of the Yorkshire District Light Railway Syndicate, which promoted the G&MLR, was none other than William Halkon. After the take-over of 1902, it fell to the L&YR to provide the locomotives for the AJR, the NER taking responsibility for the perma-nent way. The locomotives were supplied by Goole shed. Standard classes such as Barton Wright's 0-6-2Ts and 0-6-0s were used although the seniority of the 0-6-2Ts was emphasised by the fact that withdrawals had made inroads into the extensive class even before the AJR had fully opened. In later years, Aspinall's 2-4-2Ts and 0-6-0s replaced the ageing Barton Wright engines. Until the outbreak of war in 1914, passenger traffic on the line was reasonably steady, the Fockerby branch generating almost one-third of the revenue. Excursion traffic was brisk and Bank Holiday 'pilgrimages' from the industrial towns of Lancashire to Epworth became a regular feature, the L&YR actively promoting its trips 'to the Mecca of Methodism'.

At the Grouping, the newly-formed LMSR took over the L&YR's role as the supplier of motive power for the AJR. By then, the basic passenger service on the 'main line' and the Fockerby branch comprised just two trains each way, albeit with additional ones on Mondays, Wednesdays, Fridays and Saturdays; the journey times between Goole and Haxey were around 50-60min. In 1926/27, the LMSR purchased 13 two-cylinder Sentinel-Cammell steam railcars and one was allocated to the AJR. That railcar was superseded in December 1930 by a larger

Below: **A special excursion from Belton station, known as Chamberlain's Train, seems to have attracted the entire village. Evidence of the joint ownership of the Axholme line is provided by the notice-boards on the right.** Lens of Sutton

100hp six-cylinder Sentinel-Cammell car which was 65ft 8in in length and accommodated 64 passengers in the saloon with space for an extra 10 in tip-up seats in the luggage compartment. It was finished in a livery of green and cream and, in very untypical joint railway fashion, the name of the Axholme Joint Railway was emblazoned on the sides of the coach section.

As with some other rural lines, even the economies achieved by the railcar were inadequate to reverse the eventual decline in financial fortunes, and the last passenger services on the AJR ran on 15 July 1933. In the last years, services had been reduced to a bare minimum, with the Fockerby branch seeing only one train each way most weekdays. The Sentinel railcar was acquired by the LNER and, after being reconditioned at Gorton Works, remained in service elsewhere until July 1944.

The line was kept open for freight. Much of the traffic was agricultural and, therefore, seasonal but a year-round daily goods working was usually operated. Eventually, of course, the freight traffic dwindled and the first casualty was the Epworth-Haxey Junction section which was closed completely on 1 February 1956. The Hatfield Moor branch followed suit on 30 September 1963 and the rest of the system had its freight services withdrawn on 5 April 1965. During the 1950s and early 1960s, the freight workings had normally been handled by ex-LMSR '2MT' 2-6-0s.

GOSFORTH & PONTELAND LIGHT RAILWAY

see (46) PONTELAND LIGHT RAILWAY

Below: '2F' 0-6-0 No 46407 hardly seems overworked on freight duties at Reedness Junction (Axholme Joint Railway) on 22 July 1961. Hugh Davies

30 Grimsby District Light Railway

As we have already seen, the Barton & Immingham Light Railway was conceived to provide a service to and from the new dock at Immingham in northern Lincolnshire. Another light railway in the immediate area was, like the B&ILR, backed by the Great Central Railway and also homed in on Immingham. This was the Grimsby District Light Railway. The necessary Order for the GDLR was granted in January 1906 and authorised a line which was to be powered by overhead electric cables. No time was wasted in starting the construction of the line which was considered the obvious means of transporting men and materials to the site of the proposed dock at Immingham. Consequently, the priority was to lay a usable line. The installation of the electric power system could wait.

In May 1906, just four months after the Light Railway Order had been granted, the four-mile section was completed between Immingham and a triangular junction at Great Coates, the latter point being 1¼ miles west of Grimsby on the GCR's Sheffield line. At first, the GDLR was used only by the contractors who were undertaking prepatory work at Immingham Dock but, on 12 July, a contractor's locomotive hauled the train which brought assorted dignitaries to the official sod-cutting ceremony for the new dock. Prior to the arrival of the train, the heavens opened in true East Coast mid-summer fashion. Some of the waiting stewards had parked their top hats in apparent safety in the rain-lashed marquee only to find, at the crucial moment, that they were filled with rainwater. It was one of those days.

Before Immingham Dock had been completed, the GDLR's thinly-disguised parent, the Great Central Railway, considered that the 600 or so workmen who travelled each day over the line in contractor's trains warranted a regular passenger service. Consequently, a service was introduced between Grimsby and Immingham on 3 January 1910. Two small wooden platforms were built, one adjacent to the contractor's camp at Immingham and the other at Pyewipe Road, which was at the other 'end' of the Great Coates 'triangle'.

Below: **This workmen's train standing at Immingham Dock station on 28 April 1954 ran, not to Grimsby, but to New Holland. The locomotive is 'A5' class 4-6-2T No 69820.** H. C. Casserley

Four services were operated each way with 20min being the scheduled time for the four-mile journey; return fares were 1/0d (5p) first class or 6d (2½ p) third-class return, although workmens' returns were on offer for 4d (1¾ p). The services were worked by one of the GCR's trio of steam railmotors. The smart-looking railmotors had been wholly built at Gorton Works in 1904/05 and each accommodated 12 first- and 44 third-class passengers; measuring 61ft 6in in length, they were electrically lit throughout. Of the three cars, No 1 had been used on the New Holland-Barton run before its transfer to Grimsby, while Nos 2 and 3 remained in the Wrexham area for most of their lives.

The Light Railway Order for the GDLR had included authorisation for a connection with the Great Grimsby Street Tramways and, furthermore, the use of electric traction, but the existing line was neither extended nor converted. Instead, a new electrically-powered standard gauge tramway was constructed between Grimsby and Immingham, and for much of its route it ran alongside the original steam-worked line. Constitutionally, the electric tramway was part and parcel of the GDLR but the Great Central referred to it as the Grimsby District Electric Railway. Later, it was usually known as the Grimsby & Immingham Electric Tramway.

The electric tramway opened on 15 May 1912 and was later extended at the Immingham end. It had an interesting life which lasted until 1 July 1961 and, of course, it owed its origins to the Light Railway Order which authorised the GDLR, but it is nevertheless beyond the scope of this book. The opening of the tramway to the public meant that the original steam-hauled passenger services between Pyewipe Road and Immingham were redundant and, consequently, they ceased on the day the electric services commenced.

The original GDLR line remained open for freight and, as the area became increasingly industrialised, the tracks were eventually relaid for heavy-duty usage.

After the closure of the electric tramway in 1961, unadvertised workmens' specials were reintroduced on the GDLR line. Today, the route of the old GDLR serves such giants as British Steel and Tioxide UK while, near the Immingham end, there is a Railfreight terminal. Around 1,000,000 tons of freight are now carried over the line which, although capable of accommodating axle weights of 25 tons, is still referred to locally as the 'light railway'.

Harrington & Lowca Light Railway
see (38) LOWCA LIGHT RAILWAY

Isle of Axholme Light Railway
see (29) GOOLE & MARSHLAND LIGHT RAILWAY.

WORKMEN'S TICKETS
ARE ISSUED
BETWEEN CERTAIN STATIONS ON THE GREAT CENTRAL RAILWAY, FOR PARTICULARS OF WHICH SEE BILLS EXHIBITED AT THE STATIONS.

Workmen's Daily Tickets will be available for one journey in each direction in Third Class Carriages by the trains specified on the day of issue only.

Workmen's Weekly Tickets will be available for Six Days, i.e., from Monday to Saturday inclusive, and for one journey in each direction in Third Class Carriages only by the trains specified on each day while in force.

Holders of Workmen's Tickets travelling to or from Stations or by Trains other than those for which their tickets are available will be charged the full Ordinary Fare.

WORKMEN'S TICKETS are issued at a reduced rate, and in consideration thereof the ticket is accepted by the Passenger on the express condition that the liability of the Company to make compensation for injury or otherwise in respect to the Passenger shall be limited to a sum not exceeding One Hundred Pounds, and that the amount of compensation payable in respect of any such Passenger shall, subject to such limitation, be determined by an Arbitrator to be appointed by the Board of Trade, and not otherwise.

THE TICKETS ARE NOT TRANSFERABLE.

Above: **Extract from Great Central public timetable, summer 1913.**

Left: **In 1910, Great Central steam railmotor No 1 was transferred to workmens' services on the Grimsby District Light Railway, but it is believed that this picture was taken while the machine was engaged on New Holland-Barton duties prior to its transfer.**
C. T. Goode Collection

31 Kelvedon, Tiptree & Tollesbury Pier Light Railway

There was an old adage which went 'the longer the name, the shorter the railway', and many lines seemed to take heed of the saying. One was the Kelvedon, Tiptree & Tollesbury Pier Light Railway which ran for all of 10¼ miles through northeast Essex. The light railway was promoted, not only to serve a prime agricultural area, but also to provide access to the River Blackwater. Around the turn of the century, yachting was a fashionable pursuit and many amateur sailors chose to take their ozone on the trendy Essex coast. To cash in on that pursuit, the railway was intended to continue to a pier on the river, thereby serving the yotties as well.

The first section of the light railway opened on 1 October 1904, the construction costs having been just £16,000 of which one-third had been covered by grants. Built to the standard gauge, the railway started at Kelvedon, but did not use the station on the Great Eastern Railway's London-Colchester main line. Instead, it operated from a low-level station alongside the main line one; there was a sharply-graded connecting spur between the GER and the KT&TPLR lines just beyond the north-eastern end of the two stations, but this was used only for through freight traffic. A short distance beyond the south-western end

Below: **The train approaching the short-lived Pier station at Tollesbury seems to be hauled by a 2-4-0T, but the locomotive is, in fact, a 'J67' class 0-6-0T with its front coupling rods removed.**
Lens of Sutton

of the light railway platform at Kelvedon was a corrugated iron engine shed, coal stage and water column.

From Kelvedon, there were intermediate stopping places at Inworth halt (2¾ miles), Tiptree (3½ miles), Tolleshunt Knights (4¼ miles) and Tolleshunt D'Arcy (6½ miles). Feering halt (half a mile from Kelvedon) was added in the 1920s. Of those stopping places, Tiptree station had a modest goods yard and sidings into Wilkinson's jam factory; in marked contrast to the other stopping places, it also had reasonably substantial station buildings. At Inworth, Tollesbury Knights and Tollesbury D'Arcy, the accommodation was provided by old coach bodies while, at Feering, shelter was provided by the body of a disused omnibus. Throughout the line, the station platforms were only 12in high.

The other end of the line was, at first, on the eastern edge of the picturesque village of Tollesbury, the station having wooden buildings and a small goods yard. The extension to Tollesbury Pier opened on 15 May 1905, seven months after the rest of the branch. The pier itself was 1,770ft long but was merely a wooden mooring jetty and definitely not one of the traditional seaside resort variety; it failed to attract the weekend sailors and was closed on 17 July 1921.

The line had a number of sharp gradients on the Kelvedon-Tiptree section, the steepest being 1 in 50, and there were several level crossings, most of which were gated. Being worked on the 'one engine in steam' principle, the only signals were those at Kelvedon yard and a solitary distant signal near Feering on the approach to the yard. A feature of the line was its

Left: **Although built during the Alfred Hill regime at Stratford, the 'J68s' were acknowledged as the final development of Holden's 0-6-0T design of 1886. Here, 'J68' No 7045 is seen at Tollesbury in the 1930s with former Wisbech & Upwell coaches.** Lens of Sutton

Below left: **For those who think that the landscape in eastern Essex is as flat as the proverbial pancake, here's adequate evidence to the contrary. The Kelvedon-Tiptree section of the Tollesbury branch had gradients of up to 1 in 50 which were enough of a challenge for the line's most regular locomotives, the 'J67' class 0-6-0Ts. During the last summer of passenger services in 1950, 'J67' No 68608 approaches Kelvedon at the head of a motley collection of rolling stock.** Ian Allan Library

five intermediate sidings, these being provided to serve local farms.

When authorising the line, the Board of Trade had seemed unwilling to trust the KT&TPLR to operate its own services. Consequently, a stipulation of the Order had been that the Great Eastern should work the line, and so lightweight 'K9' class 0-4-2T No 25 was dispatched to Kelvedon. That locomotive was, however, scrapped in 1905 and, by then, its sisters had either been retired or were well past their prime. One of the few alternatives was a 'R24' (later LNER 'J67') class 0-6-0T, a type which later became quite familiar with light railways. For a while, the 'J67s' used on the Kelvedon-Tollesbury branch had the front section of their coupling rods removed, the consequent reduction in their rigid wheelbase helping to reduce wear and tear on the sharply-curved line. That practice did not, however, receive official approval and was therefore discontinued. Over the years, 'J68s' and 'J69s' took their share of the services, the usual procedure being for a Colchester-based locomotive to be stabled for a week at a time at Kelvedon and sent home after the last Saturday service for a boiler washout the following day.

The carriages used on the line in the early days were six-wheeled GER vehicles, but these had to be modified before being dispatched to Kelvedon. The normal procedure on branch services was for the guard to issue the tickets on the train, and to enable the guard to move freely along the train and pass from coach to coach, the compartment partitions had to be removed and end doors and steps fitted. Things were made a lit-

tle easier for the guards in 1928 when two bogie coaches from the disused Wisbech & Upwell Tramway were transferred to the Tollesbury branch. Those coaches had, at each end, open platforms and steps. The former Wisbech cars were somewhat smaller than most main line coaches and, on the Tollesbury branch, even the little 0-6-0Ts dwarfed them.

Almost from the outset, one of the line's major sources of traffic was Wilkinson's jam factory at Tiptree, but it was not only the goods traffic from the factory which was transported by rail as many of the staff also used the branch. Furthermore, fruit-picking holidays in Essex were almost as popular as hop-picking ones in Kent and, consequently, it was not unknown for up to 1,000 passengers to use the line on summer Saturdays.

The good times were not to last forever as, in the 1920s, a local bus operator started a service from Tollesbury to Kelvedon and Witham. If any single event started the line's steady decline, that was almost certainly it. By then, of course, the line had come under LNER auspices as a result of the Grouping, and the trend towards running mixed trains only added to the 'rural backwater' image. The line became popular among railway enthusiasts, largely because of the odd assortment of carriages which were used. As well as the bogie coaches, the Wisbech & Upwell Tramway provided open-ended four-wheel carriages and, although the use of of the four-wheel versions on the Tollesbury line was not common, there were occasions when a train would consist of four, six and eight-wheel coaching stock.

Although the line could not be expected to survive for ever on its curiosity value, it held out surprisingly well. Against the odds, passenger services continued until 5 May 1951 and freight facilities were retained as far as Tudwick Road Sidings (a fruit collection point half a mile beyond Tiptree) until 29 October that same year. The section serving the jam factory was retained until 1 October 1962. The final passenger working was hauled by 'J69' 0-6-0T No 68578 while the last freight train was entrusted to Hunslet 204hp diesel No D2571.

Until the early 1890s, the 'South Kent Triangle' was a railway-free zone. The communities of Tenterden and Rolvenden were hardly poverty-stricken but the major local railway company, the South Eastern Railway, had failed to provide them with a connection to the outside world. It took the efforts of a prominent Tenterden resident, Sir Myles Fenton, to prompt the locals into promoting their own railway; Sir Myles knew a little about railway matters as he was a consulting director and former general manager of the South Eastern Railway. The proposed line was to run from Tenterden to Robertsbridge, on the SER's Tonbridge-Hastings route. Under the misleading banner of the Rother Valley (Light) Railway, it was authorised by an Act of Parliament in July 1896, but the Light Railways Act was passed the following month and so, in order to construct its line more cheaply, the RVR later applied for its powers to be transferred to a *bona fide* Light Railway Order.

The engineer in charge of the Rother Valley Railway's construction was Holman Stephens, and in 1900 he was appointed as Managing Director. Of all the little lines in his empire, this one was Stephens's favourite and, in later years, enthusiasts of rural railways tended to hold it in similar esteem. The line opened to goods traffic on 26 March 1900 and to passengers on 2 April but, at first, its terminus at 'Tenterden' was over a mile from the town of that name. An extension into Tenterden itself was opened on 15 April 1903, the new

terminus being named Tenterden Town while the former one was renamed Rolvenden, despite being almost two miles from that village. On 15 May 1905, a further extension was opened and this took the line into Headcorn station on the Tonbridge-Ashford main line. By this time, the Rother Valley Railway had assumed the now-familiar title of the Kent & East Sussex Light Railway, the change of identity having been effective from 1 June 1904.

The K&ESLR's route from Robertsbridge to Headcorn was 21½ miles long. At Robertsbridge, the K&ESLR's passenger trains were allocated a bay at the rear of the SE&CR's down platform but occasionally used the main line platforms. After leaving Robertsbridge, there were intermediate stopping places at Bodiam (3½ miles), Northiam (7 miles), Wittersham Road (9½ miles) and Rolvenden (12 miles) before the line reached Tenterden Town (13½ miles). Junction Road halt (2½ miles), which nomi-

Below: **It was often remarked that the locomotive and rolling stock facilities at Rolvenden were far more extensive than were ever required on a line as rural as the Kent & East Sussex. One of the Ford railbuses waits at the platform and 'on shed' are 2-4-0T No 1 *Tenterden* and ex-LSWR 0-6-0 No 9 *Juno*. It has been suggested that this picture dates to around 1930/31.**
Bucknall Collection/Ian Allan Library

nally served the village of Hawkhurst, was added in January 1901 and Salehurst halt (1¼ miles) in 1929.

Of the stations on that section, Bodiam and Northiam had passing loops, the latter having the luxury of a second platform on its loop road. Rolvenden station was, as previously mentioned, the original terminus of the line but, despite its unimposing station facilities, it remained the home of the K&ESLR's locomotives and rolling stock until the line closed to passengers in the 1950s. At first, there was a small twin-road engine shed and limited siding accommodation but, as the years progressed, the facilities were extended in order to handle the accumulation of stock. Tenterden Town station boasted substantial buildings, two platforms and a goods yard. On the section northwards from Tenterden Town, the stations were Tenterden St Michaels (14½ miles from Robertsbridge) which opened in 1912, High Halden Road (15¾ miles), Biddenden (17½ miles), Frittenden Road (19 miles) and Headcorn (21½ miles), the only passing place on that section being at Biddenden.

At Headcorn, the K&ESLR trains used a bay at the rear of the up platform.

The original Robertsbridge-Tenterden section was laid with flat-bottomed rails of 60lb/yd and subjected to an axle-weight limit of 10 tons. It was at first lumbered with a 10mph speed limit, but that was soon raised to the 25mph which applied to the rest of the route. The use of signalling was unusually prolific for a light railway, although it was rare for either of the two sections to be worked by more than one engine in steam. The line's most significant engineering feature was a short tunnel to the north of Tenterden St Michaels station. On the southern section, there were gradients of up to 1 in 50, but the northern section had been built more to main-line standards, complete with secondhand bull-head rails, in anticipation of extending to Maidstone. That extension, like the proposed branches to Cranbrook, Appledore, Rye and even Pevensey, was never built. The differing standards of construction applied to the two sections of line were illustrated by the building costs; the south-

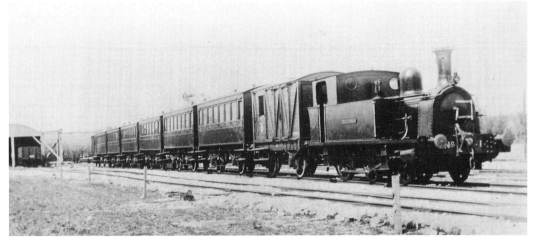

Above left: **The first 'Terrier' 0-6-0T to be purchased by the K&ES was No 3 which, although officially named *Bodiam*, seems to prefer anonymity while standing at Rolvenden shed.** Bucknall Collection/Ian Allan Library

Left: **One of the K&ESR's former LSWR 0-6-0s was No 7 *Rother*, seen here at Northiam in the 1920s.** Bucknall Collection/Ian Allan Library

Above: **One of the brand-new Hawthorn Leslie 2-4-0Ts to be purchased by the Rother Valley Railway (later the K&ESR) was No 1 *Tenterden*. The posed nature of this picture, and the length of the train, suggests a very early publicity photograph.** Bucknall Collection/Ian Allan Library

ern section cost £6,367 per mile but the northern section worked out at £13,447 per mile.

The locomotives of the K&ESLR epitomised a 'Colonel Stephens' railway, even more so as the years progressed. The company's predecessor, the Rother Valley Railway, started in dramatic fashion by purchasing two brand new Hawthorn Leslie 2-4-0Ts which became No 1 *Tenterden* and No 2 *Northiam*. The former was later rebuilt with larger driving wheels and remained on the line until the end of its days, but the latter, although unrebuilt, was passed round among other 'Col Stephens' railways. It went to the Weston, Clevedon & Portishead (qv) in 1917 and from there to the East Kent (q.v.) before returning to the K&ESLR in 1930. In 1937, it was fitted with an extremely lengthy chimney and had part of its cab removed for a role in the film *'Oh! Mr.Porter'*. The railway sequences for the film were shot on the deceased Basingstoke & Alton Light Railway (qv) and, for its role, No 2 was named *Gladstone*.

The Stephens policy of not buying anything new when something secondhand would do first manifested itself on the K&ESLR's motive power fleet in 1901. In that year, a 'Terrier' 0-6-0T was purchased from the LB&SCR for £650 and became No 3 *Bodiam*. It was retired in 1931 but, two years later, it

was rebuilt using parts from another cannibalised 'Terrier' and was to outlive the K&ESLR itself. In common with one of the K&ESLR's 2-4-0Ts, *Bodiam* took part in a film. In 1947, it was taken to Lydd for the filming of *The Loves of Joanna Godden*, an Ealing Studios' creation which fails to warrant a mention in *Halliwell's All-Time Greats*.

In 1905, 0-8-0T No 4 *Hecate* was delivered new from Hawthorn Leslie. The purchase of such a large and expensive locomotive by a small and impecunious railway company raised many eyebrows, but it had been ordered in 1904 for working over the sharp gradients of the proposed Maidstone extension. That extension was, of course, never built and so the K&ESLR found itself lumbered with, not so much a white, but a Great Eastern-style blue elephant. The locomotive set the company back £2,340 or, to be more precise, set Barclay's Bank back that amount as the loan for its purchase was not fully repaid. The locomotive had a short spell on the East Kent Railway but was returned to the K&ESR in 1919 in need of repair.

Locomotive No 5 *Rolvenden* was another ex-LB&SCR 'Terrier'. It was purchased for £700 in 1905 with over 787,000 miles already on the clock, and was cannibalised in 1933. A new vertical-boilered steam railcar was built for the K&ESLR in 1905 by Pickerings of Wishaw and later became No 6 in the stock list; it had 37 seats and a small area for luggage. Pictures of the railcar in action are scarce as it rarely ventured past the shed yard at Rolvenden until being laid up in 1931.

The flirtations with new machines were over and, in 1910, a 37-year old 'Ilfracombe Goods' 0-6-0 was purchased from the London & South Western Railway. It became No 7 *Rother* and peformed useful work until being laid aside in 1933. In 1914, a former-GWR 0-6-0ST was purchased and became No 8; it bore the name of *Ringing Rock* which had been applied by its original owners, the North Pembroke & Fishguard Railway. In 1920, No 8 was derailed on

a flood-damaged section of track and, whether as a result of of nearly becoming a wreck or of Lt-Col Stephens's interest in classical mythology, its return to traffic was marked by it being renamed *Hesperus*. Locomotive No 9 *Juno* was another ex-L&SWR 'Ilfracombe Goods' which was acquired in 1914 by a form of hire-purchase.

In 1932, the K&ESLR agreed a deal with one of its major creditors, the Southern Railway, whereby the superfluous 0-8-0T No 4 *Hecate* and three ancient six-wheeled carriages were exchanged for a 0-6-0ST and two bogie coaches. Financially, the Southern got the better part of the deal, but the K&SELR gained some highly-usable goods in return. The locomotive which was transferred to the K&ESLR was a 56-year old ex-L&SWR 0-6-0ST, and took the name and number of the departing 0-8-0T. As for the 0-8-0T, it was repaired and returned to traffic as Southern Railway No 949, still with the name of *Hecate,* and survived until 1950.

Apart from the Pickering-built railcar No 6, the K&ESLR owned three petrol railcars, each of which comprised a pair of road-omnibus bodies mounted back-to-back on sets of flanged railway wheels. Two such cars were Ford-engined and were acquired in 1923 and 1924, while the third which arrived in 1930 was Shefflex-powered. They might have been economical to operate, but passengers found them extremely noisy and uncomfortable, and all were withdrawn from service by 1939.

At first, the Rother Valley's/K&ESLR's coaching stock comprised six new four-wheeled carriages but these were later converted to bogie coaches. In subsequent years, other four-wheeled carriages were purchased from a variety of sources and it was the 1930s before bogie vehicles started a noticeable take over. The stud of assorted goods wagons comprised new and secondhand acquisitions. The K&ESLR's official livery was blue for the locomotives and dark brown or teak for the carriages, but many of the secondhand acquisitions were never reliveried and, even for those that wore the official plumage, an aversion to the use of polish at Tenterden sheds often camouflaged any hard evidence of a colour scheme.

During its early years, the K&ESLR's traffic figures were surprisingly healthy. In 1910, 88,847 passengers and 28,302 tons of freight were carried, and the gross revenue of almost £9,000 exceeded the operating costs by nearly £3,000. Unlike most small railway companies, it usually paid an annual dividend, albeit a modest one, to its shareholders. However, the 'paper' profits benefited from the company's tardiness in settling with its creditors although, to be fair, there was never any suggestion that the company deliberately tried to deceive.

Almost from the outset, the timetables for the line were full of conditional workings and, over the years, it was rare for more than three trains to traverse the entire line every weekday. Freight-only workings became increasingly rare after 1920 when the practice of running mixed trains became standard; journey times for the complete 21½ -mile trip ranged from 65 to 90min. Between 1928 and 1933, the Southern Railway advertised a through carriage from Cannon Street to Tenterden via Robertsbridge, but the most notable working on the line was in 1936 when a hop-pickers' train of 15 bogie coaches, two six-wheel coaches and one van was accommodated.

Above left: **On 7 September 1946, the 8.50am mixed train from Headcorn to Robertsbridge was entrusted to 0-6-0ST No 4 *Hecate*. Distractions from its arrival at Tenterden are offered by the unconventional signalling (left) and the LNER notice (on building on right).**
LCGB/Ken Nunn Collection

Above: **The K&ESR's 0-8-0T, No 4 *Hecate*, was sold to the Southern Railway in 1932. It spent much of its remaining life based at Nine Elms, where it was photographed in 1935.**
Rail Archive Stephenson

Right: **The final summer of passenger services on the K&ESR was 1953. On 4 July of that year, '01' class 0-6-0 No 31048 makes the most of the peace and quiet at the K&ESR platform at Headcorn.** E. H. Sawford

The K&ESLR was excluded from the Grouping and, in common with other post-1923 independents, it found the going tough. Road transport offered increasing competition and, from 1926, the final line of the balance sheets was usually in red ink. The worst year was 1930 when a loss of almost £3,300 was incurred. After the death of Lt-Col Stephens in October 1931, his long-serving assistant, W. H. Austen, took over the reins but, when the following year's losses were announced, Austen's position of General Manager had to be combined with that of Official Receiver.

Austen tried to negotiate an 'assistance' package with the Southern Railway but that was only partially successful. Nevertheless, the Southern proved willing to hire locomotives to the K&ESLR whenever necessary and these included 'Terriers', 'P' class 0-6-0Ts and assorted 0-6-0s. During the war, ex-GWR 'Dean Goods' 0-6-0s appeared on the line, but their visits were mainly for serving artillery installations at Rolvenden and Wittersham. The K&ESLR's long-standing abhorrence of discarding even the most unusable machinery brought in a few welcome pounds during the war as scrap metal became an increasingly marketable commodity.

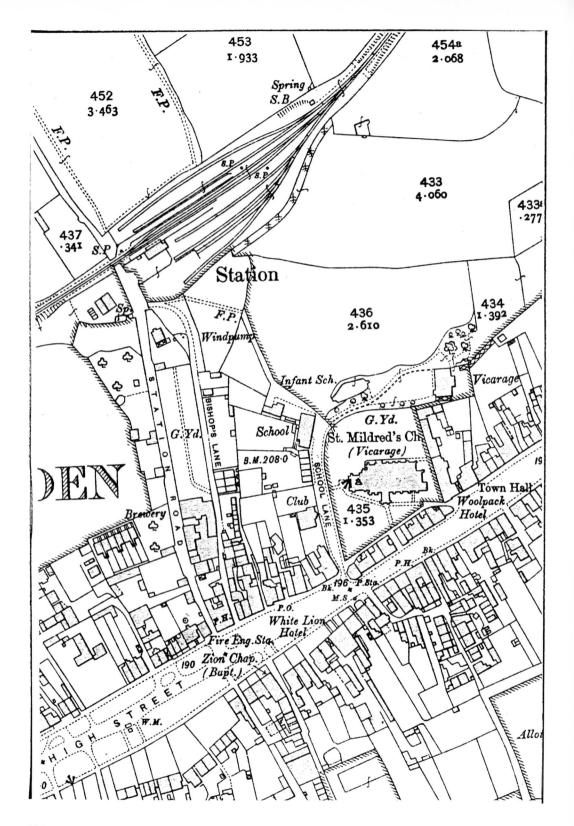

Steam Locomotives of the Kent & East Sussex Light Railway

No	Name	Type	Builder/Works No	Built	Bought	Origin	Wheels	Cyls	Weight	Wdn
1	*Tenterden*	2-4-0T	H/Leslie 2420	1899	1899	new	3ft 3in*	12in x 18in(o)	24t 2c	Scr 1941
2	*Northiam*	2-4-0T	H/Leslie 2421	1899	1899	new	3ft 3in	12in x 18in(o)	24t 2c	Scr 1941
3	*Bodiam*	0-6-0T	Brighton Works	1872	1901	L&BSC No 70	4ft 0in	13in x 20in(i)	26t 17c	Wdn 1963
4	*Hecate*	0-8-0T	H/Leslie 2587	1905	1905	new	4ft 3in	16in x 24in(o)	46t 15c	Sold 1932
4	*Hecate*	0-6-0ST	B/Peacock 1596	1876	1932	LSWR No 0335	4ft 3in	17in x 24in(i)	34t 19c	Scr 1948
5	*Rolvenden*	0-6-0T	Brighton Works	1872	1905	L&BSC No 71	4ft 0in	13in x 20in(i)	26t 17c	Scr 1933
6	-	railcar	Pickering	1905	1905	new		5½in x 8in		Wdn 1931
7	*Rother*	0-6-0	B/Peacock 1208	1873	1910	LSWR No 0349	4ft 6in	16ft x 20in(i)	26t 12c	Wdn 1933
8	*Hesperus+*	0-6-0ST	M/Wardle 630	1876	1914	GWR No 1380	3ft 7in	14in x 20in(i)	28t 4c	Wdn 1941
9	Juno	0-6-0	B/Peacock 1210	1873	1914	LSWR No 0284	4ft 6in	16in x 20in(i)	26t 12c	Wdn 1935

* Later rebuilt with 4ft diameter driving wheels.
+ Named *Ringing Rock* until 1920.

ROBERTSBRIDGE, TENTERDEN TOWN, and HEADCORN—Kent and East Sussex

Miles from Robertsbridge	Down	Week Days mrn	mrn	mrn	mrn	mrn	aft S	aft E	aft
	340 London (Char C) dep.	..	..	..	..	8 25	..	..	4A20
	340 " (Can St) "	..	..	..	..	..	..	..	..
	340 " (L Bdge) "	..	..	5 45	..	8 35	..	..	4E28
	343 Hastings "	..	..	7 40	..	1044	[illegible]	..	5 10
	Robertsbridge dep.	..	..	8 15	..	1115	..	..	5 50
1¼	Salehurst Halt	..	..	Aa	..	Aa	..	..	Aa
2½	Junction Road Halt	..	..	Aa	..	Aa	..	..	Aa
3½	Bodiam, for Staplecross	..	..	8 25	..	1130	..	..	6 0
7	Northiam A	..	..	8 35	..	1155	..	..	6 10
9½	Wittersham Road	..	..	8 42	..	1210	..	..	6 17
12	Rolvenden	640	7 45	8 49	11 5	1220	4 45	4 45	6 24
13½	Tenterden Town [Halt	645	8 J0	8 54	11J20	1225	5 J0	5V10	6 30
14¼	Tenterden St Michaels	..	Aa	..	Aa	..	Aa	Aa	..
15¾	High Halden Road	..	8 10	..	11 30	..	5 15	5 25	..
18	Biddenden	..	8 20	..	11 40	..	5 29	5 39	..
19½	Frittenden Road	..	Aa	..	Aa	..	Aa	Aa	..
21¼	Headcorn 322, 330 arr.	..	8 35	..	11 55	..	5 50	6 0	..
67½	330 London (L Bdge) arr.	..	10 8	..	1F22	..	8 16	8 16	..
68	330 " (Can St) "	..	1013	..	..	..	..	..	..
69½	330 " (Char C) "	..	..	..	1§34	..	8 26	8 26	..

Up	Week Days mrn	mrn	mrn	mrn	aft S	aft E	aft
322 London (Char C) dep.	..	..	..	1115	..	..	3§15
322 " (Can St) "	..	..	6 22	..	..	..	4E38
322 " (L Bdge) "	..	..	6 30	..	..	..	4E42
Headcorn dep.	..	..	8 50	1230	..	..	6 35
Frittenden Road	..	..	Aa	Aa	..	..	Aa
Biddenden	..	..	9 10	1243	..	..	6 47
High Halden Road	..	..	9 20	1252	..	..	6 56
Tenterden St Michaels Halt	..	..	Aa	Aa	..	..	Aa
Tenterden Town	6 55	9 20	9†40	1 8	4 20	4 40	7 12
Rolvenden	7 0	9 25	9 45	1 10	4 25	4 45	7 18
Wittersham Road	7 7	9 32	..	..	4 35	4 55	..
Northiam A	7 17	9 44	..	..	4 45	5 5	..
Bodiam, fr Staplecross	7 27	9 56	..	..	4 55	5 15	..
Junction Road Halt	Aa	Aa	..	..	Aa	Aa	..
Salehurst Halt	Aa	Aa	..	..	Aa	Aa	..
Robertsb'dge 340, 343 arr.	7 40	1010	..	..	5 10	5 30	..
340 Hastings arr.	8 25	1047	..	..	5 48	6 14	..
343 London (L Bdge) "	9‡47	1§22	..	..	7 29	7 29	..
343 " (Can St) "	9 51	..	..	..	..	..	..
343 " (Char C) "	..	1§34	..	..	7 40	7 40	..

Left: **Tenterden station and surrounds, 25in Ordnance Survey map of 1908.** Crown Copyright

Above: **Bradshaw's, March 1940.** Author's files

At Nationalisation in 1948, the K&ESLR was vested in British Railways, and big brother must have wondered what on earth it had acquired. Although the little company had had a staff of 47 at the end of 1947, precious few improvements had been made to the line for many years. Only one of the K&ESLR locomotives, 'Terrier' No 3 *Bodiam*, and a handful of rolling stock escaped being scrapped by BR, the 'Terrier' becoming No 32670 and surviving until November 1963 after having spent some years working on the Hayling Island branch. Happily, it was later preserved. To help ease the motive power situation on the old K&ESLR line, BR started to use various pre-Grouping Southern Region 0-6-0Ts and 0-6-0s more frequently.

Under state ownership, the line was operated in two sections and through trains were all but discontinued. It became inevitable that passenger services would be withdrawn altogether, and the last passenger train was the 5.50pm from Robertsbridge on 2 January 1954. In justified anticipation of 'last-day' crowds, a six-coach set was brought from Ashford for the occasion, and two 'Terriers', Nos 32655/78, were required to work the train, one pulling and the other pushing. From Rolvenden, 'O1' class 0-6-0 No 31064 took over from the leading engine. The shed at Rolvenden which had, in its day, housed the remains of a bewildering miscellany of locomotives and coaches, closed after the cessation of passenger services.

The section between Tenterden and Headcorn was lifted soon afterwards but the southern section remained open for the occasional freight and, until 1958, summer 'hop-pickers' specials'. There were, of course, enthusiasts' specials as well. In June 1957, lightweight 204hp Drewry diesels started to be used on the line, and No D2253 became the regular performer. The complete closure of the remaining section to public traffic took place on 12 June 1961, and only the privately-worked spur from Robertsbridge to Hodson's flour mill remained open, an ex-SE&CR 'P' class 0-6-0T having been purchased by the flour company for shunting duties.

But that was not the end of the story. A preservation organisation promptly stepped in and has since restored and reopened the section between Tenterden and Northiam, the ultimate intention being to reopen through to Robertsbridge. At Tenterden, the town's museum is some 500yd from the preserved railway station and, most interestingly, houses an impressive range of exhibits from the 'Colonel Stephens' empire.

33 Kingsnorth Light Railway

The town of Chatham in Kent had, until the 'economies' of recent years, a lengthy association with the Royal Navy. Consequently, several military-orientated installations were established near the town, one being a munitions depot at Lodge Hill, some 2½ miles north of Strood. In 1901/02, a single-track standard gauge railway to the depot was laid westwards from Sharnal Street station, on the South Eastern & Chatham Railway's Port Victoria branch, with the ultimate plan of extending eastwards from Sharnal Street to a pier on the River Medway. Thoughts of the pier extension were consigned to the shelf until 1915 when the building of a new munitions factory and a cluster of airship hangers near Stoke Saltings resulted in a revival of the original plan. The outcome

was that a two-mile line was laid from Sharnal Street to Kingsnorth, and was later extended to Abbott's Court Pier to provide an alternative to Upnor for the supply ships.

After World War 1 the munitions factory became redundant and the site was taken over by Messrs Holm & Co for use as a chemical works. The railway from Sharnal Street to the pier was part of the deal and, in November 1926, the company obtained a Light Railway Order so that the line could be used for public passenger and goods traffic. In July 1929, a nominal subsidiary company, the Kingsnorth Light Railway, was created to administer the line and, when Messrs Berry Wiggins opened a sizeable factory near Sharnal Street, traffic figures on the light railway became quite healthy.

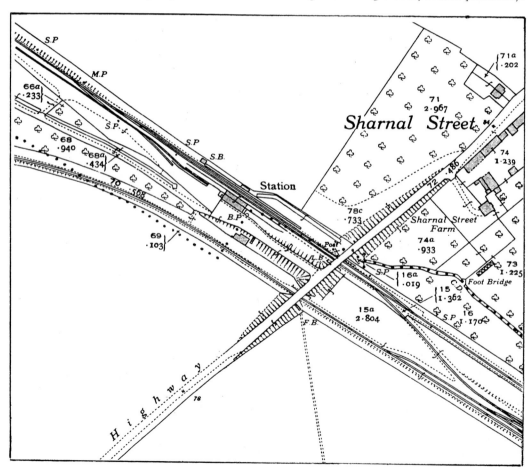

Above: **Former SER '01' class No A7 ('A' denoting 'Ashford', the post-Grouping home of Eastern Section locomotives) hauls a mixed goods train from the interchange sidings at Sharnal Street station on 29 April 1932.** R. W. Kidner

Left: **Sharnal Street station, showing the Admiralty line (left) and the start of the exchange sidings for Admiralty and, at one time, Kingsnorth traffic (right). Ordnance Survey 25in map of 1940.** Crown Copyright

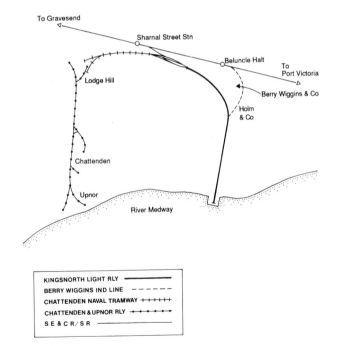

There is no evidence that passengers were ever officially carried on the Kingsnorth Light Railway. Even the freight traffic was comparatively short-lived as, after a dispute between Berry Wiggins and the light railway company in the early 1930s, the former built its own service line. This resulted in the decline of the KLR, and it was finally closed in 1940. The flat-bottomed rails were lifted by the Military soon afterwards. As far as can be determined, the KLR's motive power consisted of a 1921 Kerr Stuart 0-4-0ST, Works No 4227, which was later transferred to Woolwich Arsenal, and a pair of Hardy petrol locomotives.

34 Lampeter, Aberayron & New Quay Light Railway

Southwest Wales was not a prime target for railway promoters. The population tended to be very thinly scattered and, furthermore, the local terrain was rarely conducive to simple and inexpensive railway construction. Consequently, the usual motive behind any proposed railway in the area was to gain access to a port which might conceivably attract Irish or even trans-Atlantic steamers. Nevertheless, there were exceptions, one being the Manchester & Milford Railway's line from Pencader, 15 miles north of Carmarthen, to Aberystwyth. It opened throughout in 1867 and was intended primarily as a through route, the only significant intermediate town it served being Lampeter which, even a century after the railway arrived, had a population of little over 2,000.

Roughly 12 crow-miles northwest of Lampeter lies Aberayron which, during the 19th century, had a modest ship-building industry, over 60 vessels being constructed there between the 1830s and the 1880s; seven road-miles from Aberayron lies New Quay which was, and still is, acknowledged as one of the prettiest small fishing ports in Cardiganshire. The idea of a branch line to Aberayron and New Quay was frequently mooted, but it took the Light Railways Act of 1896 to prompt serious thoughts that the construction of such a line could be viable. The narrow gauge Vale of Rheidol Railway was an early contender with its proposal for a line from Aberystwyth, but the scheme which eventually passed go was that for a standard gauge line from Lampeter. The company behind the proposal was the Lampeter, Aberayron & New Quay Light Railway, and its favoured route was to follow river valleys for much of its length, but a reminder of the local landscape was the 1,127ft summit of Trichrug, not a stone's throw from the valley of the River Aeron.

The LA&NQLR opened its single-track line between the first two towns of its title on 10 April 1911; the last-named town was never to see a railway. For the first month, only freight was handled, passenger services not commencing until 12 May. From Lampeter, the intermediate stopping places on the line were Silian halt (1¾ miles), Blaenplwyf halt (4 miles), Talsarn halt (6 miles), Ystrad (7¼ miles), which was renamed Felin Fach in 1913, Ciliau-Aeron halt (9¾ miles) and Llanerch-Ayron halt (11½ miles); in 1929, Ciliau-Aeron was upgraded to the status of a proper station and, to its north, Crossways halt (10¾ miles) was added. At Aberayron, 13½ miles from Lampeter, the terminus comprised a single platform, and there was a small goods yard and single-road

engine shed. The original timber-built shed was destroyed by fire and was replaced, in 1926, by the corrugated-iron shed building from Wrexham which had been dismantled and transported for re-erection at Aberayron. In post-Grouping days, the shed became a sub shed of Machynlleth.

The line was leased to and worked by the GWR. On opening day, the locomotive in charge was No 1356 *Will Scarlett*, a Fletcher Jennings 0-6-0T which had started life in 1873 with the Severn & Wye Railway. For most of the line's life, however, auto-trains were used and these were clearly marked in the public timetables as carrying one class only; the usual locomotives on auto workings were '517' and, later, '48XX' class 0-4-2Ts. Over the years, the usual pattern was for the summer services to comprise four

LAMPETER AND ABERAYRON. (Week Days only.) (Third class only.)

		a.m.		p.m.	p.m.		p.m.			a.m.	a.m.		a.m.	p.m.		p.m.
Lampeter	dep.	8 25	...	12 20	4 35	Saturdays only	7 50	Aberayron	dep.	7 15	9 20	Saturdays excepted	10 55	3 0	Saturdays only	5 35
Silian Halt		8 32	...	12 27	4 43		7 57	Llanerch-Ayron Halt		7 21	9 26		11 1	3 6		5 41
Blaenplwyf Halt		8 40	...	12 35	4 50		8 5	Crossways Halt		7 25	9 30		11 5	3 10		5 45
Talsarn Halt		8 47	...	12 42	4 57		8 12	Ciliau-Aeron		7 30	9 35		11 10	3 15		5 50
Felin Fach		8 53	...	12 48	5 3		8 18	Felin Fach		7 38	9 43		11 18	3 23		5 58
Ciliau-Aeron		9 1	...	12 56	5 11		8 26	Talsarn Halt		7 45	9 50		11 25	3 30		6 5
Crossways Halt		9 5	...	1 0	5 15		8 30	Blaenplwyf Halt		7 52	9 58		11 33	3 38		6 13
Llanerch-Ayron Halt		9 9	...	1 4	5 19		8 34	Silian Halt		8 1	10 6		11 41	3 47		6 21
Aberayron	arr.	9 15	...	1 10	5 25		8 40	Lampeter	arr.	8 7	10 12		11 47	3 53		6 27

Above: **The very last GWR public timetable (6 October 1947) showed these services on the Aberayron branch.** Author's files

Left: **This picture of Aberayron station has the hallmarks of an 'opening day special', but that notion is apparently incorrect as the first passenger train on the line was hauled by a side tank locomotive, not a saddle-tank working double-headed.** Lens of Sutton

Below left: **The Lampeter-Aberayron line closed to passengers from 2 February 1951, but this working on 28 August 1956 is not an hallucination. The service entrusted to '74XX' class 0-6-0PT No 7402 is, in fact, a milk train and, despite the lightweight loading, the locomotive has to work hard on the gradient between Ciliau-Aeron and Felin Fach.** G. F. Bannister

trains each way on weekdays while the winter services were reduced to three; journey times for the 13½-mile journey remained at around 50min throughout the branch's existence.

A more positive idea of the locomotives which worked the line can be gleaned from Aberayron shed's allocation lists. In January 1921, the resident locomotives were '517' class 0-4-2Ts Nos 205 and 548 although, mysteriously, the latter is known not to have been fitted with auto apparatus until 1923; the January 1934 allocation was a pair of similar engines, Nos 219 and 848. The first post-Nationalisation allocation list of January 1948 shows that the shed's resident was '14XX' (originally '48XX') class 0-4-2T No 1474.

After the novelty value of the railway had passed, the line settled down to a steady existence and in the pre-Grouping years, the gross receipts hovered between £3,000 and £3,500 per annum. After expenses, this usually resulted in an annual loss for the LA&NQLR of

between £100 and £400. During the 1920s and 1930s the line suffered from motor-bus competition, and the national recession did little to help the declining traffic figures. During World War 2, an Army camp was established between Aberayron and New Quay, but the additional traffic generated by the troops came to a predictable end when peace was restored.

After Nationalisation, the Western Region of British Railways transferred the line from the juristiction of the Swansea District to the Oswestry District, motive power being supplied by Aberystwyth shed but maintained, somewhat illogically, at Carmarthen. The traffic figures for 1950 showed that just 7,000 passengers used the branch that year and, predictably, British Railways chose to 'review' the line's future. The inevitable notices went up and passenger services were withdrawn from 2 February 1951.

Freight services were retained, and the opening of a milk factory near Felin Fach in May 1951 did much to provide regular goods traffic. The usual locomotives for freight duties during the 1950s were '74XX' class 0-6-0PTs, Nos 7402/07/17/44 being among those known to have worked the branch. Public freight facilities were withdrawn from Aberayron on 5 April 1965, after which date only the section to Green Grove Siding, which served the milk factory at Felin Fach, remained operational. That closed on 30 September 1973. The little engine shed at Aberayron, which had become a sub-shed of Carmarthen in January 1961, had not closed until April 1962, by which time it had outlived the passenger services by over 10 years.

Below: **0-6-0PT No 7444 marshals its train at Aberayron on 18 June 1963, the station and small yard being visible in the distance.** H. C. Casserley

35 Lauder Light Railway

The first proposal for a railway from Fountainhall, on the North British Railway's legendary 'Waverley Route' between Carlisle and Edinburgh, to Lauder surfaced in 1852 although, just seven years earlier, a report had commented on the seemingly satisfactory road services to and from Lauder. The report had referred to the four 'public carriages' which had served Lauder in 1845, but the main observation was: *'Very ample means of communication are enjoyed by the Parish. It has a post office in the town, and a daily mail, brought by the curricle which runs through Lauderdale between Edinburgh and London'*. As things turned out, the 1852 proposal for a railway came to nothing, as did revived plans in 1883, but the North British Railway later subsidised a privately-operated omnibus service on the six-mile route between Stow station and Lauder.

The idea for a railway to Lauder was revived after the passing of the Light Railways Act. Under the provisions of the Act, it was possible for local authorities to subscribe to a light railway company and so, fearing that the Lauder area might become a commercial wilderness if it failed to gain a rail connection, Berwickshire County Council and Lauder Town Council provided, between them, one-third of the £45,000 capital for the Lauder Light Railway Co.

The first sod for the railway was cut on 3 June 1899 and it opened on 2 July 1901. The line started at Fountainhall station, 22½ miles south of Edinburgh and 700ft above sea level; it terminated 10½ -miles away at the sparsely-equipped station in Lauder, 600ft above sea level, with just one intermediate station at Oxton, 6½ miles out from Fountainhall. The Fountainhall–Oxton section involved crossing the hills in the shadow of the 1,254ft high Collie Law, the highest point of the railway being 944ft near Eastertown. The Oxton–Lauder section had an easier time of it by following close to Leader Water. That river was popular with trout fishermen, and many anglers soon regarded the railway as a convenient mode of transport to the locations which were to provide their sport.

The Lauder Light Railway was worked by the North British, the latter taking a 50% cut of receipts

Below: **Although the 'J67' class 0-6-0Ts were versatile locomotives, they ran with empty tanks on the Lauder branch, the water being carried in a six-wheeled tender in order to minimise axle-weights. The branch was serviced by the sub-shed at Galashiels, which is where No 8492 rests on 26 June 1947.** Ian Allan Library

NORTH BRITISH RAILWAY.

Opening of Lauder Light Railway for Traffic, on Tuesday, 2nd July, 1901.

The Lauder Light Railway will be Opened for Traffic, on Tuesday, 2nd July, 1901, and the following will be the Train Service until further notice.

WEEK-DAYS.

	A.M.	A.M	P.M.	P.M.
Edinburgh (Wav.) leave	6 20	9 27	4 25	6 45
Galashiels ,,	6 50	7 42	3 29	8 0
Fountainhall, leave	7 40	10 28	5 10	8 25
Oxton,	8 14	11 2	5 44	8 59
Lauder, arrive	8 27	11 15	5 57	9 12

WEEK-DAYS.

	A.M.	A M.	P.M.	P M.
Lauder, leave	6 25	9 30	3 3	7 3
Oxton, ,,	6 38	9 43	3 16	7 16
Fountainhall, arrive	7 12	10 17	3 50	7 50
Galashiels, arrive	7 56	10 43	4 55	8 19
Edinburgh (Wav.), ,,	8 26	12 58	4 57	9 p3

W. F. JACKSON, General Manager.

Edinburgh, June, 1901.

Above: **The first timetable for the Lauder Light Railway issued in 1901.**

Below: ***Bradshaw's Shareholders' Guide,*** **1915 edition.** Author's files

for its troubles. At first, small Drummond 0-6-0Ts were the usual locomotives, but when the last representatives were retired in the mid-1920s, ex-NBR 'D51' class 4-4-0Ts took over on passenger and mixed trains. The passenger services, which had started off as four trains each way on weekdays, eventually stabilised at three with an additional each way working on Saturdays. Journey times were usually between 40 and 45min. The Lauder Light Railway Co retained nominal independence until the Grouping when it was taken into the LNER fold. By then, the line's lack of passenger revenue was already causing some concern, and things deteriorated more sharply during the rest of the 1920s. Consequently, the LNER withdrew the passenger services from 12 September 1932.

Freight services were retained, an ex-NER 'J24' class 0-6-0 often being in charge of proceedings until August 1948, the Border County area was hit by severe floods and the Lauder branch had to be closed. In many circles, it was felt that British Railways would use that as an excuse for permanent closure, but the line reopened for freight traffic on 2 November 1950. The branch was serviced by

---

LAUDER LIGHT.
DIRECTORS:
Chairman—The Most Hon. the Marquis of TWEEDDALE, Yester, Gifford.

Harry G. Younger, Esq., 21, Grosvenor Crescent, Edinburgh.

Robert Dickinson, Esq., Longcroft, Oxton, Berwickshire.

OFFICERS—Secretary, C. F. Umpherston; Auditors, Richard S. Aitchison and John Martin; Solicitors, Robson and McLean, W.S.

Offices—25, Queen Street, Edinburgh.

Incorporated in 1898. Authorised capital, 63,000*l.*, including loans. Capital issued, 47,090*l.* in 10*l.* ordinary shares, fully paid up, and 13,500*l.* in 3¼ per cent. loans. Length of line, 10 miles 1 furlong. Opened 2nd July, 1901, and is worked by the North British. Under the North British (General Powers) Order, 1904, power was obtained to make a small deviation from the original plans, which has been done. Accounts made up half-yearly to 30th June and 31st December, and meetings held October and April. For half-year ended 30th June, 1902, the dividend was at the rate of 2 per cent. per annum, for each half-year from December, 1902, to December, 1905, it was at the rate of 1¼ per cent. per annum; for each half-year to December, 1907, at the rate of 1¼ per cent. per annum; for the years 1908, 1909, 1910, and 1911, 1¼ per cent. per annum. For 1912, at the rate of 1 per cent. per annum, for 1913, 1¼ per cent. per annum, and for the half-year to June, 1914, at the rate of 1 per cent. per annum.

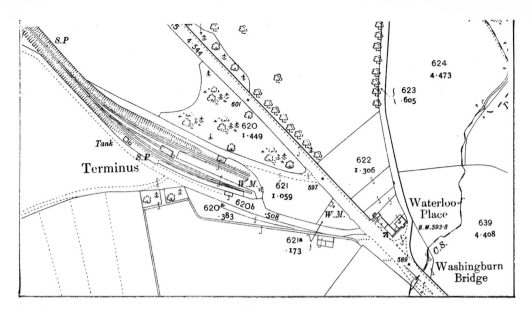

Galashiels depot, a sub-shed of St Margaret's in Edinburgh, and by the time of Nationalisation in 1948, St Margaret's had acquired two ex-Great Eastern 'J67' class 0-6-0Ts, Nos 68492 and 68511, one of which was usually out-stationed at Galashiels for working the freight services to Lauder. The axle weight of a 'J67' in full working order was 14 tons and so, on Lauder duties, they ran with empty tanks with their water being supplied by a six-wheeled tender attached behind. It might have been neither conventional nor pretty, but it worked.

The freight workings continued until the end of September 1958, the official date for the total closure of the line being 1 October. Despite being a remarkably attractive route through some of the best Border

Above: **Lauder station, 25in Ordnance Survey map of 1908.** Crown Copyright

Below: **Extract from NBR Appendix dated 2 October 1922.** Charles Meacher

Country scenery, the Lauder branch seems to have grabbed the attention of very few historians and, furthermore, official records seem largely to ignore the existence of the line. One of the very few publications which include anything at all about the branch is *Lauder and Lauderdale*, written by a certain A. Thomson in 1902, However, that book should not be regarded as a definitive railway history as, among the author's statements are: '...*the gage* (sic) *is 4ft 4½ in...the speed varies with the gradient...*'.

No. 20—FOUNTAINHALL JUNCTION TO LAUDER.

STATION, JUNCTION, SIGNAL-BOX, &c.	Local Speed Restriction.		Refuge Sidings and Loops.	Engine Turntable Diameter.	Water Columns or Tanks.	Catch Points.	Ramps.	Ambulance.		LOCALITY OF Speed Restriction, Refuge Sidings and Loops, Engine Turntables, Water Columns or Tanks, Catch Points, Ramps and Ambulance Equipment.	Signals from which Trainmen do not require to proceed to Signal-box to carry out Rule 55.	
	Miles per Hour.		Wagon Capacity in addition to E. and V.	(Ft.)	W	C		No. of Sets.	First Aid.	Stretchers.		Signals.	Description, &c.
	Up.	Down.							A	B			
Fountainhall Jct.	15	15	...	...	...	...	...		...	...	Between Fountainhall Junction and a point about a mile South of Oxton.		
Oxton	25	25	...	...	...	...	...		...	...	Between a Point about a mile South of Oxton and Lauder.		
	3	3	...	...	...	...	...		...	...	All Trains carrying Passengers, passing over Facing Points at Oxton.		
Lauder	...	...	...	...	W	...	...		...	...	North End of Station.		
Lauder Line	15	15	...	...	...	...	...		...	...	Tender Engines running Tender foremost over any part of the Lauder Light Railway.		

											Speed Restrictions at Level Crossings, Lauder Branch.	Distance from Fount'h'l Jct.	
												Mls.	Chs.
Threeburnf'd No. 1	10	10	...	...	...	...	...		...	...	Within 300 yards of Public Level Crossing.	3	33
Threeburnf'd No. 2	10	10	...	...	...	...	...		...	...	Within 300 yards of Public Level Crossing.	3	51
Hartside	10	10	...	...	...	...	...		...	...	Within 300 yards of Public Level Crossing.	4	53
Path	10	10	...	...	...	...	...		...	...	Within 300 yards of Public Level Crossing.	5	72
Oxton	10	10	...	...	...	...	...		...	...	Within 300 yards of Public Level Crossing.	6	37
Shieldfield	10	10	...	...	...	...	...		...	...	Within 300 yards of Public Level Crossing.	7	77
Trabrown	10	10	...	...	...	...	...		...	...	Within 300 yards of Public Level Crossing.	9	38

No Engine, Carriage, or Truck, bringing a greater weight than 12 tons upon the Rails by any one pair of Wheels, will be allowed to run upon this Railway.
There are no gates at these Crossings, but there are Cattle Guards, and Drivers must approach them with great caution and be prepared to stop at a moment's notice if necessary: They must also sound the Engine Whistle when nearing the Crossings.

36 Leadhills & Wanlockhead Light Railway

In the magnificent bleak expanses of south Lanark-shire, the Lowther Hills have been mined for lead since at least the 13th century and, possibly, as far back as Roman times. In 1710, a consortium of local businessmen trading under the title of The Quaker Co took a lease on the mines, that lease later passing to the Leadhills Mining Co. The gradual decline of protectionism in the early 19th century enabled cheap foreign ore to be imported and, consequently, the prosperity of the Leadhills mines diminished. Nevertheless, a fresh lease on the mines was taken out in 1903 and, in an effort to revitalise the area's fortunes, new machinery was installed and the smelt mill rebuilt.

Even before the plans to re-establish the local mining industry had been under serious consideration, thoughts had turned to providing a railway for transporting the lead, but the local terrain had presented a formidable challenge to even the most ambitious railway promoter. However, in 1897 the Caledonian Railway was plucky enough to pick up the gauntlet and a nominal subsidiary, the Leadhills & Wanlockhead Light Railway, was created for the purpose. It confounded the sceptics by completing its line. The decision to build the line to the standard gauge had been questioned, as it had been estimated that a narrow gauge line would have saved 18% of the cost of earthworks, 48% on culverts and a massive 64% on overbridges and viaducts, but a fair proportion of those hypothetical savings would have been nullified by the need for purpose-built locomotives and rolling stock.

The single-track light railway started at Elvanfoot, 50 miles south of Glasgow on the Caledonian's main line to Carlisle. The first 5¾-mile section to Leadhills was opened on 1 October 1901 and the 1½ -mile extension to Wanlockhead was ready for business exactly one year later. The railway reached a height of 1,498ft above sea level, which was the highest summit on any standard gauge line in Britain, the celebrated summit at Druimuachdar on the Perth-Inverness line being 14ft lower. Leadhills station itself was 1,405ft above sea level, and a nearby house was claimed to be the highest in Scotland. The timber-built engine shed at Leadhills was, however, without doubt the highest standard gauge shed in Britain.

As could be expected, the engineering works required to build the line were considerably greater than those for most other light railways. After leaving Elvanfoot, the line climbed the hills above Elvan Water and Shortcleuch Water, passing on its route

Above: **The staff of Wanlockhead station show off the line's first regular locomotive, Caley '171' class 0-4-4T No 172.** Lens of Sutton

the abandoned gold mines at the foot of Howkwood where gold was once extracted for use in the Scottish Crown jewels. Shortly after passing the old gold workings, the line was carried over Risping Cleuch by means of a magnificent viaduct before negotiating the 1 in 40 climb to Leadhills, where the simple station was at the south end of the village. The engine shed and its water tower were situated about ¼-mile east of the station, on the south side of the track. The community of Leadhills bore all the hallmarks of a mining area, the surrounding hills being liberally dotted with scars and spoil-heaps. A horse-worked tramway connected Wilson's and Glengonnar Shafts, to the south of the village, with the washing mill, a spur from the light railway providing the outlet from the mill. From Leadhills, the line continued 1½ -miles southwestwards to Wanlockhead which was just over the border in Dumfries-shire, the station being on the south side of the village. There were no raised platforms on the line, even the facilities for branch trains at Elvanfoot being on rail level.

The Caledonian locomotives initially used on the Wanlockhead route were Drummond's '171' class 0-4-4Ts which had solid trailing wheels; the first regular engine was No 172, sister No 192 appearing later and, for duties on the branch, they were normally fitted with cowcatchers. A pair of vintage four-wheel

ELVANFOOT, LEADHILLS, and WANLOCKHEAD.—Caledonian.

Miles		Week Days only.							Miles		Week Days only.							
				S	**E**	**S**								**S**	**E**	**S**		
		mrn	aft	aft	aft	aft					mrn	mrn	aft	aft	aft	aft		
—	Elvanfoot ....dep	9 10	12 45	2 35	6 25	7 35	....	....	—	Wanlockhead ......dep.	7 15	10 0	1 35	3 10	5 30	6 40	....	....
5¼	Leadhills...............	9 40	1 15	3 5	6 55	8 5	....	....	1¼	Leadhills.................	7 25	10 10	1 45	3 20	5 40	6 50	....	....
7¼	Wanlockhead ....arr.	9 50	1 25	3 15	7 5	8 15	....	....	7¼	Elvanfoot 824, 831 arr.	7 50	10 35	2 15	3 50	6 5	7 20	....	....

E Except Saturdays.   **S** Saturdays only.

Above: **Public timetable, Summer 1922.**

Right: **Ex-Caledonian '2P' 0-4-4T No 15181 (later BR No 55181) leaves Elvanfoot on 30 July 1931 with the 12.19pm mixed train for Wanlockhead.** H. C. Casserley

Below right: **During the mid-1930s, passenger services on the Wanlockhead branch were usually worked by the LMSR's economical Sentinel-Cammell steam railcars, but even they couldn't save the line.** Real Photographs/Ian Allan Library

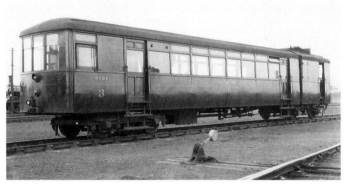

coaches was adapted for use on the line and offered compartments for first-class passengers. By 1910, the passenger services comprised three trains each way on weekdays while, by 1922, the timetables showed an additional up working each day and an each-way Saturday Only service. At the Grouping, the line came under LMSR auspices and McIntosh '439' class 0-4-4Ts soon replaced the older Drummond 0-4-4Ts. In 1929, the LMSR transferred a Sentinel-Cammell steam railcar to the line in an attempt to achieve much-needed economies and, during the mid-1930s, services usually comprised three or four passenger workings each way on weekdays, a Sunday service being introduced in 1935, and two weekly freight services. It is known that Sentinel cars Nos 29910/13 were used on the branch while, for freight turns, 0-4-4Ts Nos 15181 and 15217/38 did the honours during the 1930s, larger locomotives not being permitted on to the line.

Disconcertingly, the anticipated lead traffic failed to materialise in sufficient quantities to make the railway profitable. The major problem was the high cost of pumping ore from veins almost 500ft below sea level and, of course, the economic depression of the 1920s and its aftermath had only made things harder for the local mines to be competitive. Glengonnar Shaft at Leadhills closed in 1929 and the Wanlockhead Mining Co went into liquidation in 1936 and, predictably, that placed the proverbial question mark over the usefulness of the railway. After the mines'

closure, the railway was used sporadically by hikers during the summer months but the vital year-round passenger and goods traffic became all too sparse. The inevitable closure took place on 2 January 1939.

In 1951, an attempt was made to resurrect the mining industry at Wanlockhead but that came to nothing and, afterwards, there were threats of a Closing Order being served on the entire village. However, the Order was staved off and, despite the period of severe hardship which ensued, the community is now starting to emerge from the economic gloom. In recent years, the Museum of Scottish Lead Mining was established at Wanlockhead and it houses an impressive collection of exhibits relating to local industrial history. Furthermore, in 1986 the Lowthers Railway Society started work on constructing a 2ft gauge diesel-worked line between Leadhills and Wanlockhead, and the first quarter-mile is already up and running.

37 Leek & Manifold Light Railway

In the 1890s, the valleys of the River Manifold and River Hamps in northeast Staffordshire supported some quarrying and light agriculture. Most of the area's produce was taken to Leek for onward transportation by the North Staffordshire Railway and, although the NSR hardly made a fortune from that source, the company became concerned when the London & North Western Railway started constructing a branch from Buxton to Ashbourne in western Derbyshire. The feeling was that the LNWR branch would prove more convenient for the people and produce of the Manifold Valley area.

However, it was not the NSR which initially took the bull by the horns. The businessfolk of Leek formulated plans for a local light railway but nevertheless wisely consulted the NSR. The outcome was the formation of the Leek, Caldon Low & Hartington Light Railways which gained authorisation to construct a 9¾-mile standard gauge line from Leek to Waterhouses, a standard gauge branch to Caldon Low Quarries, and a 2ft 6in gauge 8¼-mile line from Waterhouses to Hulme End. Under the terms of the Light Railway Order, the NSR was empowered to construct and work the lines. The corporate distinctions between the different sections of line were confusing. The narrow gauge section had, in fact, been promoted independently of the standard gauge lines and, although the whole lot was authorised under the same Order, the narrow gauge line was referred to separately as the Leek & Manifold Valley Light Railway. The other company which added to the confusion, the Leek, Caldon Low & Hartington Light Railways, was regarded as a form of 'holding' company and was soon officially absorbed by the NSR; its standard gauge line to Waterhouses did not open until over a year after the L&MVLR had commenced operating.

In 1900, while construction of the L&MVLR had still to commence, Everard Richard Calthrop was appointed as chief engineer. Calthrop was one of Britain's greatest proponents of narrow gauge railways, and the vast experience which he had gained abroad was to manifest itself in many ways. During the construction stage, for example, Calthrop laid the rails facing inwards at three degrees from vertical so that their surfaces would correspond with the angles of the wheels. That was one of several features which contributed to the rails' renowned smoothness and longevity.

The railway opened on 27 June 1904. It was single-track throughout and started at Waterhouses where, until the arrival of the standard gauge NSR branch from Leek the following year, the narrow gauge trains used a temporary platform some 300yds east of the uncompleted NSR station. When the

Below: **L&MVR No 1 *E. R. Calthrop* hauls a mixed train across the river bridge at Redhurst.**
Bucknall Collection/Ian Allan Library

MANIFOLD VALLEY.

proper station was opened, NSR trains used the south side of its platform and the L&MVLR trains the north side; to the west of the station was a goods yard. After leaving Waterhouses, there were intermediate stopping places at Sparrowlee (1½ miles), Beeston Tor (3½ miles), Grindon (4 miles), Thor's Cave (4¾ miles), Wetton Mill (5½ miles), Butterton (6¾ miles) and Ecton (7¼ miles) before the terminus at Hulme End, (8¼ miles) was reached. Redhurst (5¼ miles) was added in 1915. At Hulme End, the terminus comprised a single platform for passengers and a double-faced one for goods; the engine and carriage sheds, each with two roads, were in the station yard. In common with all stations along the route, the platform at Hulme End was just 6in high. On its journey

through the picturesque valleys, the line had gradients of up to 1 in 41 and its major engineering feature was the 154yd Swainsley tunnel, just to the south of Butterton station. The passing places on the line were at Wetton Mill and Ecton.

The L&MVLR possessed two locomotives. They were identical 2-6-4Ts built by Kitsons and were christened No 1 *E. R. Calthrop* and No 2 *J. B. Earle*, the latter name being that of the company's resident engineer. It has often been remarked that they were, in effect, scaled-down versions of 4-8-4Ts which Kitsons had built to Calthrop's specifications for use on the Barsi Light Railway in India. The L&MVLR's locomotives had Walschaerts valve gear, outside cylinders of 11½ in x 16in, and 2ft 6in diameter driv-

Right: **Showing off its smart lined livery of early L&MVR years, No 1 *E. R. Calthrop* rests in the shed yard at Hulme End.** Bucknall Collection/Ian Allan Library

Below: **Two of the L&MVR's transporter trucks carry a pair of standard gauge tank wagons.** Bucknall Collection/Ian Allan Library

118

ing wheels which were contained in a rigid wheelbase of just 6ft. The locomotives weighed in at 26tons 13cwt apiece. Passenger rolling stock comprised just four bogie carriages. Two were fitted with covered platforms at each end, while the other pair had similar platforms but at only one end; all four had steps at each end, these being necessary in view of the low platform heights along the line. The L&MVLR's stud of freight wagons eventually numbered eight, four of which were ingenious Calthrop-inspired transporter wagons on to which standard gauge trucks could be loaded for stations beyond Waterhouses. As well as the two terminii, five of the intermediate stations on the narrow gauge line had facilities for loading and off-loading standard gauge trucks.

At first, the company's locomotive livery was light chocolate brown, but the NSR's livery of lake was applied in 1919. At the Grouping, the locomotives became LMSR property and, although they were not allotted new numbers, they received the obligatory lined crimson liveries. Later, however, that gave way to unlined black. The coaches were, at first, given a primrose yellow livery but, from 1919, they followed the lead of the locomotives by being repainted, first in NSR lake and later in LMSR crimson.

The NSR's standard gauge line from Leek to Waterhouses did not open until 1 July 1905, the delay being due to heavy rain causing havoc with the earthworks. As an interim measure, the NSR ran a pair of 20-seat coke-fired buses between Waterhouses, Leek and Ashbourne and, although they were not the most comfortable or reliable of contraptions, their usefulness was immeasurable as they prevented the L&MVLR from starting life with a totally isolated

line. Before the L&MVLR had opened, it had been intended to build an extension from Hulme End to Buxton but, when the corporate coffers failed to fill as quickly as required, that plan was abandoned. Despite the expertise of E. R. Calthrop and the support of the NSR, the little L&MVLR found revenue hard to come by. The L&MVLR generated a small amount of holiday traffic but the essential year-round passenger trade failed to materialise in the necessary quantity and, to a great extent, the railway was kept solvent by its milk traffic. The establishment of a dairy processing plant alongside Ecton station in 1921 provided the line with welcome extra traffic but, by then, the balance sheets were showing losses of around £2,000 annually.

At first, the passenger services on the line comprised four trains each way with an additional one on Thursdays and Saturdays; the third-class return fare for the entire journey was, at that time, 1/3d (6½ p). By 1922, one of the weekday services had been dropped, but even the remaining services were more than was required as, outside of holiday periods, the loadings of many trains were only half a dozen passengers. In common with many little light railways, the usual practice was to run mixed trains.

After the Grouping, the LMSR took stock of the L&MVLR. Viability was rated more highly than charisma or sentiment and, consequently, the L&MVLR was treated to minimal investment; it had to be admitted that, in view of the increasing popularity of road transport during the 1920s, that policy made economic sense. A major nail in the L&MVLR's coffin was the closure in 1932 of the creamery at Ecton, the railway's principal source of steady traffic. The line clung on grimly but, in 1934, the inevitable closure was formally announced. The last scheduled train ran on 10 March 1934 and, as if to emphasise the local apathy, it carried just seven passengers. Passenger services on the standard gauge Leek-Waterhouses line were withdrawn on 28 September 1935, thereby putting paid to any chances that the L&MVLR might ever be

Left: **No 2 *J. B. Earle* pulls into Waterhouses with the 3.45pm from Hulme End on 29 April 1933, less than a year before the line's closure. The standard gauge ex-NSR station is behind the railings on the right.**
H. C. Casserley

Above: **The 3.45pm for Waterhouses waits to leave Hulme End on 29 April 1933.** H. C. Casserley

Below: **The L&MVR narrow gauge line from Hulme End enters from the right while the NSR standard gauge line to Leek exits left. The interchange sidings are clearly marked on this 25in Ordnance Survey map.** Crown Copyright

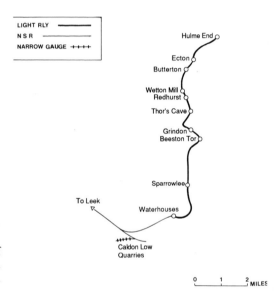

revived. Of the two locomotives, No 2 *J. B. Earle* was taken to Crewe where it remained until being sold for scrap in 1937; No 1 *E. R. Calthrop* remained on site and was last used to haul the demolition trains in 1937. It was cut up at Waterhouses later that year.

In the fields of mechanical and civil engineering, the L&MVLR was streets ahead of most of its contemporaries, and the line's lack of support and ultimate fate was a poor tribute to E. R. Calthrop, the man who did so much to make it the showpiece of British narrow gauge railways. Calthrop had passed away in March 1927 and so was at least spared from witnessing the decline of his progeny.

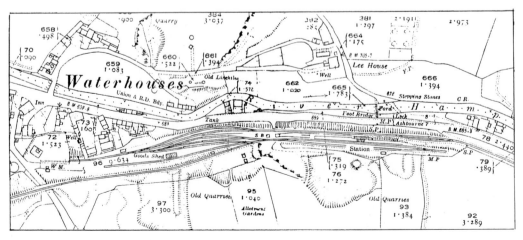

38 Lowca Light Railway

Of all the little lines in Britain, the Lowca Light Railway in Cumberland must rate as one of the most obscure. It started life as one of the many privately-owned mineral railways which served the industrialised parts of Cumberland; laid in the early 1870s, the two-mile line served James Bain & Co's colliery at Lowca, to the south of Workington. When the Cleator & Workington Junction Railway was formed in 1876, part of its powers were to construct a 1½-mile line from the Derwent Ironworks at Workington to Rosehill where a connection would be made with the Lowca colliery line.

In 1909, the Workington Iron & Steel Co was formed. It took over Derwent ironworks and Lowca colliery, the latter being expanded and a coke and by-products plant being established. The problem of transporting staff to the cliff-top site at Lowca was solved in 1911 when the steel company was granted permission to operate its own workmen's trains over the tracks of the Cleator & Workington Junction Railway. The services were successful, and in order to introduce public passenger services, formal authorisation was obtained for the Lowca Light Railway.

The public services commenced on 2 June 1913 and comprised four trains each way between Lowca and Workington Central; until 1919, one of those in each direction ran through to, or from, Seaton. From Workington, the trains used C&WJR metals as far as Rosehill, the rest of the journey to Lowca being over the light railway's own tracks. On the C&WJR section, spartan halts were provided at Harrington (Church Road) and Rosehill (Archer Street) while

the LLR erected similar-style 'minimalist' halts at Copperas Hill, Micklam and Lowca itself. The normal practise for services on the line was for one third-class coach to be allocated for public use while the workmen had their own coaches, and woe betide any workman who tried to mingle with the public.

The line was extremely difficult to work. Southbound trains had to negotiate a short stretch of 1 in 17 immediately after leaving Rosehill and the ferocity of the winds off the Irish Sea could mean that any sand intended to aid adhesion was blown away before it even touched the rails. Nominally, the C&WJR worked the trains but the company had, at that time, only ten engines and so even its own scheduled passenger services were handled by Furness Railway locomotives. The Furness locomotives used on the passenger services to Lowca were usually Sharp Stewart 0-6-0s which were paired with distinctive four-wheeled 1,500gal tenders.

While the passenger trains were operating on the LLR, the electric tablet block system was used and there were signalboxes at Rosehill and Lowca. How-

Below: **The Furness Railway 0-6-0s which usually hauled the passenger trains on the Lowca Light Railway were very smart-looking machines. A total of 55 such locomotives were built by Sharp Stewart between 1866 and 1884, No 63 being one of the 1871 batch. No 63 was rebuilt in 1899 and fitted with its modern cab; the locomotive was retired in 1918, its class becoming extinct just ten years later.** Bucknall Collection/ Ian Allan Library

Miles	LOWCA, WORKINGTON, and SEATON (3rd class only).—Cleator and Workington Junction. Up	Week Days only.							Miles	Down	Week Days only.					
		mrn aft aft	S E aft	S aft							mrn mrn aft	S E aft	S aft			
	Lowca ....dep.	6 10 1 5 1 37	.... 5 35 9 10						Seaton ....dep.							
¼	Micklam ¶	6 12 1 7 1 39	.... 9 12					2¼	Workington (Central) ¶	.... 5 10 11 30 12 40	.... 5 0 8 40					
5	Workington (Central) ¶	6 29 1 27 1 56	.... 5 54 9 27					7	Micklam	.... 5 27 11 47 12 57	.... 8 57					
7¼	Seaton .... arr.							7¼	Lowca .... arr.	5 29 11 49 12 59	.... 5 20 8 59					

E Except Saturdays.   S Saturdays only.   ¶ "Halts" at Rosehill (Archer Street) and Harrington (Church Road), between Micklam and Workington.

ever, after the Lowca-Workington passenger services were withdrawn on 31 May 1925, all that remained were the freight workings which comprised coal from the colliery, the coke and tar from its by-products plant and bricks from a works at nearby Micklam. Micklam Brick Works, incidentally, specialised in bricks for lining the blast furnaces of the steel works.

The tracks of the LLR were subsequently taken over by the United Steel Co, that concern having absorbed the Workington Iron & Steel Co in 1919. The colliery at Lowca became part of the National Coal Board in 1947, and the coal was transported southwards to the Partington-Distington line which had once been owned by the Whitehaven, Cleator & Egremont Railway. The NCB and British Steel (which took over the United Steel Co in 1967) used their own locomotives and, at Lowca, the two industrial sections met end-on. As a purely industrial line, the route of the old light railway continued to operate until 23 May 1973.

Although the Lowca Light Railway might have been one of life's unsung lines, the name of Lowca should not be totally unfamiliar. In the 1700s, the famous Lowca Engineering Works was founded at Parton and, in 1830, that company became Messrs Tulk & Ley. The new proprietors built steam locomotives, not only for local railway companies, but for customers worldwide; its successor in 1857, Fletcher Jennings & Co, continued the local tradition of locomotive building until the early 1920s.

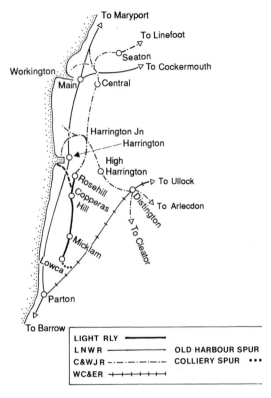

Top: *Bradshaw's*, July 1922.

Left: **The view of the 1 in 17 incline between Copperas Hill and Rosehill Junction is seen from the cab of an United Steels Co diesel locomotive on 6 June 1968. Moss Bay Steelworks is in the distance.** Ian Allan Library

39 Maidens & Dunure Light Railway

The Glasgow & South Western Railway's route from Ayr to Girvan was opened throughout in 1860. Since the coastal area between Ayr and Girvan had only a few small villages, the G&SWR had decided to ignore the indisputable scenic delights of the coast-line and, instead, build its line inland via Maybole. In 1901, however, the railway company took another look at Turnberry, one of those small coastal villages, and subsequently established a large luxury hotel there complete with the seemingly obligatory golf courses. As Turnberry was four miles from the existing railway line, the G&SWR promoted a nominally-independent light railway to provide rail access to the new hotel.

The so-called independent company was the Maidens & Dunure Light Railway. Its line opened on 17 May 1906, the same day as the public opening of Turnberry Hotel, and left the Ayr-Girvan route at Alloway Junction, two miles south of Ayr. There were stations at Alloway (3 miles from Ayr), Heads of Ayr (6¼ miles), Dunure (8 miles), Knoweside (11 miles), Glenside (13 miles), Maidens (15¼ miles) and Turnberry (16¾ miles) before rejoining the existing line just north of Girvan (21¾ miles); a halt was added at Balchriston Level Crossing (11¾ miles) in the 1920s. As well as the passenger stations, there were goods depots at Greenan Castle and Dipple. At first, there were passing loops only at Alloway, Dunure and Maidens and, as the line was subjected to the usual light railway speed limit of 25mph, severe delays soon resulted. Matters came to a head in July 1913 when it was revealed that the total delays on the route during the month amounted to an abysmal 88hr; consequently, loops at Dipple and Heads of Ayr were added the following year.

The route was worked by the G&SWR whose crews referred to that duty as 'The Turnberry', although the public later came to refer to it as the 'Heads of Ayr' line. For duties on sharply-curved lines such as the Maidens & Dunure route, the G&SWR's locomotive superintendent, James Manson, designed the '266' class 0-4-4Ts. The G&SWR had never favoured tank locomotives and, even with the completion of the six members of the '266' class, only 40 of the company's engines were of the tank variety; of those 40, a mere 14 were intended for passenger duties. Two of the '266s' were usually used on the Maidens & Dunure line, but were later superseded by standard types which included veteran 4-4-0s.

Above: **The general appearance of Maidens station on the Heads of Ayr route gives no real clues that the line was built to light railway standards.** Lens of Sutton

Below: **The use of locomotives with 7ft 1in driving wheels on a secondary line such as the Maidens & Dunure route might have sounded ambitious, but the Manson renewals of older Stirling 4-4-0s nevertheless worked the line, that being proved by No 14234 in charge of an Ayr to Girvan local at Heads of Ayr in the late 1920s.** Ian Allan Library

Above: **The new platform serving the holiday camp at Heads of Ayr opened in 1947. Ex-LMSR '2P' 4-4-0 No 40640 runs round its train at the station on 6 July 1957.** H. C. Casserley

28. The period limited by the Glasgow and South Western Railway (Maidens and Dunure Light Railway) Order 1899 for making and completing the railway by that Order authorised is hereby extended for a period of two years from the thirtieth day of September one thousand nine hundred and four and sections 24 and 25 of the said Order shall be read and construed accordingly and the Company may during such extended period exercise the powers granted to the Company by the said Order with respect to the said railway.

Extension of time (Maidens and Dunure Light Railway).

If the said railway be not completed within the said period then on the expiration of that period the powers by the said Order of 1899 granted to the Company for making and completing the said railway or otherwise in relation thereto shall cease except as to so much thereof as shall be then completed.

Left: **This extract from the G&SWR's Confirmation Act of July 1904 refers to the Maidens & Dunure Light Railway.** Author's files

TURNBERRY, Ayrshire.

TURNBERRY STATION HOTEL.

(G. & S. W. Rly. Co.)   Tels.: "Souwestern, Turnberry."   Telephone: "Girvan," 59 and 60.

Electric Light.   Lift.   Lounge.   Sea-water Baths.   Billiards (3 Tables).   Conservatory
Garage.   Stables.   Two Magnificent Golf Courses (Professional).   Seaside.

At the Grouping in 1923, the line became part of the LMSR empire, the old light railway company having been officially absorbed by the G&SWR some years earlier. By the summer of 1930, the passenger service comprised a basic six down and five up trains on weekdays, although there were additional workings on Wednesdays and Saturdays. Included in the services were the 7.22am Girvan-Glasgow Pullman restaurant car train which had a 5.10pm return working, and a through carriage and first-class sleeping car leaving Turnberry for Euston at 6.42pm and connecting with the 9.40pm Larne

Boat Express from Stranraer. A balanced working left Euston at 8pm.

Despite the impressive standard and variety of services, the line was not over-patronised; it was closed between Alloway Junction and Turnberry on 1 December 1930, services to Turnberry subsequently being rerouted via Girvan. However, the section northwards from Turnberry was reopened on 4 July 1932 when a twice-daily service to and from Kilmarnock was introduced, although the six intermediate stations remained closed to passengers. This service fared little better and lasted only until 31 May

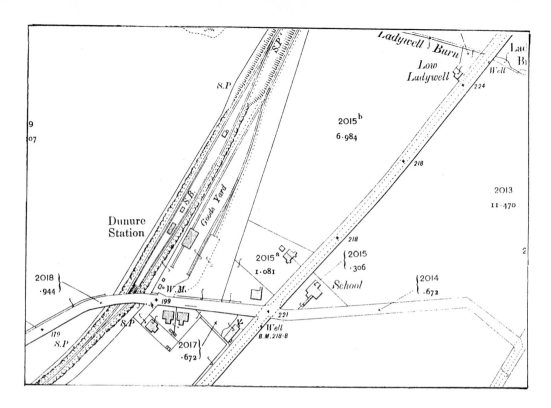

Above: **25in Ordnance Survey map, 1909.** Crown Copyright

PASSENGER STATIONS ON THE MAIDENS & DUNURE LIGHT RAILWAY

STATION	Distance from Alloway Junct.	Gradients		Platform length
		on approach	on leaving	
Alloway	1m 25ch	1 in 80 fall	level	550ft
Heads of Ayr	4m 36ch	1 in 300 rise	1 in 80 rise	400ft
Dunure	6m 19ch	1 in 80 fall	1 in 150 rise	400ft
Knoweside	9m 29ch	1 in 200 rise	1 in 90 rise	150ft
Glenside	11m 17ch	1 in 100 fall	1 in 100 fall	150ft
Maidens	13m 36ch	1 in 70 fall	1 in 70 fall	400ft
Turnberry	14m 78ch	1 in 100 fall	1 in 100 fall	400ft

Information sourced and kindly supplied by the Glasgow & South Western Railway Association.

1933. Once again, services to Turnberry Hotel were rerouted via Girvan but those were withdrawn after 28 February 1942, the hotel trade having been severely affected by the economies of the war years. During the last summer before the war, passenger services between Girvan and Turnberry had comprised nine trains each way on weekdays, with an additional one on Saturdays, the sleeping-car facilities having, by then, been extended to accommodate third-class passengers. Despite the cessation of passenger workings, public freight traffic was accommodated on the entire line until 28 February 1955, the facilities at Alloway lingering on until 7 December 1959.

On 17 May 1947, the LMSR reopened the section between Alloway Junction and Heads of Ayr in order to serve Butlin's holiday camp, the camp having started life during the war as a naval training base. To service the holiday camp, a new platform was pro-vided just to the north of the original Heads of Ayr station. An anomaly of the new platform was that, although it was listed in the public timetables from 31 May 1948, it was available for use only by visitors to the holiday camp. By the summer of 1954, Saturday services to Heads of Ayr comprised eight down trains and five in the up direction, a few of which ran through to or from Kilmarnock. As mass car-ownership grew during the 1950s and 1960s, fewer holidaymakers used the railway to the camp and the last train ran on 7 September 1968.

40 Mawddwy Light Railway

The original Mawddwy Railway opened on 1 October 1867. Like so many other small railways in North Wales it was built primarily to tap the slate traffic from local quarries, although a passenger service was offered as well. The Mawddwy's Act of Parliament, granted in 1865, referred to the company as the *Mowddwy* Railway, but it remains unconfirmed as to how the incorrect spelling came about.

The lightly-laid standard gauge line opened on 1 October 1867 and, virtually from the outset, the Mawddwy upheld the tradition of small localised Victorian railway companies by struggling to make ends meet. The freight traffic failed to reach the anticipated levels and, of course, passenger traffic was minimal. Nevertheless, a daily freight service was provided until 8 April 1908 when the line was closed completely, passenger services having been withdrawn on 17 April 1901. Despite having been operational for just over 40 years, the company had not paid even a groat to its directors or in dividends.

That was the end for the original company but, in

1910, the remnants of the line were bought by David Davies, a director of the Cambrian Railways who, perhaps philanthropically, was keen to add the line to his company's map. Davies obtained a Light Railway Order for the reconstruction of the line and, with the help of a £9,000 Treasury grant, assistance from the Cambrian Railways' civil engineers, and the assurance of a working agreement with the Cambrian, the line reopened to the public on 31 July 1911. Working agreements were commonplace in Britain but, usually, the operating company's cut was around 50-55% of gross receipts. In the case of the revived Mawddwy Railway, however, the Cambrian demanded 70% as fair recompense for having undertaken most of the reconstruction work itself and, considering the deplorable state of the track which had been inherited from the old company, the Cambrian certainly earned its money.

The single-track light railway followed the route of its predecessor. It started at the isolated outpost of Cemmes Road station, in Montgomeryshire, on the Cambrian Railways' Welshpool-Machynlleth line, where branch trains used a bay at the rear of the main-line platform. The terminus at the northern end of the branch was 6¾ miles away at Dinas Mawddwy, just over the border in Merionethshire; the terminus

Below: **Lt-Col Stephens would probably have fancied Cemmaes station, but the Mawddwy Railway was not part of his empire.** Real Photographic/IAL

Above: **One of the original Mawddwy Railway's two locomotives was Manning Wardle 0-6-0ST *Mawddwy*. It outlived the old company and was taken in hand by the Cambrian Railways to became No 30; at the Grouping, it was given GWR No 824 and was not retired until September 1940.** Real Photographic/IAL

comprised a single platform, basic goods facilities and a single-road engine shed. Between Cemmes Road and Dinas Mawddwy, the line followed the valley of the Afon Dyfi or, for the benefit of the English, the River Dovey. The intermediate stations were best described as primitive; they were at Cemmaes (1¼ miles), Aberangell (4 miles) and Mallwyd (5½ miles), and none served any real centre of population. The first two could boast a siding each but Mallwyd consisted of merely a platform. The freight facilities at Aberangell were used mainly for the transfer of slate from the Hendre-ddu quarry, the quarry having its own narrow gauge tramways which, in its early years, were horse-operated but after World War 1, were worked by an ex-WD Simplex diesel shunter.

When the original railway had been purchased for conversion to a light railway, the deal had included the old company's two locomotives. Both were standard Manning Wardle 0-6-0STs and were named *Mawddwy* and *Disraeli*. The former had a square-topped tank, 3ft 1in diameter wheels and inside cylinders of 12in x 17in; it had been built in 1864 for a contractor, and had been bought by Sir Edmund Buckley for the Mawddwy Railway three years later. The latter, a slightly larger locomotive, had a round-topped tank, 3ft 6in diameter wheels and 13in x 18in cylinders; purchased new in 1869, the funds had been made available, once again, by Sir Edmund Buckley.

After acquiring the two ageing locomotives, the Cambrian Railways thought it best to have a close look at them before trusting them in service. They were both taken to Oswestry Works for inspection, and *Disraeli* made such an impression that it was promptly condemned. However, *Mawddwy* was considered worth reconditioning and, after the necessary surgery, was taken into Cambrian stock as No 30; until the Grouping. It usually shared branch duties

with Cambrian Railways' 2-4-0 No 28. As for coaching stock, the Cambrian transferred some of its own four and six-wheel carriages to the branch to replace the former-Mawddwy stock which, according to locals, had qualified as museum pieces even when first purchased in 1867.

Despite the Cambrian's valiant efforts to improve and promote the line, the traffic figures failed to impress. The optimistic passenger service of 1911 had comprised four trains each way on weekdays but, by the early 1920s, that had been reduced to just two. At the Grouping, the Cambrian became part of the GWR empire but, predictably, the new proprietors were equally unable to produce the necessary miracle. In the 1920s, the usual branch locomotive was '517' class 0-4-2T No 846 but, by 1930, '14XX' class 0-4-2T No 1434 and ex-Lambourn Valley Railway 0-6-0T No 819 had taken over.

Passenger services were withdrawn from 1 January 1931 but the line remained open to freight and a return service operated on Mondays, Wednesdays and Fridays, principally to serve Hendre-ddu quarry. The closure of the quarry in 1939 placed a question mark over the line's future but, at the outbreak of war that year, the quarry was used for storing explosives and not only was a daily freight service required but, on occasions, a Sunday working was also needed. A veteran 'Dean Goods' 0-6-0 was sometimes put in charge of the freight workings and, during the war,

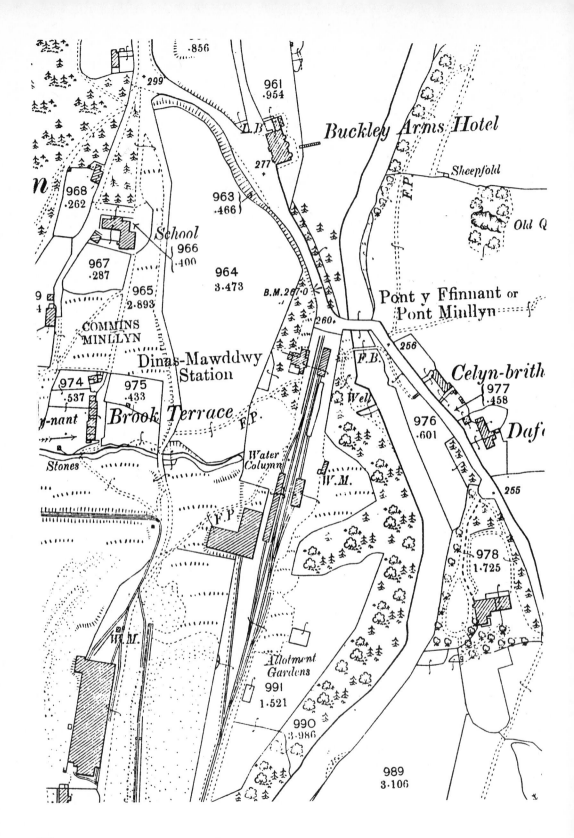

Left: **Dinas Mawddwy station and surrounds, 25in Ordnance Survey map.** Crown Copyright

Top: **Veteran 'Dean Goods' 0-6-0 No 2322 stands at Aberangell in September 1949, the overgrown nature of the trackbed providing evidence that the Mawddwy branch was, at that time, not exactly over-used.**
R. W. Kidner

Above: **The delightful setting of Dinas Mawddwy terminus is clearly seen in this picture of 24 September 1948 the locomotive is '14XX' class 0-4-2T No 1434.**
R. S. Carpenter Collection

'Duke' class 4-4-0 No 3265 *Tre Pol and Pen* was observed on the branch.

When peace was restored, the line saw little usage and, once again, its future was questioned. Officially, the date for total closure of the partly-overgrown line was 1 July 1951 but, since the previous autumn, the condition of the bridge over the River Dovey near Cemmaes had caused concern, and the last recorded revenue-earning working had, in fact, taken place on 5 September 1950. As for the veteran locomotive *Mawddwy*, it had been taken into GWR stock at the Grouping to become No 824. It had not been retired until September 1940, its later years having been spent on the Tanat Valley and Van branches in North Wales.

41 Mid-Suffolk Light Railway

Railway history is full of conflicting tales of grandiose aspirations and rude awakenings. The story of the Mid-Suffolk Light Railway contains both. Conceived as a 50-odd mile network of lines which would cross eastern Suffolk linking Haughley in the west, Halesworth in the east, and Westerfield and Needham Market in the south, the MSLR finished up, instead, with a rambling branch to nowhere in particular. Nevertheless, it eventually achieved the status of one of Britain's truly charismatic light railways.

The area which the MSLR wanted to exploit had been left alone by major railway companies. By the late 1890s, the MSLR's anticipated catchment area had less than 15,000 inhabitants, and to say that the population was scattered was an understatement since few individual villages could boast more than 1,000 residents. As for potential freight traffic, the only real industry was agriculture. Hoping to become established as a through route, rather than one which generated most of its own traffic, preparatory work went

Left: **The Mid-Suffolk's 0-6-0T No 2 was, in theory, named** *Kenton* **but there is little evidence of any nameplate in this early picture.**
Lens of Sutton

Below: **Mid-Suffolk No 3 provides visible evidence of the not-uncommon light railway practice of disconnecting the front coupled wheels of 0-6-0Ts in order to reduce the wear on the tracks. The locomotive appears to be towing No 2, as the latter has no coupling rods at all.**
Bucknall Collection/Ian Allan Library

ahead, and a Light Railway Order was gained for the construction of a line from Haughley to Halesworth, complete with a branch from Kenton to Westerfield.

After more than the usual quota of problems faced by light railways, the MSLR opened the 19-mile section between Haughley and Laxfield to goods traffic on 20 September 1904, the line being extended to Cratfield two years later. By 1905, a basic freight service had commenced on the branch which was intended to reach Westerfield, but the rails had not even reached the first station at Debenham. Passenger services did not commence until 29 September 1908, but ran solely on the 'main line' from Haughley, and then only as far as Laxfield.

The MSLR's line started at Haughley, which was served by the Great Eastern Railway's Ipswich-Norwich main line and a meandering branch to Cambridge. The MSLR's trains, however, had to use their own separate station some 100yd from that of the GER. The buildings on the single platform at the MSLR's station were faced in zinc sheet which, curiously, was painted to resemble brickwork. Freight facilities at the station were negligible as most of the goods traffic generated by the MSLR was for onward transportation and, therefore, was taken direct to the GER's yard via a connecting spur.

After leaving Haughley, there were intermediate stations at Mendlesham (4½ miles), Brockford & Wetheringsett (6 miles), and Aspall & Thorndon (8½ miles). The mid-point of the journey was Kenton (10 miles) which, in deference to its intended status as the junction for the Westerfield branch, boasted a second platform on its passing loop and, until the 1920s, a single-road engine shed. Continuing from Kenton, the stations were at Worlingworth (12 miles from

Haughley), Horham (14 miles) and Stradbroke (15 miles) before the passenger terminus at Laxfield (19 miles) was reached. Eastwards from Laxfield, the line continued for two miles to Cratfield, but that section was used only for freight. An additional station was later opened at (or, rather, one mile from) Wilby, between Stradbroke and Laxfield, and a goods 'station' provided at Gipping, 1½ miles from Haughley.

Laxfield was the centre of the MSLR's operations. The station itself comprised little more than a single-platform with basic facilities for passengers and only a couple of sidings for freight, but the administrative offices were alongside the station and the locomotive department beyond it. To put things into perspective, however, the locomotive department consisted of a single-road shed which was so small that, it was alleged, the mice went round on their hind legs. Nevertheless, routine repairs to the company's locomotives were carried out at the shed.

As for motive power, the MSLR ordered a Hudswell Clarke 0-6-0T for the opening of the line but, due to the railway company's financial problems, the builders refused to release the machine until some sort of payment was forthcoming. Consequently, the inaugural freight services were handled by the contractor's engine, a Manning Wardle 0-6-0ST named *Lady Stephenson*.

In October 1904, a few weeks after the opening to freight, the MSLR's Hudswell Clarke 0-6-0T arrived;

Below: **The wagons have been detached from the 11.15am Haughley-Laxfield mixed train at Kenton on 5 July 1952, and 'J15' class 0-6-0 No 65447 prepares to continue its journey.** G. R. Mortimer

weighing in at 29tons 12cwt, it was christened No 1 *Haughley*. A more powerful Hudswell Clarke 0-6-0T, No 2 *Kenton*, was purchased in 1905, and it has been suggested that the locomotive arrived in the form of a 2-4-0T. A third Hudswell Clarke 0-6-0T, No 3 *Lax-field*, was delivered in 1909 but, while the names quoted above for the MSLR's three locomotives appear in offi-cial documents, there is a lack of photographic evidence of the names actually being applied. Occasionally, the MSLR found it necessary to hire an additional locomo-tive from the Great Eastern, and those supplied were usually 'E22' (later 'J65') class 0-6-0Ts. The MSLR's locomotive livery was lined crimson lake with polished copper and brass appendages. The company's coaching stock consisted of new and secondhand vehicles; freight stock comprised a mixture of open wagons and vans, although a significant proportion of cattle trucks and horse boxes revealed much about the line's principal sources of traffic.

Reverting to the commencement of services, the four-year gap between inaugurating the freight and the passenger services was down to several factors,

most of which revolved around the company's appalling financial state. Receivers were first appointed as early as 1907 and that set the tone for much of the company's future existence. The passenger services initially comprised two trains each way on weekdays, but that was soon increased to three; Sunday services were only an intermittent feature of operations on the MSLR. After the first few years, the practice was to run mixed trains with the locomotives performing their own shunting en route. That might have been a wise economy but it did little for speeding up the ser-vices, the fastest of which took all of 63min for the 19-mile trip between Haughley and Laxfield.

By 1912, the MSLR had conceded that its grand plans to reach Halesworth and Westerfield were never likely to materialise. Furthermore, that year saw the truncation of the Cratfield extension at Laxfield Mills, only half a mile beyond Laxfield itself, and the formal abandonment of the still-uncompleted Kenton–West-erfield branch which had yet to reach Debenham. Although still in a poor financial position, the nadir in the MSLR's fortunes had passed and, in the following years, traffic figures showed a slight increase. Never-theless, the clause in the company's public timetable which stated: *'Passengers booking at intermediate stations can only do so conditionally upon there being room on the Train'*, was not taken too seriously.

At the Grouping, the LNER was forced to take in the MSLR, debts and all. The three locomotives, Nos

Below: **The last scheduled passenger services on the Mid-Suffolk Light Railway were on Saturday 26 July 1952. On that final day, the 1.45pm Laxfield-Haughley train arrives at Mendlesham in the charge of well-scrubbed 'J15' No 65447.** G. R. Mortimer

Table 32 HAUGHLEY and LAXFIELD (Light Railway)

Miles from Haughley		a.m	S	E
3	London (Liverpool St.)..dep	8 30	1 30	1 30
3	COLCHESTER .... "	9 47	2 47	2 47
3	IPSWICH .... "	1022	3 16	3 16
3	NORWICH (Thorpe)........ "	9 55	1 45	2 55
42	BURY ST. EDMUNDS....... "	1021	3 5	3 55
—	Haughley ....dep	1115	3 55	4 42
4½	Mendlesham..................	1128	4 8	4 55
6	Brockford and Wetheringsett..	1137	4 17	5 4
8½	Aspall and Thorndon A......	1152	4 29	5 16
10	Kenton......................	12 4	4 41	5 28
12	Worlingworth...............	1216	4 52	5 39
14	Horham.....................	1223	4 58	5 45
15	Stradbroke.................	1228	5 3	5 50
16½	Wilby......................	1233	5 8	5 55
19	Laxfield.................arr	1241	5 19	6 6

Miles		a.m	p.m
	Laxfield..................dep	7 21	1 45
2½	Wilby	7 33	1 58
4	Stradbroke	7 38	2 4
5	Horham	7 43	2 10
7	Worlingworth	7 49	2 16
9	Kenton	8 4	2 35
10½	Aspall and Thorndon A	8 10	2 41
13	Brockford and Wetheringsett	8 22	2 53
14½	Mendlesham	8 33	3 4
19	Haughley .... arr	8 48	3 18
31½	42 BURY ST. EDMUNDS.....arr	9 35	4 11
51	3 NORWICH (Thorpe)...... "	9 43	7 10
33½	3 IPSWICH................ "	9 22	3 53
50½	3 COLCHESTER............ "	10 52	5 19
102	3 London (Liverpool St.).. "	11 18	6 33

A Station for Debenham. **E** Except Saturdays **L** Arr. 5 34 p.m. on Saturdays **P** Via Stowmarket.
S Saturdays only. **U** Arr. 7 5 p.m. on Saturdays

Above: **Eastern Region timetable, 18 June to 23 September 1951.** Author's files

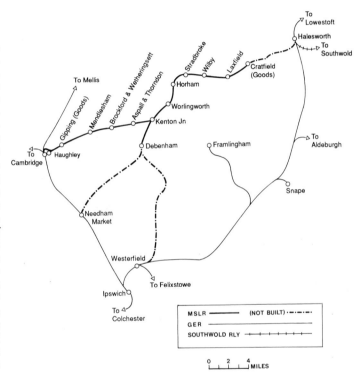

1, 2 and 3, became LNER Nos 8316/17/15 respectively and, despite their detail differences, were all classified 'J64'; it was most unusual for the LNER's engineers to miss an opportunity to create a couple of sub-classes. All three locomotives were retired by December 1929, the last to go being No 8317 (MSLR No 2), and ex-Great Eastern 'J65' class 0-6-0Ts were drafted in as replacements. During the 1920s, the familiar spectre of motor-bus competition reared its head, and the effect of the buses was clearly illustrated by the Mid-Suffolk line's returns for 1930. In that year, only £990 of its £8,337 receipts resulted from passenger traffic and, additionally, the national depression of the period began to have a marked effect on the freight figures. Apart from a brief recovery during World War 2, when the line was well patronised by personnel from the Air Force bases at Horham and Mendlesham, traffic was poor. Nevertheless, almost the entire line was relaid with LNER bull-head rails, and this allowed ex-Great Eastern 'J15' class 0-6-0s to work the line.

As the threat of closure loomed in the early 1950s, countless enthusiasts made pilgramages to witness the leisurely goings-on on one of Britain's few surviving light railways. Part of the line's appeal was that, by then, its six-wheel carriages were the only ones of their type in normal British Railways service. It was eventually announced that the last trains would run on 26 July 1952, and the final day's services were handled by 'J15' class 0-6-0 No 65447, a locomotive that was no stranger to the line. After closure, the tracks were lifted and much of the route of the old MSLR was sold off for farmland. During the 40-odd years since then, a thorough job has been done on eridicating almost all traces of the line. This writer, who smugly prides himself on being able to sniff out a disused trackbed at 1,000 paces, spent a frustrating few hours in 1991 trying to find some discernible relic of the line, but the trip was a total failure. Next time, a large-scale Ordnance Survey map will be taken along for guidance.

42 Nidd Valley Light Railway

During the industrial boom of the 19th century, many towns and cities in Yorkshire and Lancashire prospered from the textile industry. One of those was Bradford where, in the last half of the century, the population more than tripled. Inevitably, Bradford Corporation became hard-pressed to cope with such growth, and among its problems was that of an adequate water supply. Consequently, work started in 1893 on the construction of a new reservoir at Gouthwaite, in the valley of the River Nidd some 25 miles to the north of the city, but even before that reservoir was completed, plans were being made for an additional one at Angram, beyond the head of the Nidd Valley.

In 1901, an independent 2ft 6in gauge light railway through part of the Nidd Valley was promoted, primarily for the goods and staff traffic anticipated from the construction of Angram reservoir. The reservoir was to be built on bleak moorland, and so Bradford Corporation viewed the proposed railway as the only feasible means of transport to and from the site. However, the promoters found that funds to build the railway were not forthcoming and so, when the proposed line looked set for abandonment, Bradford Corporation had little option but to step in and take over the plans. Since the Light Railways Act made specific reference to local authorities becoming involved in the building of new lines, the transfer of the plans to the Corporation was little more than a formality. While the transfer was being sewn up, Bradford Corporation had the plans amended so that, instead of a narrow gauge line, a standard gauge one could be built in order to facilitate through running from the North Eastern Railway's branch from Harrogate which terminated part way up the Nidd Valley at Pateley Bridge.

Under the title of the Nidd Valley Light Railway, the Corporation-backed line from Pateley Bridge to Lofthouse-in-Nidderdale was opened to the public on 12 September 1907. The two intermediate stations on the six-mile line were at Wath-in-Nidderdale (1½ miles) and Ramsgill (4 miles), both of which had passing loops. At Pateley Bridge, the NVLR station was about a quarter of a mile beyond the NER station but they were connected by a through line, principally for the benefit of freight traffic to the construction site at Angram. The NVLR station at Pateley Bridge had two platforms, one built in stone and the other in timber, and there was a modest goods yard; beyond the

Top: **The departure of the ex-GWR steam railmotor from Lofthouse appears to be held up for photographic purposes.** Ian Allan Library

Above: **One of the handsome ex-Metropolitan 4-4-0Ts waits to depart from Lofthouse station. The other locomotive is, it seems, a contractors' engine and it appears to be setting off along the spur which leads to the site of Angram Reservoir.** Lens of Sutton

Left: **Avonside 0-6-0ST Blythe belonged to the contractor, John Best, but was nevertheless used to haul workmens' train to and from Pateley Bridge. The different materials used for the construction of each platform at Pateley Bridge station are clearly visible in this 1928 photograph.** Rail Archive Stephenson

station were the twin-road engine and carriage sheds. The passenger terminus at Lofthouse-in-Nidderdale had one platform, a passing loop, siding accommodation and a single-road engine shed.

Beyond the platform at Lofthouse, the line continued for six miles to the site of Angram reservoir but that section was used only by the contractors engaged on the construction work. Nevertheless, a passenger service between Lofthouse and a temporary wooden

platform at Angram was operated by the contractors for the workers and their families. The Lofthouse-Angram section had gradients of up to 1 in 40 and a number of tight curves; at Goyden Pot, a 180yd tunnel was built in the 1920s to circumvent one of the sharpest curves but, later, the original course was relaid for use as a passing loop. The precise opening date of the contractor's railway seems to be unrecorded, but it is known to have been operational by 14 July 1904 when a party of civic dignitaries from Bradford visited Angram. The contractors used their own locomotives, mostly industrial-type 0-6-0STs, and it is believed that up to 15 different engines were in use beyond Lofthouse at one time or another.

On the Nidd Valley Light Railway itself, motive power was at first provided by two ex-Metropolitan Railway Beyer Peacock 4-4-0Ts which had been made redundant on their old home territory by the spread of electrification. In their younger days, the Metropolitan's 4-4-0Ts had been held in high regard but, when the time came to pension them off, few buyers were found despite the circulation, in 1905, of around 3,000 sale catalogues, some of which went as far away as China. Apart from the two purchased for the NVLR, the only public railway companies in Britain to buy any of the 4-4-0Ts were the Cambrian, the Mersey and the West Somerset Mineral Railways. One of the NVLR's pair had been the Metropolitan's 'A' class No 20 and the other 'B' class No 34; the NVLR christened them No 1 *Holdsworth* and No 2 *Milner* respectively. Prior to their move to Yorkshire, they had undergone heavy repairs at Neasden Works, during which their condensing apparatus had been removed but their lined red liveries retained.

It seems that the ex-Metropolitan locomotives did not take too kindly to their new duties, as No 2 was withdrawn in 1909 and No 1 in 1912; the former was

Miles		Week Days only.						Miles		Week Days only.					
		mrn	mrn	aft	aft	aft				mrn	mrn	aft	aft	aft	
	Pateley Bridge..........dep.	8 30	1020	1 30	3 30	5 0	....		Lofthouse-in-Nidderdale..dep.	9 10	11 02	0 4	1 05	5 30	....
1¼	Wath-in-Nidderdale..........	8 35	1025	1 35	3 35	5 5	....	2	Ramsgill	9 15	11 52	5 4	1 55	5 35	....
4	Ramsgill	8 48	1038	1 48	3 48	5 18	....	4¼	Wath-in-Nidderdale..........	9 25	1115	2 15	4 25	5 45	....
6	Lofthouse-in-Nidderdale.. arr.	8 55	1045	1 55	3 55	5 25	....	6	Pateley Bridge 752........arr.	9 30	1120	2 20	4 30	5 50	....

Top: **Public timetable, summer 1922.**

Above: **The Nidd Valley's second locomotive to carry the name *Milner* was a Hudswell Clarke 0-6-0T of 1909. It is seen near Lofthouse in this photograph of 1928.** Rail Archive Stephenson

Above right: **Engine sheds and locomotive facilities on light railways were rarely state-of-the-art affairs. This was the mpd at Pateley Bridge on the Nidd Valley Light Railway circa 1928, with contractor's 0-6-0ST *Blythe* on the right and the NVLR's ex-GWR steam railmotor on the left.** Rail Archive Stephenson

sold for industrial use and is known to have finished up at a North Wales quarry where it survived until 1930, but the latter was scrapped. The replacement for No 2 was a new Hudswell Clarke 0-6-0T which, although unnumbered by the NVLR, took the name of its predecessor, *Milner*; initially it proved quite unreliable, recording its first breakdown after just three weeks in service. Another Hudswell Clarke locomotive, this time a 0-4-0ST, was purchased in 1920; originally named *Gadie* but later christened *Craven*, it worked mainly on the contractors' lines serving another new reservoir site near Angram.

The NVLR's most interesting acquisition was an ex-Great Western Railway 48-seat railmotor; purchased in 1921, it was one of 14 GWR cars which had had their power units built by Kerr Stuart. The NVLR's final acquisition was an Andrew Barclay 0-6-0ST which took the name of *Gadie* from the Hudswell Clarke 0-4-0ST. As far as can be determined, routine repairs to the NVLR's locomotives were carried out, in later years, at the waterworks repair shop at Scar House but, almost certainly, anything more extensive than the fitting of new cylinders or fireboxes would have involved a return to the relevant manufacturer.

The NVLR's passenger rolling stock comprised 10 ex-Metropolitan Railway four-wheel coaches, a single-deck 20-seat tramcar-style trailer which was used as the VIP's coach and was later sold to the Wantage Tramway in Berkshire, and a four-wheel carriage with an open observation platform. Freight stock consisted of a small mixture of vans and opens, most of the construction traffic on the line being taken through in NER wagons.

The initial passenger service on the NVLR comprised four trains each way on weekdays, the average time for a single six-mile journey being 20min. A third-class excursion fare of 9d (3¾p) return was introduced and, before long, the picturesque Nidd valley area became popular for day trips from the

Locomotives of the Nidd Valley Light Railway

No	Name	Type	Maker/Works No.	Date	Bought	Origin	Wheels	Cyls	Weight	Disposal
1	Holdsworth	4-4-0T	B/Peacock 707	1866	1907	Met Ry No 20	5ft 10in	17¼in x 24in(o)	45t 0c	Wdn 1912
2	Milner	4-4-0T	B/Peacock 1878	1879	1907	Met Ry No 34	5ft 10in	17¼in x 24in(o)	46t 15c	Sold 1909
-	Milner	0-6-0T	H/Clarke 882	1909	new	new	3ft 8in	12in x 18in(o)	30t 10c	Sold 1936
-	Gadie*	0-4-0ST	H/Clarke 1411	1920	new	new	3ft 7in	14in x 20in(o)	29t 10c	Sold 1929
-	Gadie	0-6-0ST	Barclay 1866	1925	new	new	3ft 5in	14in x 22in(o)	28t 0c	Sold 1937
-	Hill	railcar	K/Stuart 906	1905	1921	GWR car no 15	3ft 3in	9in x 15in(o)	32t 0c	Sold 1937

* Renamed *Craven* in 1925.

industrial conurbations in West Yorkshire. For several years, traffic on the NVLR remained steady but profits were hard to come by. The outbreak of World War 1 caused a hiatus in the construction of Angram reservoir and, consequently, weekday services between Pateley Bridge and Lofthouse were eventually reduced to three mixed trains each way.

After peace had been restored, Bradford Corporation started work on another reservoir beyond Lofthouse. It was located at Scar House, near Angram, but work on the project did not bring great fortunes to the NVLR. By then, Angram reservoir was all but finished and, for the new workforce at Scar House, the contractors soon established a self-contained 'village' which accommodated over 1,000 people; therefore, those workers who had previously lodged in the Nidd Valley area had no need to catch a train to work. The effect was clearly seen in the NVLR's returns which showed a drop in the annual passenger figure from almost 150,000 to little over 60,000, and one consequence of this was that the intermediate stations at Ramsgill and Wath-in-Nidderdale became merely unstaffed request stops. At the Grouping in 1923, the NVLR found itself excluded from the master plan. During the 1920s, there were occasional grandiose suggestions that the NVLR should be con-

verted to electric traction using power generated by Angram or Scar House Reservoirs, but as the decade wore on, it became very obvious that the line's present or potential traffic hardly justified such a move.

The tourist traffic to the Nidd valley area continued but, of course, the 1920s saw the emergence of competition in the form of road transport. The inevitable withdrawal of scheduled passenger services between Pateley Bridge and Lofthouse took place without ceremony on 31 December 1929. The line remained open for construction traffic, the site at Scar House becoming something of a tourist attraction and, consequently, a number of special excursion trains took visitors to see how work was progressing. The completion of Scar House Reservoir in September 1936 brought an end to, not only the construction traffic, but also the visiting parties and so the NVLR's purposes in life disappeared. The precise date of the last working on the NVLR remains a mystery, although it has been suggested that contractors' debris was still being brought down via the line until early 1937. The NVLR's remaining two locomotives and assorted hardware were auctioned in June that year, the Barclay 0-6-0ST going to an iron foundry in Scotland and the ex-GWR railmotor being sold for scrap.

As we have already seen, the London & South Western Railway was a dab hand at establishing subsidiary companies for the purpose of obtaining Light Railway Orders. In Southwest England, it perpetuated its habit with the North Devon & Cornwall Junction Light Railway which was authorised in 1914. At the time of the Grouping in 1923, very little had been done towards building the line but, without even a blush, the newly-formed Southern Railway happily took the project on board. The line was to claim the distinction of being the last of any length to be completed in the southwest and, furthermore, the last new standard gauge light railway to be opened in Britain.

The engineer employed to oversee the line's construction was our old friend, Lt-Col Stephens. The engineering work itself went fairly smoothly, but there was constant trouble among the workforce, riots and even a murder taking place among the band of navvies who were hired for the duration of the contract. While such lawlessness had become legend during the mass railway-building of the mid-19th century, it was not expected in the 1920s.

The single-track line was opened on 27 July 1925 and ran between Torrington and Halwill in North Devon. The route was 20½-miles long and had intermediate stopping places at Watergate halt (1¾ miles from Torrington), Yarde halt (4½ miles), Dunsbear halt (5¾ miles), Petrockstow (8 miles), Meeth halt (10¾ miles), Hatherleigh (12¾ miles) and Hole (17¾ miles). Its main purpose was to provide a new outlet

for the heavy ball clay which was extracted around Peters Marland and, just before the opening of the line, additional clay workings were developed at Meeth. Although Devon is usually disregarded as an industrial county, the area south of Torrington was, in fact, one of the three largest sources of ball clay in Britain.

The Marland Brick & Clay Works (later the North Devon Clay Co) had opened its own 3ft gauge railway system in 1880, and the line was extended to Torrington where the L&SWR had arrived in 1872. During its long life, the narrow gauge system was worked by a total of 15 different locomotives. At the nearby workings at Meeth, a 2ft gauge system was used and this, too, was locomotive-operated but, sadly, the interesting histories of these two industrial railways are outside the scope of this book.

As far as Dunsbear, the Southern's new 'light railway' from Torrington to Halwill was built on the route of Marland's narrow gauge railway, and this necessitated several alterations to the latter. These included a realignment in order to connect with the new line near Dunsbear halt, the construction of a new standard gauge exchange siding at Peters Marland and the purchase of two secondhand standard gauge locomotives for working the exchange traffic.

The expectation of passenger traffic on the Torrington-Halwill line had never been great as the only significant community it allegedly served was Hatherleigh, which was a good two miles from the railway. Once again, it made a mockery of the light railway

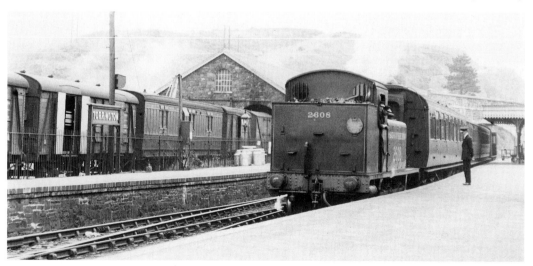

Above: **The reason why '2MT' 2-6-2Ts Nos 41216 and 41283 were required to work double-headed with a mixed train from Torrington to Halwill is unknown to the author. One matter which is a little more certain, however, is that beneath the viaduct over the River Torridge are the remains of the old part-timber viaduct which once carried the narrow gauge line from Peters Marland clay works to Torrington.** J. C. Beckett

Below left: **'E1/R' class 0-6-2T No 2608 (later BR No 32608) waits alongside the up platform at Torrington on 24 May 1935.** H. C. Casserley

legislation. The intermediate stations on the line showed ample evidence of the Southern's love affair with ferro-concrete but, as if to emphasise their anticipated lack of usage, they were sparsely equipped. The older stations at each end of the line were, however, a little more substantial.

At Torrington, the station had been opened as a terminus in 1872, and the facilities and buildings befitted the important market town. A single-road engine shed and turntable stood on the eastern side of the station. The original 42ft turntable was replaced by a 50ft model in the late 1890s. The unveiling of the line to Halwill required the rebuilding of Torrington station for through running. Just to the south of Torrington station, an iron viaduct was built to take the new line over the River Torridge, the timber viaduct of the narrow gauge Marland industrial line being considered far too insubstantial for the heavier axle weights.

The other end of the line was at Halwill. The station had opened in 1879 when the L&SWR line had been been extended as far as Holsworthy (later to Bude), and it had become a junction in 1886 when the first stretch of the line to Padstow had been com-

pleted. Originally named Halwill & Beaworthy, it had been renamed Halwill Junction in 1887, but the word 'Junction' had been officially dropped in 1923. With the arrival of the line from Torrington in 1925, Halwill became a three-way junction and, despite the three lines being far from the world's busiest, it was often remarked that something always seemed to be happening at the station.

For passenger services, the Torrington-Halwill line was worked as a completely separate unit. The axle weight limit was 16 tons and so the Southern Railway had to think long and hard about suitable motive power. At first, seven of the Adams '460' class 4-4-0s were dispatched to Barnstaple, the parent shed of Torrington, although it became usual to find three out-stationed at the latter. They proved perfectly capable of working the line, but problems arose at Halwill where the turntable was situated on the down side of the line. When Wadebridge and Bude trains occupied the other lines at Halwill simultaneously, as was often the case at peak times, access to the turntable was blocked and so the only solution was to undertake the run to Torrington tender-first. It was an unsatisfactory situation.

The long-term answer to the line's motive power problem was provided by rebuilding a number of surplus ex-London, Brighton & South Coast Railway 'E1' class 0-6-0Ts as 0-6-2Ts. The transformations were carried out at Brighton Works and the new trailing axles, which were to the design of the pony trucks of the 'N' class 2-6-0s, were added to enable the fitting of larger bunkers and additional 348gal tanks. The design proved to be so well thought out that fully-enclosed cabs could also be fitted while still keeping the axle weights down to just 14¼ tons. Originally, the rebuilds were due to be reclassified as

SECTION OF LINE.		Maximum Load inclusive of Van.					REMARKS.
		Class of Engine.					
From	To	E.216.	B.94.	C.757.	C.395.	K.	
		Equivalent to Loaded Goods Wagons.					
Torrington	Marland Clay Siding ...	10	16	16	15	10	
Marland Clay Siding ...	Petrockstow	16	20	20	18	13	
Petrockstow	Halwill	*See Note A.*	20	20	18	13	
Halwill	Hatherleigh		25	25	35	25	
Hatherleigh	Meeth Clay Siding		20	20	18	13	
Meeth Clay Siding ...	Petrockstow		25	25	30	20	
Petrockstow	Marland Clay Co.'s Siding ...	16	20	20	18	13	
Marland Clay Co.'s Siding ...	Torrington	10	16	16	14	10	

A—E.216 class of engine will only work between Torrington and Petrockstow.

Above: **The loading limits for the Torrington-Halwill line were spelt out in the SR's Western Division working timetable for July 1932.**

'E7s' but, in recognition of their new radial tanks, the classification of 'E1R' was applied instead.

In all, 10 'E1s' were rebuilt as 'E1R' 0-6-2Ts in 1927/28 and eight of them were allocated to Barnstaple and Torrington. They proved powerful enough to tackle most tasks, even on wet rails, but there were regular complaints from passengers of rough riding. That problem was tackled in 1936/37 when the five members of the class usually employed on the line were taken to Eastleigh Works for rebalancing. The 'E1Rs' went on to retain a monopoly of duties on the Torrington-Halwill line until 1953, when ex-LMSR Ivatt '2MT' 2-6-2Ts took over; after that, only No 32696 kept the 'E1R' flag flying in North Devon, the remainder moving to Exmouth Junction.

By 1932, the working timetable for the line showed two mixed trains each way on weekdays. There was also one through freight each way, an additional freight working from the clay works at Peters Marland, and a mixed 'workmens' train each way between Torrington and Hatherleigh in the mornings. The timetables for 1940 and 1952 revealed a similar pattern, although the latter showed changes to the timings of the 'workmens' trains. The scheduled times for a complete journey remained at a leisurely 86min. As late as 1957, over 8,000 head of cattle were being taken from Hatherleigh by rail, but as for the passenger services, astonishment was often expressed that they were retained as, for many years, the single-coach trains had often run completely empty on the southern section of the line. Nevertheless, it was often remarked that the station at Hatherleigh always seemed very well kept, despite its lack of passengers.

The first of the inevitable cuts came in 1959 when the small engine shed at Torrington was closed, the locomotives subsequently being sent from Barnstaple on a day-to-day basis. In 1964, a 65-seat diesel railcar took over from steam traction on the Torrington-Halwill line, but even that failed to bring about the required economies and, on 1 March 1965, passenger services were formally withdrawn. The section between Torrington and Meeth was kept open for outwards clay traffic, some of the clay being exported through Fremington Quay, between Bideford and Barnstaple. By then, motive power for the clay trains often took the form of North British Type 2 diesel-hydraulics or Type 3 Hymeks. The clay trains ceased operating on 13 September 1982, by which time Fremington Quay and the Barnstaple-Torrington passenger services had also both become memories.

Below: **On 14 August 1963, '2MT' 2-6-2T No 41283 pauses at Hatherleigh with the 4pm from Torrington to Halwill Junction.** P. Paye

At the beginning of the 20th century, northwest Lincolnshire became the target for several light railway schemes but only a few came to fruition. One of the non-starters was the Trent Valley Light Railway which, in 1906, was reconstituted as the Blyton & Frodingham Light Railway. The proposed railway was intended to serve the new ironstone areas which had been leased by the Frodingham Iron & Steel Co, but even with the backing of the Great Central Railway, the light railway company's seemingly perpetual entry in 'Bradshaw's Manual' always had the bottom line of: 'The construction of the line has not yet commenced'.

Nevertheless, neither the Great Central nor the community of Frodingham were to be excluded from the world of light railways. The North Lindsey Light Railway had been incorporated in 1900 and, from the outset, the GCR had promised a working agreement. The NLLR had been promoted by the Yorkshire Light Railway Syndicate, some of the directors of which had interests in the ironstone fields of Lincolnshire.

The first section of the North Lindsey Light Railway opened on 3 September 1906. It started just to the east of Frodingham & Scunthorpe station which, until October 1886, had masqueraded under the shorter title of Frodingham. The line passed through the station goods yard to its own station in Dawes Lane which, confusingly for all, was named Scunthorpe. From there, it continued to Thealby (5 miles) which, in July 1907 was renamed Winterton & Thealby, before reaching West Halton (6 miles). On 15 July 1907, a 2½-mile extension was officially opened from West Halton to Winteringham simultaneously with a half a mile feight spur to Winteringham Haven.

The final section of the NLLR was the 2½-mile extension from Winteringham to Whitton, and this was opened on 1 December 1910 to complete the 11-mile long single-track route. At Winteringham Haven, there was a small wharf which had two chutes for handling coal and slag. A ferry service to and from Hull was etablished at the wharf, the outward trips being on Mondays and the returns on Wednesdays. At Whitton, there was a pier where the Hull-Gainsborough packet steamer called three times a week.

When the railway opened as far as Winteringham in 1907, the passenger service comprised three trains each way on weekdays. The Whitton extension, which was opened in 1912, was served at first by just two trains each way. Even those meagre services were more than was required and, by 1922, the timetables showed two trains each way to Winteringham, only one of those in each direction venturing as far as Whitton. The order of the day was third class only. The Great Central worked all the services on the NLLR with standard stock, the former's cut of the takings being 60% plus 'a proportion of surplus profits'.

Freight traffic on the NLLR perked up in 1912 when John Lysaght & Co commissioned two blast furnaces at Normanby Park near Scunthorpe. A goods station at Normanby Park, 1¾ miles along the line from Frodingham & Scunthorpe station, was opened on 1 August that year to handle the extra traffic. Access to the NLLR's line was improved in 1913 with the laying of a new curve at the Frodingham end, thereby avoiding the station's goods yard. In 1910-12 there had been plans to double the line as far as Normanby Park and to extend the other end of the line from Winteringham to Barton, but although much of the necessary land had been acquired, the plans died a death. The freight traffic to and from the blast furnaces at Frodingham increased, but passenger traffic on the NLLR line dwindled almost in inverse proportion. The line passed to the LNER at the Grouping and the new proprietors had little hesitation in dispensing with the passenger workings. The official date of their withdrawal was 13 July 1925.

Nevertheless, there was no question of closing the line to freight, and as the Frodingham/Scunthorpe area became increasingly industrialised, the local railway network was modernised accordingly. North of Frodingham and Scunthorpe, freight services continued on the old NLLR line until the official total closure on 20 July 1964. Public goods facilities had been withdrawn from Winteringham and Whitton in October 1951, and those at West Halton had followed suit in May 1961. Today, a small section of the former NLLR route immediately to the north of Scunthorpe still survives as part of the heavy-duty freight line serving the local industrial concerns.

Miles	SCUNTHORPE and WHITTON (3rd class only).—Great Central.					Miles				
		Week Days only.						Week Days only.		
		mrn| aft		[aft					mrn| aft	[aft	
	Scunthorpe..........dep.	7 55	20	6 0	......		Whitton............dep.	......	2 0	......	......
5	Winterton and Thealby...	8 10	35	6 15	......	2½	Winteringham...........	8 25	2 10	6 30	......
6	West Halton............	8 13	38	6 18	......	5	West Halton............	8 32	2 17	6 37	......
8½	Winteringham..........	8 19	45	6 24	......	6	Winterton and Thealby...	8 35	2 20	6 40	......
11	Whitton.............arr.	.....	1 55		......	11	Scunthorpe ....arr.	8 50	2 35	6 55	......

Left: Bradshaw's, July 1922.

To most Southerners, the old county of Northumberland remains a mystery and, quite often, the most informed description of the area is 'the bit between Newcastle and Scotland'. Away from the industrialised areas to the immediate north of Tyneside, Northumberland boasts some magnificent scenery and a wealth of history but the area is rarely explored by tourists. The lack of visitors is largely explained by the climate, the author,for one, having many memories of walking the Northumberland coast while clad in thick jumpers, waterproofs and two pairs of socks, even in July.

Bearing in mind that this is meant to be a railway book and not a travel guide, let's proceed with the nitty-gritty. North of the Blyth and Newbiggin areas, there are several small fishing ports on the Northumberland coast, but only two ever had a direct rail link. One was Amble and the other was Seahouses. The North Eastern Railway had condescendingly opened a branch to Amble but the locals around Seahouses had to sort out their own railway.

It took a completely independent concern, the North Sunderland Railway, to promote, construct and operate the short branch from Chathill, on the North Eastern Railway's main line 46 miles north of Newcastle, to Seahouses. The community in the corporate title, North Sunderland, was only a stone's throw short of Seahouses. The NSR was incorporated in 1892 but, when the Light Railways Act was passed in 1896, the company promptly amended its plan to that of a light railway and subsequently became one of the very first to have a line sanctioned under the new legislation. Nevertheless, the word 'Light' was never to appear in the company's title.

The North Sunderland Railway opened to freight traffic on 1 August 1898 and to passengers on 14 December. It started from a bay on the up side of Chathill station but, originally, the intention had been for the NSR to have its own platform there. The line ended four miles away at Seahouses where there was a single platform, a small goods yard and the company's engine shed. The only intermediate stopping place was at North Sunderland, just outside Seahouses. The NSR was a standard gauge line and had no significant engineering features; its ruling gradient was 1 in 80 and it was laid with 63lb/yd flat bottomed rails which, apart from a section at the Chathill end, were to remain until the end of its days. The final construction bill for the line worked out at a modest £6,205 per mile. Almost as soon as the line had opened, a

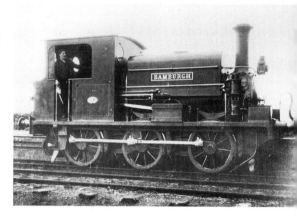

Above: **The North Sunderland's first (and only) steam locomotive was Manning Wardle 0-6-0ST *Bamburgh*, seen here in its original glory at Seahouses.**
Real Photographs/Ian Allan Library

two-mile extension branch from Seahouses northwards to Bamburgh was proposed but, when it became clear that the company wasn't going to turn its directors into millionaires, the proposal was dropped.

For working the line, the 'one engine in steam' principle was the obvious one to adopt because, quite simply, the NSR possessed only one engine. It was a Manning Wardle 0-6-0ST (Works No 1394) named *Bamburgh* which had 3ft 6in driving wheels, 12in x 18in inside cylinders and a boiler pressure of 140lb; it was fitted with a Westinghouse brake, the donkey-pump being situated on the driver's side of the smokebox. The locomotive was finished in a mid-green livery. When, in 1920, *Bamburgh* was sent to Manning Wardle's for major repairs, North Eastern Railway 0-6-0T No 407 was hired as a stand-in. During its life, that temporary replacement also saw service on the Easingwold and the Cawood, Wistow & Selby Light Railways, both of which are featured elsewhere in this book.

At first, the NSR had five carriages, all four-wheeled vehicles which had been purchased from the Highland Railway. In later years, other coaches were acquired and, in its final years, the NSR operated with a pair of ex-Great Eastern six-wheel carriages and one ex-North Eastern Railway four-wheel vehicle. The NSR's official coaching livery was medium brown with yellow lettering. The company's passenger services were not exactly over-subscribed but the freight figures were reasonably steady. As had been anticipated, almost all of the freight was fish from Seahouses although, between 1909 and 1912, some stone traffic was generated by the small rail-connected quarry at Pasture Hill. There was also a small amount of inwards goods traffic. The NSR's returns for 1910 showed that 22,848 passengers and 14,961 tons of freight were carried, producing gross receipts of £2,262 and a working profit of over £1,200.

For the summer of 1922, the public timetables showed six trains each way on weekdays although, mysteriously, the first one of the day in each direction was marked 'Gov'. That abbreviation normally denoted services which were operated to the well-meaning, but nevertheless infamous, 'Parliamentary' conditions of the 1844 Railway Act which had compelled railway companies to run at least one daily train which stopped at every station en route and offered cheap fares. It can only be assumed that the NSR's 'Parliamentary' was a workmen's cut-price special.

The early 1920s were the heyday of the line. At its peak, the NSR employed a staff of nine and, occasionally, accommodated excursion trains from Newcastle. However, the familiar spectre of road transport loomed in the mid and late-1920s and, although around 20,000 passengers used the line annually in the middle of the decade, the freight traffic had, by then, dropped to around 8,000 tons per year. On the financial side, the gross receipts during the mid-1920s were usually around £2,400, ie hardly any more than in 1910, but expenses had more than doubled.

By the early 1930s, the NSR was in serious trouble. Its permanent way and rolling stock were in very poor repair but there were no funds available to bring

things up to scratch. In an attempt to reduce overheads, the company acquired an Armstrong-Whitworth 95hp diesel-electric locomotive; carrying Works No D25 and the name of *Lady Armstrong*, it entered service in 1934. The 'Armstrong' connection was explained by the fact that one of the NSR's directors was Lord Armstrong who had two homes in the area, the first being Bamburgh Castle and the second being Cragside, near Rothbury. The little locomotive performed sterling work but it was not the speediest creature in the land. Evidence of this is found in the timetables which, by spring 1940, showed five trains each way on weekdays but with a journey time of 25min for the four-mile trip. In 1922, the scheduled journey times had been 15 min.

The NSR's worsening financial situation prevented a prompt, let alone total, settlement of its bills with the LNER and so, in 1939, the LNER took over the management of the ailing company. By then, *Lady Armstrong* had suffered several breakdowns and the hiring of replacement motive power from the LNER had become almost a regular occurence. That situation continued into the 1940s and among the locomotives hired were an ex-NER 'J71' class 0-6-0T and Sentinels of the 'Y1' and 'Y3' classes.

In 1945, a permanent replacement for the mortally ill diesel arrived; it was 'Y7' class 0-4-0T No 986 which boasted an axle weight of just 13 tons. The locomotive

Below: **Diesel traction was not the norm for impecunious light railway companies, but the North Sunderland nevertheless acquired *Lady Armstrong* in 1934. The facts that it was built by Armstrong-Whitworth, and that one of the railway company's directors was a certain Lord Armstrong were not entirely coincidental. The picture was taken at Seahouses on 5 June 1934.**
H. C. Casserley

Above: **In the final years of the North Sunderland Railway, services were entrusted to 'Y7' class 0-4-0T No 68089, seen here at Seahouses engine shed.**
Lens of Sutton

had been built at Darlington in 1923 and was one of seven survivors of a class which had once numbered 24; prior to its transfer to the Seahouses line, the locomotive had been fitted with a vacuum ejector. In November 1948, the 'Y7' received its BR No 68089 and was officially transferred to the parent shed at Tweedmouth, having previously remained on the books of Tyne Dock shed despite its new sphere of duty. The two NSR locomotives, *Bamburgh* and *Lady Armstrong*, were sold for scrap in 1949, the sales providing £61/9/11d (£61.50p) for the coffers.

The NSR retained its nominal independence after Nationalisation in 1948, but the Railway Executive quickly realised that there was no way the little company could stand on its own

Right: **The 'Who's Who' and 'Who Owns What' of the NSR was detailed in** *Bradshaw's Shareholders' Guide,* **1915 edition.** Author's files

corporate feet. The Executive was not prepared to continue supplying locomotives for the line and so the only alternative was closure. The last trains ran on 27 October 1951. 'Y7' class No 68089 was in charge of proceedings and, to mark the occasion, was fitted with headboards bearing the legend 'The Farne Islander'.

Plymouth, Devonport & South Western Junction Railway

See (9) BERE ALSTON & CALSTOCK LIGHT RAILWAY.

NORTH SUNDERLAND.

DIRECTORS:

Chairman—EDWARD SISTERSON, Esq., J.P., Woodley Field, Hexham.

The Right Hon. Lord Armstrong of Bamburgh and Cragside, Northumberland.

Major George J. W. Noble, Jesmond Dene House, Newcastle-on-Tyne
Captain S. M. Rowlandson, The College, Durham.

OFFICER.—Sec., Richard Smith, 61, Westgate Road, Newcastle-upon-Tyne.

Incorporated in 1892, to construct a line about four miles in length. Opened for goods traffic 1st August, 1898, and for passenger traffic 14th December, 1898. Authorised capital, 41,333*l.*, including 10,333*l.* loans. Capital issued, 14,900*l.* in 10*l.* ordinary shares fully paid; 9,920*l.* 4 per cent. 10*l.* preference shares fully paid; 5 per cent. debenture stock, 3,300*l.*; loan, 760*l.*; Lloyds bonds, 400*l.*; and rent-charges 315*l.* per annum. To June, 1908, there was a debit to revenue after charging interest of 1,051*l.*; to 30th June, 1909, the debit balance, after charging interest, was 929*l.*; to June, 1910, it was 636*l.*; and to June, 1911, it was 38*l.* To June, 1912, there was a credit balance of 63*l.*; and to December, 1912, 130*l.* No dividend yet paid on ordinary or preference.

Director's Qualification: 20 shares.

Transfer form, common; fee, 2*s.* 6*d.*

46 Ponteland Light Railway

To the northwest of Newcastle, proposed housing developments around Ponteland prompted the North Eastern Railway to promote a light railway from South Gosforth. The Order was in the name of the Ponteland Light Railway, and the line opened to freight on 1 March 1905 and to passengers on 1 June 1905. The original intention was to electrify the line as soon as it had become established — the Tyneside electrification had been undertaken in 1904 — but the outbreak of World War 1 in 1914 brought a hiatus to the development work at Ponteland and, consequently, the line never saw enough passenger traffic to warrant electrification.

The Ponteland branch left the main line at South Gosforth and had intermediate stations at West Gosforth (¾-mile), Coxlodge (2 miles), Kenton (3½ miles) and Callerton (4¾ miles) before the line reached Ponteland (7 miles). A 1¼-mile extension to Darras Hall, known locally as the 'Little Callerton Railway', was opened in 1913, freight traffic commencing on 27 September and passenger ser-

vices on 1 October, but the extension was authorised by an Act of Parliament and not a Light Railway Order. Like the Ponteland line, the Darras Hall extension was built with the intention of tapping potential traffic from a projected housing development.

For much of the branch's life, the usual locomotives were Fletcher 'BTP' (later LNER 'G6') class 0-4-4Ts, No 1019 being the locomotive in charge of the first passenger service in 1905 with No 605 becoming a regular performer in subsequent years. A total of 124 'BTPs' had been built between 1874 and 1883 and were considered, by many, to be the NER's only worthwhile passenger tanks. In 1905, a start was made on fitting the class with auto apparatus and this did much to boost their usefulness even further.

Below: **Fletcher 'BTP' (later LNER 'G6') class 0-4-4T No 323 arrives at Ponteland.** Lens of Sutton

There was a small engine shed at South Gosforth which opened in 1902 and closed just two years later, but it appears that it was not used by Ponteland branch engines. The line was serviced, instead, by the more durable shed at Heaton and, at the end of 1923, three of the push-pull 0-4-4Ts were allocated there. However, the Ponteland run was not their only duty as they were also used on the hop between Newcastle and Dunston which, with its route of 2m 22ch, is reputed to have been the NER's shortest branch working.

By 1922, the timetables showed a weekday service of nine trains each way between South Gosforth and Ponteland, three in each direction continuing to, or originating at, Darras Hall. At the southern end of the route, one or two trains in each direction ran through to, or from, Manors North station in Newcastle. Also advertised was a 10.20pm Saturday train from South Gosforth to Ponteland. The journey times were 20min to or from Ponteland, with an extra three minutes being allowed for the trot from there to Darras Hall.

In the late 1920s, the 0-4-4Ts were superseded on many light branch services throughout the northeast by the Sentinel-Cammell steam railcars. One of the LNER's first Sentinels, the two-cylinder chain-driven No 22 (later named *Brilliant*), was sent new to Heaton shed in May 1927 and was used on the Ponteland line. Among the other duties undertaken by the 64-seat car were the trips to Lintz Green and North Wylam. In July 1927, 60-seat Clayton steam railcar No 41 (later named *Pilot*) was dispatched to Heaton after trials and, in mid-1928, six new Clayton cars were sent there; at the end of 1928, they were joined by a pair of six-cylinder Sentinel-Cammell cars. Official LNER records contain ample documentary evidence that Sentinel No 22 *Brilliant* was used on the Ponteland branch, but they do not reveal which other railcars were used. For the public, however, the timetables confirmed that some railcar or other was to be expected on the line, the annotation of 'One Class Only' being a sure giveaway.

In more recent years, the names of the LNER's Sentinel and Clayton railcars have occasionally raised a few eyebrows. The idea of naming the cars was publicly announced in the LNER Magazine of January 1928, an in-house competition being held to find a suitable name theme with a prize of £10 being offered for the winning suggestion. The competition attracted 404 entries and the name themes suggested ranged from dog breeds to playing cards, but the LNER chose to ignore all the entries by naming the railcars after old horse-drawn stage-coach services. A finishing touch was that each rail-car was subsequently fitted with a framed poster giving known details of the stage-coach service after which it was named, a five shilling (25p) reward being made available for further information about

the relevant service. The railcars were originally finished in a teak livery; a vermillion and cream livery was later introduced but that eventually gave way to green and cream.

At Ponteland and Darras Hall, the housing developments failed to become as extensive as had originally been intended and, consequently, traffic on the railway did not reach the expected levels. Even the economies achieved by the railcars were not enough to make the line viable, and so passenger services were withdrawn from 17 June 1929. Facilities for parcels traffic were retained only until 5 January 1935, but public freight facilities were maintained at Ponteland until 14 August 1967, the other stations along the line having already succumbed to total closure.

As for other railway activities around the South Gosforth-Ponteland-Darras Hall line, a 8¾-mile extension was laid in the 1920s from Darras Hall to Kirkheaton Colliery and an ex-Glasgow & South Western Railway inside-cylindered 0-6-0 was purchased by the colliery company in 1926 for interchange duties. The locomotive had been built at Kilmarnock Works in 1898; originally G&SWR No 173, it had been renumbered 171 in 1919 and, at the Grouping, had been designated LMS No 17196. Kirkheaton Colliery closed in 1930 and the locomotive was left to rust in peace on site until 1942 when it was acquired by the Board of Trade. After being overhauled at Darlington, it was given No MD525 and was used at Cambois opencast disposal point and then at Backworth Colliery before being scrapped as No 20 by the National Coal Board in July 1953.

During the 1960s, Ponteland and Callerton were used for the storage of redundant North Tyneside electric stock, while Railfreight workings from the ICI explosives factory at Callerton and the Rowntrees factory near Kingston Park continued until 28 July 1988. Nowadays, the Tyne and Wear Metro uses much of the old Ponteland branch. The Metro's line from South Gosforth to Bank Foot station (which replaced Kenton) was unveiled in May 1981, but as freight workings to the Rowntrees and ICI premises were still undertaken at that time, the overhead wires on that section of the Metro had to be raised from the standard 12ft 1in to 13ft 7in in order to give adequate clearance for the freight trains which, usually, were hauled by Tyne Yard's Class 31 or Class 37 diesels. In November 1991, the Metro's extension from Bank Foot to Newcastle Airport was opened and, apart from short diversions at Wooslington and the airport itself, the extension followed the alignment of the Ponteland branch.

Rother Valley (Light) Railway
See (32) KENT & EAST SUSSEX RAILWAY.

146

Above: **Much of the Ponteland line is now incorporated in the Tyne & Wear Metro network, but conventional freight workings continued until 1988 and operated, in effect, alongside the Metro's services. One of the line's freight** customers was the ICI factory at Callerton, and Class 31 No 31231 is seen hauling a van ex-Callerton at Wheatsheaf Level Crossing on 30 August 1985.
Ian S. Carr

So far, we have come across several narrow gauge light railways, although only a small number used a gauge of less than 2ft. There were, of course, *bonafide* light railways which worked on narrower gauges, one example being the Romney, Hythe & Dymchurch Light Railway, but they have been excluded from this book due to their generally accepted status as 'miniature' railways. The cut-off point at which a light railway becomes classified as a miniature railway is open to debate and so, in an attempt to keep both camps relatively happy, the 1ft 6in gauge Sand Hutton Light Railway warrants a mention.

The Sand Hutton Railway, in its original form, was born in order to serve Maj Sir Robert Walker's sizeable estate a few miles east of York. In 1912, Sir Robert had started building an experimental 1ft 3in gauge miniature railway but, in 1920, he obtained a Light Railway Order for the purpose of upgrading the line for public traffic. The new light railway was built to a gauge of 1ft 6in using ex-War Department rails, much of the redundant 1ft 3in gauge stock being sold to the Ravenglass & Eskdale Railway in Cumberland.

The light railway was neither a toy nor a philanthropic gesture, as Sir Robert considered that the line would enable the produce of his estate to be transported more easily and cheaply, thereby bringing about a greater effiency in the working of his lands. Furthermore, he later expounded his theories about light railways in a lengthy, but well argued, article in the *Railway Magazine* of May 1924 although, sadly, it remains unknown how many of the magazine's readers had scope for similar railways on their own estates.

The revamped railway was opened in December 1923, passenger services (mainly for tourists) commencing on 4 October 1924. The route started at

Warthill station which was a separate entity from the LNER's station of that name on the York-Market Weighton line but, nevertheless, had facilities for tipping freight directly into LNER wagons. A proliferation of 'stations' was provided along the route of the SHLR. From Warthill, there was Warthill Cottage halt, White Sike Cottages, White Sike Junction, Sand Hutton Depot, Sand Hutton Central, Sand Hutton Gardens, Memorial, Kissthorns and Belle Vue halt, the other terminus being at the village of Bossall, some three miles from Warthill. A half mile goods-only spur continued from Bossall to Barnby House while, at White Sike Junction, a 1½-mile branch ran to Claxton, primarily to serve a brickworks.

In the days of the 1ft 3in gauge railway, a Bassett Lowke 4-4-2 named *Synolda* had been used but, for 1ft 6in gauge operations, four small outside-cylindered Hunslet 0-4-0WTs were purchased form the War Surplus Board. They had previously been used on a temporary wartime line to a meat depot at Deptford where they had been oil-fired, and it has sometimes been remarked that they were almost identical in appearance to some of the locomotives used at Woolwich Arsenal. Three of the Sand Hutton trio became known as Nos 2/3/4, the fourth being named *Esme* after Sir Robert Walker's second wife, but it is known that at least two of the quartet retained their former-WD numberplates.

The SHLR's passenger rolling stock consisted of just one coach, a parcels van having to be pressed into use at holiday times. The coach had seats for 30 passengers and, with measurements of 32ft 9in long and 5ft 8in wide over its steps, it was a very bulky vehicle to operate on a gauge of only 1ft 6in. Nevertheless, its comparatively spacious accommodation was welcome when, during the line's early years, it had to carry not only the passengers but also a mobile buffet. The coach was finished in a livery of burnt sienna with black underframes and a white roof. After the demise of the railway, the coach body was bought by the nearby Harton Ladies Cricket Club where it served as the official pavilion for well over 30 years. The SHLR's freight stock comprised a remarkable total of 75 wagons, all being ex-WD four-wheel trucks with 2½-ton capacities. Around 13,000 tons of freight was carried annually during the 1920s and, apart from agricultural produce, the main source of traffic was the brickworks at Claxton where 20,000 bricks were made daily. The volume of freight traffic sometimes necessitated three locomotives being kept in steam each day.

Usually, the SHLR was open for public passenger traffic only on Saturdays but, occasionally, a Wednesday service was operated. Those services were moderately successful but, after the death of Sir Robert Walker in 1930, the enthusiasm for maintaining them soon dwindled and, consequently, the line was closed to passengers on 5 July. It continued a partial operation for goods only until June 1932 when it closed completely.

Left: **The Sand Hutton Light Railway puchased four small 0-4-0WTs from the War Surplus Board, at least two retaining their ex-WD numberplates. This is ex-WD No 12 photographed at Sand Hutton in 1927.** Rail Archive Stephenson

Above: **One of the Sand Hutton's War Surplus 0-4-0WTs, *Esme*, stands outside the engine shed in the summer of 1927.** Rail Archive Stephensen

48 Sheppey Light Railway

In a fit of late-Victorian optimism, a railway was proposed between Queenborough, on the London, Chatham & Dover Railway's Sittingbourne–Sheerness branch in Kent, to Leysdown. The theory was that the railway would help Leysdown to develop as a fashionable seaside resort and residential centre, but a few sceptics were swift to question the potential appeal of the low-lying marshland of the Isle of Sheppey.

Under the banner of the Sheppey Light Railway, the independent company had the support of the LC&DR although, by the time the necessary Order was obtained in May 1899, the LC&DR had joined forces with the South Eastern Railway to become the South Eastern & Chatham. The SLR appointed Holman Stephens to oversee the line's construction, and Stephens found himself on territory which was to become very familiar in subsequent years. The plans for the line incorporated a number of typical light railway characteristics such as an absence of proper platforms, signals only at passing places and, if trains of three coaches or less were to be used, no requirement for continuous brakes.

Mainly due to the relatively flat terrain which the route crossed, construction was swift and the line was

Below: **Eastchurch was the last station on the Sheppey Light Railway before the terminus at Leysdown. Spacious but unpretentious seems to be a fair assessment of the facilities.** Lens of Sutton

formally opened on 1 August 1901. After leaving Queenborough, where SLR trains used a bay at the rear of the up platform, there were intermediate stopping places at Sheerness East (1½ miles), East Minster-on-Sea (2½ miles), Minster (Sheppey) (3¼ miles), Brambledown halt (4 miles) and Eastchurch (5½ miles) before the terminus at Leysdown (8¾ miles) was reached. Harty Road halt (7 miles) was added in March 1905 and, in May 1906, Minster (Sheppey) was retitled Minster-on-Sea. Along the route, the station buildings were built from corrugated iron and, in view of the anticipated agricultural traffic, each station had siding accommodation. The line was single track but there was a passing loop at Eastchurch, while at Leysdown a run-round loop was provided. Rails of 64lb/yd were used and the usual light railway restrictions of a 25mph speed limit and a maximum axle load of 14 tons prevailed.

The line was worked by the SE&CR. One of the early locomotives was an immaculately-kept 2-4-0T, No 533, which owed its origins to a R. & W. Hawthorn 4-4-0 of 1860 that had been built for a South American railway but, on cancellation of the order, had been purchased by the LC&DR; it had been broken up in 1873 but the boiler had been reused in the construction of the 2-4-0T. That locomotive, originally named *Comus*, worked the Leysdown line until the arrival of a Wainright-designed steam railcar in 1905. The railcar was powered by a Kitson-built 0-4-0T 'engine' which had wheels of 3ft

7in and cylinders of 10in x 15in; it incorporated a Belpaire firebox and Walschaerts valve gear which were, at that time, novel features on the SE&CR. Eight such units were built in 1904/05, their 56-seat single-class coach bodies being constructed by the Metropolitan Carriage & Wagon Works, but all were withdrawn in 1911-14 and the coach portions subsequently converted for use as conventional push-pull sets. Two of the sets were articulated and were used on the Leysdown branch.

When a freight locomotive was required for the SLR line, the SE&CR purchased 'Terrier' 0-6-0T

Above: **Kirtley 'R' class 0-4-4T No 1673 (later BR No 31673) stands alongside the water crane at Queenborough before making another trip along the Leysdown branch. The branch tracks are those behind the engine, the tracks on the left of the picture being those of the Sheerness line.** Ian Allan Library

Below: **Former LCDR 'R' class 0-4-4T No 1673 pulls out of Leysdown station.** Ian Allan Library

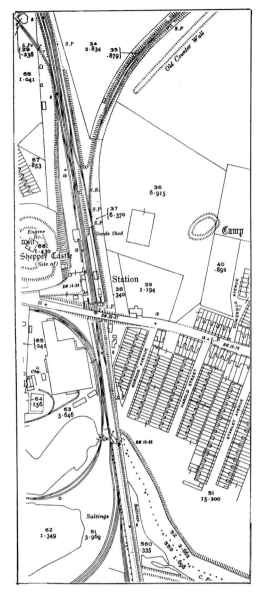

Left: **Queenborough station and surrounds; 25in Ordnance Survey map of 1933.** Crown Copyright

rier', by then SE&CR No 751, was to be found at the head of a rake of five ancient four-wheel coaches on the branch as the railcar could not cope with peak-season loadings. The 'Terrier' proved popular with local crews and became known as 'Little Tich', the stage name of the Kentish music hall entertainer, Harry Relph. In 1910, newly-built 'P' class 0-6-0T No 27 was dispatched to work the push-pull services on the Leysdown line and the railcars disappeared from the Isle of Sheppey two years later. The 'Terrier' was transferred to other duties and, when the 'P' class locomotive was shipped to France in 1918 to help with the war effort, ex-LC&DR 'R' and 'R1' class 0-4-4Ts took over the passenger workings to Leysdown.

The Sheppey Light Railway was officially absorbed by the SE&CR on 1 August 1905. As for services on the line, the passenger timetables for 1906 showed seven trains each way on weekdays and, although no scheduled branch passenger workings ran through beyond Queenborough, five of those seven daily trains were timed to connect with London trains. From London, the only through workings were specials which brought prospective residents to view potential building plots. The projected estate at Minster had only limited success, but a more-substantial development was undertaken at Leysdown.

During the 1920s and 1930s, the residential developments at Minster and Leysdown grew slowly, but with the random scattering of bungalows, huts and bus-bodies alongside the unmade roads, it was painfully apparent that the original dreams of prosperous purpose-built communities were not going to come true. At one time, there had been plans to build a 7,000ft long steamer pier at Minster and a further scheme had proposed a luxurious hotel at Leysdown to accommodate 1,200 guests, but the harsh reality of the local situation put paid to those ideas once and for all. Even the holidaymakers provided little trade for the railway, and the agricultural traffic gradually defected to road transport. Nevertheless, the RAF Station at Eastchurch generated a degree of traffic and, after the war, the Southern Railway looked at the possibility of converting the premises into a holiday camp. Instead, the RAF base became an open Borstal.

After Nationalisation, there was little hope that British Railways would treat the line to any investment and, in view of the poor traffic figures, it was not long before closure was announced. The last public services ran on 2 December 1950 with 'R1' class 0-4-4T No 31705 in charge of proceedings at the head of articulated set No 514...the very set which had been created almost 40 years earlier from the coach sections of the steam railcars.

No 654 *Waddon* from the LB&SCR for £670; the locomotive had been built in 1874 and had notched up 578,421 miles in LB&SCR service. Before being let loose on the Leysdown run, the 'Terrier' was sent to Ashford Works for the removal of its Westinghouse equipment and feed pumps, the fitting of vacuum ejectors, and painting in SE&CR green livery. The 'Terrier' was actually purchased by the SE&CR in September 1904, but it was 12 February 1905 before the locomotive commenced freight duties on the Leysdown line. It was not long before the 'Ter-

49 Shropshire & Montgomeryshire Light Railway

In this book, there have been many examples of how light railways cut out every last frill in order to reduce overheads to a bare minimum. We have seen stories of locomotives and rolling stock of dubious parentage and even more dubious vintage, and stations and facilities which turned sparsity into an art form but, of all the ramshackle little lines in Britain, few were as rustic as the Shropshire & Montgomeryshire Light Railway.

The would-be route of the S&MLR existed long before the days of any Light Railways Act. On 13 August 1866, a 20-mile double-track line was opened between Abbey station in Shrewsbury and Llanymynech, an extension at the latter point being opened in 1872 through Llanyblodwel (renamed Blodwell Junction in 1904) to quarries at Nantmawr. The Shrewsbury-Llanymynech line belonged to the Potteries, Shrewsbury & North Wales Railway — usually referred to as 'The Potts' — which envisaged it as the first stage in the master plan for a new route between Stoke-on-Trent and Portmadoc. In 1871, the existing line was augmented by a six-mile branch to Criggion which was intended to serve the quarries at Brieden Hill and, for a while, the traffic on 'The Potts' increased from a droplet to a trickle. But that was the most 'The Potts' ever achieved.

No further sections of the Stoke-Portmadoc route were built and, consequently, the existing Shrews-

Below: **Without any doubt at all, the gem in the S&M's motive power stud was the diminutive 0-4-2WT** *Gazelle* **which, quite properly, has been preserved. The location of this picture appears to be Abbey station in Shrewsbury.** Bucknall Collection/Ian Allan Library

Above: **Hawthorn Leslie 0-6-2T No 6** *Thisbe* **spent only five years on the S&M before being dispatched to the Longmoor Military Railway. This picture, which shows the deceptively proud company livery, was almost certainly taken at Kinnerley Junction.** Bucknall Collection/ Ian Allan Library

Below: **One of the S&M's ex-LSWR 'Ilfracombe Goods' 0-6-0s arrives at Kinnerley Junction in the 1930s.** Lens of Sutton

bury-Llanymynech section proved about as useful as a lifeboat station in Birmingham. It stumbled on in an appalling state of repair until 22 June 1880, when the Board of Trade ordered the closure of everything except the Nantmawr Quarry branch, that section later being acquired by the Cambrian Railways which laid a new connecting spur. Over the next 29 years, the route of 'The Potts' became virtually derelict and when, in 1909, a Light Railway Order was granted for its reopening as the Shropshire & Montgomeryshire Light Railway, there was a strong feeling in some circles that the promoter was decidedly out to lunch. However, those who were a little more informed felt differently because the man behind the proposed reopening was one Holman Frederick Stephens. He was not unfamiliar with underprivileged railways.

Despite the abysmal state of the old abandoned line, the 75lb bull-headed rails which had been laid 45 years previously were deemed serviceable and, after being resleepered, were relaid. In all, the renovation of the line was not as difficult as had been feared and so it was ready for the ceremonial reopening on 13 April 1911.

The S&MLR's line started at Abbey station in Shrewsbury, a single-platform terminus which was almost half a mile south of, and unconnected to, the joint main line station in the town. The intermediate stopping places on the route were Shrewsbury West (1 mile), Meole Brace (1¾ miles), Red Hill (3 miles), Hanwood Road (4 miles), Cruckton (5¼ miles), Shoot Hill halt (6¾ miles), Ford & Crossgates (7¼ miles), Shrawadine (11½ miles), Nesscliff (13¼ miles), Kinnerley Junction (15¼ miles) which had two through platforms and a branch bay, Wern Las (18 miles) and Maesbrook (19 miles). The other end of the line was at Llanymynech (20 miles from Shrewsbury), where the S&MLR had its own spartan platform to the rear of the Cambrian's station. Of those stations, Nesscliffe was suffixed 'and Pentre' in 1913 while Red Hill and Hanwood Road were renamed in 1921 as Hookagate and Edgebold respectively; Red Hill station was, incidentally, resited about 100yd to the east when the line was being prepared for reopening as a light railway. Eleven of the 14 stations on the S&MLR's 'main line' had been inherited from the old 'Potts' company, the new ones being Meole Brace, Cruckton and Wern Las. The first-named of those served as the freight interchange point with the GWR, as the old connecting spur between 'The Potts' and the GWR at Shrewsbury had not been replaced.

On 22 July 1912, the old branch from Kinnerley Junction to Criggion reopened for passenger traffic, freight having been accommodated since the previous February. The branch had intermediate stopping places at Chapel Lane (1 mile from Kinnerley), Melverley (2 miles), Crewe Green (5¼ miles) and Llandrinio Road (6¼ miles) before reaching the terminus at Criggion (7¼ miles); of the branch stations, all but Chapel Lane had been built in 'Potts' days. The only renaming was a minor one, and merely involved altering the spelling of CREWE Green to CREW Green.

As for motive power, S&MLR No 1 was a remarkable little 2-2-2WT named *Gazelle* which had been built in 1896 by Alfred Dodman & Co of Kings Lynn. It originally had wooden driving wheels of 3ft 9in diameter and weighed in at a mere 5tons 6cwt. The much-repeated story about *Gazelle* is that it had been built for a Norfolk seed merchant who used it as a means of personal transport, for which it was equipped with a partly-covered platform at the rear. Over the years, the merchant travelled over several main lines in the locomotive, the driving being undertaken by a qualified man from the Great Eastern Railway's shed at Kings Lynn. It is believed that, in 1897, the locomotive travelled as far as Chesterfield and notched up 210 main line miles on the round trip. Shortly after Holman Stephens acquired *Gazelle* for the S&MLR, the machine was dispatched to William Bagnall's for rebuilding as a 0-4-2WT, this time with solid cast-iron driving wheels.

The second engine bought in time for the opening of the S&MLR was 0-4-2ST No 2 *Hecate*. Built as a 0-4-0 tender engine for the L&NWR in 1848, it had been sold to 'The Potts' in 1872 and then resold for use at a colliery near Nuneaton where it had been fitted with its trailing axle and saddle tank. Also on hand for opening day was S&MLR No 3, an ex-L&SWR 'Ilfracombe Goods' 0-6-0 of 1875 vintage; after being purchased by Holman Stephens in 1911, it was named *Hesperus*. Late in 1911, an 0-6-0ST which had been built in 1866 by T. R. Crampton and rebuilt by Manning Wardle in 1896 was purchased from the Stratford-on-Avon & Midland Junction Railway. It became No 4 *Morous*. At the same time, a pair of brand new Hawthorn Leslie 0-6-2Ts arrived and became No 5 *Pyramus* and No 6 *Thisbe*; they were smaller versions of the impressive 0-6-2Ts which the same manufacturer had built for the Plymouth, Devonport & South Western Junction Railway in 1907/08. A short-term acquisition was that of 0-6-0ST *Walton Park* which was transferred from the Weston, Clevedon & Portishead Light Railway in 1913, only to be dispatched to the East Kent Light Railway three years later.

At first, the S&MLR's coaching stock comprised four bogie coaches and a pair of four-wheeled brake vans, all purchased from the Midland Railway, and six former-L&SWR four-wheel brake thirds. In later years, additional coaches were acquired and, among them, were three four-wheelers from the North Staffordshire Railway and a converted London tramcar, the latter normally being used behind *Gazelle*.

Above: **The L&SWR's 'Ilfracombe Goods' 0-6-0s were favoured by Holman Stephens, and three such locomotives finished up on the S&M. This is No 3 *Hesperus*, built in 1875, bought by the S&M in 1911 and scrapped in 1941.** Bucknall Collection/Ian Allan Library

Right: **The WD presence on the S&M is very evident in this 1949 picture of Kinnerley Junction. It has often been remarked that the only time the S&M looked even half-tidy was after the WD had given things a good sprucing-up.** W. M. West

The motive power department was at Kinnerley Junction which boasted a twin-road timber-built engine shed, and it was not very long before there were changes among the regular residents. In 1914, three-year old 0-6-2T No 5 *Pyramus* was requisitioned for use on the Longmoor Military Railway in Hampshire and in 1916 its sister, No 6 *Thisbe* , took the same path. The S&MLR's replacements for both were 40-odd year old ex-L&SWR 'Ilfracombe Goods' 0-6-0s which acquired the names and numbers of the two 0-6-2Ts. Three of the ubiquitous ex-LB&SCR 'Terriers' were purchased for £470 apiece from the War Disposals Board in 1921 and 1923. They had all been sold to the Admiralty in 1918 and had been used at Inverness; on arriving at the S&MLR, they became No 7 *Hecate*, No 8 *Dido* and No 9 *Daphne*. The S&MLR's final acquisitions arrived in 1930-32. They were Webb-designed ex-L&NWR 0-6-0s, 500 of which had been built between 1873 and 1892; some of the class survived until Nationalisation and the class leader, by then BR No 58321, was not withdrawn until after its 80th birthday in 1953. The three which ended up on the S&MLR retained their LMSR numbers of 8108, 8182 and 8236.

In true 'Colonel Stephens' fashion, internal-combustion traction was not ignored. In 1923, a new three-car Ford railbus was purchased, each of the end cars being powered and accommodating 19 passengers while the unpowered middle car had seating for 24. It was often remarked that the noise generated by the contraption's solid wheels could be heard from one station to the next. A new Wolseley-Siddeley railbus was purchased in 1923 and a secondhand single-car Ford machine was acquired in 1925.

For the summer of 1922, the timetables showed a host of conditional workings. Basically, the weekday-only services comprised four through trains from Shrewsbury to Llanymynech daily while, in the opposite direction there were three every day, but additional services operated on Wednesdays and Saturdays. Scheduled times for the 20-mile journey

ranged from 65 to 95min. The Criggion branch was served by three trains each way with additional ones on Thursdays and Saturdays; journey times on the 7¼-mile branch were 20-30min.

The potential traffic available for the S&MLR had been doubtful enough to start with, and when road transport started to take a slice of the already sparse action during the 1920s, the railway company found the going very tough indeed. The first casualty of the company's lack of pennies was the Criggion branch, passenger workings ceasing beyond Melverley in October 1932 after doubts had been raised about the safety of the viaduct. The withdrawal of passenger services over the rest of the S&MLR followed just over a year later, 6 November 1933 being the official date of their cessation. A freight service continued to be offered, and the opening in 1934 of an oil depot in the yard of Abbey station at Shrewsbury provided a little of the occasional traffic.

The S&MLR's lines were given a new lease of life

157

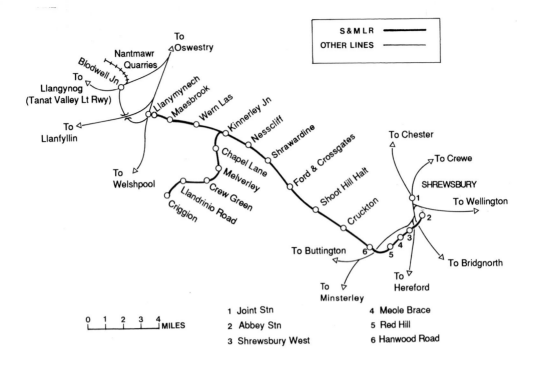

S&M L R ━━━━━━
OTHER LINES ─────────

To Oswestry

To Nantmawr Quarries

Blodwell Jn

To Llangynog (Tanat Valley Lt Rwy)

Llanymynech
Maesbrook
Wern Las

To Llanfyllin

Kinnerley Jn
Nesscliff

Shrawardine

Chapel Lane

Ford & Crossgates

To Welshpool

Melverley

Crew Green

Llandrinio Road

Criggion

Shoot Hill Halt

Cruckton

To Chester

To Crewe

SHREWSBURY

To Wellington

To Bridgnorth

To Buttington

To Hereford

To Minsterley

0 1 2 3 4 MILES	
1 Joint Stn	4 Meole Brace
2 Abbey Stn	5 Red Hill
3 Shrewsbury West	6 Hanwood Road

in 1941 when they were requisitioned by the War Department for the purpose of serving large ammunition stores, the quiet Shropshire countryside being considered far safer from enemy air raids than urban areas. The WD relaid most of the track with 75lb flat-bottomed rails and added several loops and spurs, one of them leading to a four-platform station at Lonsdale which served the main camp at Nesscliffe. Several additional platforms were also erected along the line for the benefit of the troops. When the Army first arrived, even the most hardened railway enthusiast among the ranks found it hard to take everything in. To all outward purposes the S&MLR had been, until then, a working railway but the overgrown tracks and a clutch of rusting locomotives did little to confirm that notion. The only remaining locomotives were No 1 *Gazelle* which was discovered still attached to its customary former tramcar, the three former-LNWR 0-6-0s and ex-'Ilfracombe Goods' 0-6-0 No 3 *Hesperus*.

Of those, *Gazelle* was at least usable, and the Army dispensed with the locomotive's covered platform in order to improve visibility. The ex-LNWR 0-6-0s were all dispatched to Crewe for overhauls and two similar locomotives, LMSR Nos 28204 and 28308, were supplied as temporary replacements. As for *Hesperus*, it was inspected by the Army's chief fitter who had been trained by the LNER at Doncaster and, as a matter of pride, he vowed that he would get the

machine moving again. After a weekend's strenuous efforts, *Hesperus* managed to raise steam, but none reached as far as the cylinders. Admitting defeat, the Army had the locomotive towed to Shrewsbury for scrap.

During the Army occupation, a multitude of 'foreign' locomotives were used on the S&MLR lines. They included one which is believed to have originally been destined for the Turkish Government, assorted industrial saddle tanks, LNWR works shunters, veteran tank and tender 0-6-0s from the LNER and GWR, and a 150hp diesel which was sometimes used in conjunction with the S&MLR's Royal Saloon as the VIP's train. Before the mention of a Royal Saloon coach conjures up images of modernity and grandeur, it should be pointed out that it was a four-wheeled carriage which had been built in 1844 as part of the L&SWR's Royal Train. Although Queen Victoria may have travelled in an adjacent coach, there was no positive evidence that any Royal posterior had graced the seats of the S&MLR's vehicle.

The freight traffic carried annually over the S&MLR's tracks during the war reached a remarkable peak of over 390,000 tons in 1943, and over 40,000 tons of that was non-WD merchandise. The quarry near Criggion provided some of the outwards traffic, the quarry company's Sentinel shunter working the line beyond the flood-damaged viaduct at Melverley.

To ease the flow of traffic to and from the S&MLR, Hookagate station was largely demolished to make room for a crossing loop and marshalling yard, interchange traffic with the GWR subsequently being handled there instead of at Meole Brace. When troops were given nights off, passenger trains were often operated to Shrewsbury but, in view of the 1 in 40 climb away from Abbey station on the return trips, three coaches were the maximum loading permitted.

The S&MLR's lines remained under WD control until the time of Nationalisation in 1948. British Railways' financial arrangement was to pay S&MLR shareholders 6d (2½p) per £10 share, and that placed a nominal value on the little company of £25.

Below: **Bradshaw's, July 1922.**

Despite BR's ownership of the old S&MLR, the WD continued to use the line, albeit mainly for the piecemeal removal of stores and equipment, and the last military depot was not closed until 1959, the same year that the stone traffic from Criggion finally ceased.

The official closure of the old S&MLR to all traffic took place on 29 February 1960, the last trains having run three days previously. An enthusiasts' special negotiated the line on 20 March to claim the distinction of being the final passenger working. At the oil depot at Abbey station in Shrewsbury, a new spur was laid, and this lasted until closure well into the 1980s, but one particular relic of the S&MLR survives today. In 1950, the distinctive little 0-4-2WT *Gazelle* was taken to the Longmoor Military Railway in Hampshire for static preservation, and it now lives at the Army Transport Museum.

Bradshaw's timetable.

Shrewsbury and Llanymynech.] 591 [S. and M.

SHREWSBURY, CRIGGION, and LLANYMYNECH.—Shropshire and Montgomeryshire.
Man. Director, Eng., and Loco. Supt., H. F. Stephens, Tonbridge, Kent.   Supt., J. L. White, Shrewsbury.

Down. — Week Days only.

	mrn	mrn	mrn	mrn		aft	aft		aft	aft		aft	aft	aft	aft	aft	aft	
Abbey Station,																		
Shrewsbury......dep.				9 40			1 20		1 40			3 50		6 45		9 30		
Shrewsbury West......				c			c		c			c		c				
Meole Brace......				9 50			1 30		1 50			3 55		6 50		c		
Hookagate				c			1 37		1 57			4 0		c		a		
Edgebold				c			1 42		2 2			4 4		c		a		
Cruckton ¶				c			c		c			c		c				
Ford and Crossgates......				1015			1 55		2 15			4 10		7 7		9 50		
Shrawardine......				c			2 5		2 25			4 20		c		a		
Nesscliff and Pentre....				1030			2 10		2 30			4 30		7 25		10 5		
Kinnerley Junction arr.				1038			2 18		2 38			4 38		7 30		1020		
Kinnerley Junc.dep.	7 0			1040		1215						3 45	4 20		4 40		7 32	
Chapel Lane				a		a			c		c		c		c			
Melverley	7 7			a		a			3 52	4 25		4 47		7 40			
Crew Green*	7 12			a		a			4 0	c		4 52		7 45			
Llandrinio Road	7 20			a		a			4 5	c		4 57		7 50			
Criggion	arr. 7 25			1115		1250			4 15	4 45		5 0		7 55			
Kinnerley Junction dep.		7 30	8 30	1040			1 35		2 20		2 40		4 40		7 32			
Wern Las......		c	c	c							c		c		c			
Maesbrook........[580		7 40	8 40	1050					2 35		2 55		4 45		7 40			
Llanymynech 578, arr.		7 45	8 45	11 0			1 50		2 40		3 0		4 55		7 45			

Up. — Week Days only.

	mrn	mrn	mrn	aft	aft		aft	aft	aft		aft	aft		aft
Llanymynech......dep.	8 10	8 50	1125				2 25	3 16	4 5		5 25	8 10		
Maesbrook......	8 15	8 55	1132				c	3 21	4 10		c	8 15		
Wern Las......	c	c	c				c				c	a		
Kinnerley Junction arr.	8 23	9 5	1140				2 38	3 30	4 20		5 43	8 25		
Criggion......dep.	8 0						1 5				5 5		8 0	
Llandrinio Road	8 5						1 8				c		c	
Crew Green*	8 10						1 13				5 12		c	
Melverley	8 17						1 18				5 16		c	
Chapel Lane	c						c				c		c	
Kinnerley Junc. arr.	8 24						1 25				5 22		8 24	
Kinnerley Junction dep.	8 30		1144	1 50			2 40		5 45			8 25		
Nesscliff and Pentre...	8 40	b	1150	1 55			2 45		5 52			8 32		
Shrawardine...	8 45		1156	2 5			2 52		c			a		
Ford and Crossgates ¶..	8 55		12 7	2 10	2 45		3 0		6 8			8 50		
Cruckton ¶	c		c		c		c		c			c		
Edgebold	9 5		1220		c		3 12		6 20			a		
Hookagate	9 10		1230		c		c		6 25			a		
Meole Brace...	9 15		1235		3 10		3 20		6 30			c		
Shrewsbury West [452	c		c		c		c		c					
Shrewsbury † 450, arr.	9 25		1245		3 15		3 30		6 37			9 15		

Stop to set down.
Runs to Nesscliffe and Pentre if required.
Stop when required.

* Station for Alberbury, Coedway.
† Abbey Station; about ¼ mile to General Station (G.W. and L. & N.W.).

¶ "Halts" at Shoot Hill, between Cruckton and Ford and Crossgates.

159

50 South Shields, Marsden & Whitburn Colliery Railway

The northeast of England was at the forefront of railway development, that being largely due to the early industrialisation of the area. Coal mining was, of course, one of the major local industries, a large fish in that industrial pond being the Harton Coal Co which was founded in 1842. The HCC gradually took over a number of other colliery companies in the locality and sunk new pits itself, one of those being Whitburn colliery which opened in 1879. A 3¼-mile long railway was laid from Whitburn colliery to a junction with the North Eastern Railway's Stanhope and Tyne branch; the line was known as the Marsden Railway and, despite being formally entitled the South Shields, Marsden & Whitburn Colliery Railway in later years, it was still usually referred to locally under its old title or, more familiarly, 'The Rattler'.

Miners were carried on the Marsden Railway almost from the outset and a primitive public service commenced in March 1885 although, in the absence of Board of Trade approval, fare-paying passengers had to sign a disclaimer. Officialdom did not take kindly to the 'bending' of the rules and so the public services soon ceased, but an upgrading of the line and the installation of signals met with BoT approval; public services were formally reintroduced on 19 March 1888, this time with official blessing. Those services,

however, ran only to Marsden, the section from there to Whitburn colliery being solely for the benefit of miners and other staff. The Harton Coal Co continued to expand and modernise. In 1908, its line linking Harton and Westoe collieries to staiths on the Tyne was electrified using the 500V dc overhead system, 10 locomotives and the ancilliary equipment being purchased from the German company of Siemens. The Marsden Railway, however, continued using steam traction although, over the years, an increasing number of coal trains from Whitburn swopped their steam locomotives for electric ones for the last leg of the journey to Harton Low Staiths. Furthermore, the passenger workings routinely traversed electrified tracks on the section around Westoe Lane station.

In the mid-1920s, plans were announced for a new coastal road at Marsden which necessitated a diversion of the railway; the diversion was authorised by a Light Railway Order and was completed in 1929. The former public terminus at Marsden had been reasonably popular with visitors to the beach, but there had been

Below: **One of the SSM&WCR's ex-LNER 'J21' class 0-6-0s, No 8, hauls a precarious-looking train near Marsden in August 1932.** Rail Archive Stephenson

Above: **At Westoe Lane, the steam-hauled services of the SSM&WCR ran 'under the wires'. Here, 0-6-0 No 8 stands with a mixture of ex-North British and former-Great Eastern six-wheeled coaches prior to its departure for Marsden at 12.45pm.** H. C. Casserley

little danger of Marsden developing into a major seaside resort and so a replacement station was not provided on the new alignment. As a compromise of dubious usefulness, public trains were permitted to run through to Whitburn colliery station, but *Bradshaw's* referred to the station there as 'Marsden'. There were only two other stopping places on the line, one being Marsden Cottage halt, also known locally as Salmon's halt, the other being Westoe Lane, which was near the northern end of the line close to the junction with the LNER. A fair description of Westoe Lane station appeared in the October 1953 issue of *The Railway Magazine:* '... about ¾-mile by road from South Shields or High Shields stations, its nearest neighbours on British Railways ... no public notices, no nameboard ... no advertisements ... no platform seats and no porters'.

The line was affected by Nationalisation, but not that of the country's railways; when the National Coal Board came into being on 1 January 1947, the Harton Coal Co and the old Marsden Railway became NCB property, the line thereby gaining the status of the first state-owned passenger railway in Britain. The NCB continued to operate public passenger services on the route until 21 November 1953 although, by then, the trains often ran almost empty. On the demise of the SSM&WCR's passenger workings, a new bus service between South Shields and Whitburn was introduced, the single fare of 4d (2p) being the same as, not only the final railway fares, but also those of the first 'official' railway services of

1888. This writer will refrain from commenting on the comparative inflation rates of recent times.

Throughout the line's life, passenger services were geared to shift times at Whitburn colliery although, in the early years, excursions to Marsden became so popular that, by the summer of 1890, Sunday services actually outnumbered the weekday workmens' trains. In later years, the July 1922 timetables showed 11 trains each way on weekdays and 10 on Sundays, while the March 1940 timetables listed 16 trains each way on Mondays to Fridays, and eight on Saturdays and Sundays. The last timetables before the withdrawal of passenger services listed 12 each way on Mondays to Fridays only. At the time passenger workings ceased, there was no question that the line would close completely as it carried some 11,000 tons of coal each week from Whitburn colliery. That, however, did not last indefinitely as Whitburn colliery closed on 7 June 1968. Devoid of any purpose in life, the railway was dismantled soon afterwards.

The locomotive history of the South Shields, Marsden & Whitburn Colliery Railway is extremely confused. It is believed that the early locomotives included a Manning Wardle 0-4-0T, three Black Hawthorn 0-6-0STs and a Stephenson 0-6-0ST, all industrial types. Comparatively little is known about their subse-

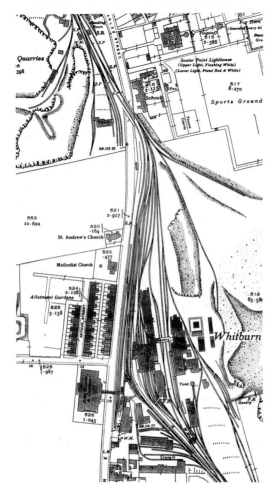

claim. It has been confirmed that two ex-Blyth & Tyne Railway 0-6-0s were acquired for the Marsden Railway, their building dates being 1857 and 1862, and so it might seem that one of those would be the '90-year old engine'. However, those two were SSM&WCR Nos 9 and 10 and, it is believed, retired around 1913. The locomotive carrying No 5 in 1953 was, it appears, an ex-NER '398' class 0-6-0 which, having been built in 1881, was a mere junior by comparison. The other locomotives which found their way on to the SSM&WCR fleet were a Chapman & Furneaux 0-6-2T of 1898, a Manning Wardle 0-4-0ST of indeterminate vintage, and an ex-Furness Railway 2-2-2WT which had been built in 1864. A Barclay 0-6-0ST was borrowed from Boldon colliery from 1929 to 1938, and one Hunslet and three Stephenson Hawthorn WD-type 0-6-0STs were purchased after World War 2 and fitted with air brakes to enable them to work the passenger services. During the last years of the coal traffic, NCB diesel locomotives were used, the SSM&WCR's WD 0-6-0STs ultimately being transferred to other NCB sites in the North Durham Area.

The coaching stock of the SSM&WCR comprised a mixture of four and six-wheel vehicles which came from companies as diverse as the Great Eastern, the North British, the Great North of Scotland, the North Eastern and, later, the Southern. In later years, their original interiors were removed and longitudinal seating installed, although one coach escaped the austerity treatment so that it was more 'suitable' for use by white-collar workers and the general public.

Left: **25in Ordnance Survey map, 1942. The passenger platform at Whitburn Colliery is at the end of the footbridge leading from the bath house and canteen.** Crown Copyright

quent histories. The SSM & WCR eventually developed a taste for NER and, later, LNER cast-offs, the first of six Fletcher '398' class 0-6-0s being purchased in 1907 and four 'J21' 0-6-0s in 1930-35; the 'J21s', incidentally, had started life as NER 'C' class compounds, but had later been rebuilt as simples. The last of the SSM&WCR's veteran 0-6-0s were retired shortly before the withdrawal of passenger services in 1953.

Newspaper accounts of the cessation of passenger services made much of the fact that one locomotive, allegedly SSM & WCR No 5, was around 90 years old, but the known facts seem not to substantiate that

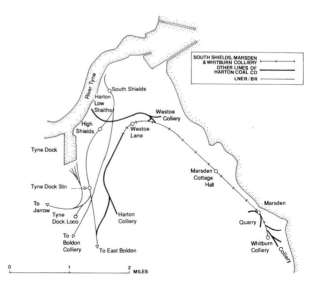

51 Tanat Valley Light Railway

The Afon Tanat rises in the Berwyn Mountains in northern Montgomeryshire and joins the River Severn in western Shropshire. Mining was first undertaken in the Tanat Valley in the 17th century, lead and slate being extracted near the upper reaches and, eventually, thoughts turned to providing a railway to facilitate the transportation of the minerals.

The Tanat Valley Railway was incorporated in 1897, which was very late in the day compared to the other mineral railways in North Wales. The negotiations which preceded the formation of the company involved the Cambrian Railways, which undertook to work the proposed railway, and Liverpool Corporation which, having set its sights on building Lake Vyrnwy reservoir, viewed the line as a useful means of transporting men and materials towards the construction site.

The cutting of the first sod was the easy bit as, before very long, the seemingly obligatory obstacles manifested themselves. It became painfully evident that initial estimates of construction costs had been somewhat optimistic, and so new financial powers had to be obtained. Even when that had been done, a prolonged spell of abysmal weather played havoc with the construction work. A further problem was encountered with the contractor who, among his unofficial activities, operated his own 'market day special' train on the uncompleted line without the permission of the rail-

way company's directors. In an attempt to make the peace, the contractor offered to work on Sundays, but that only offended the Chapel-going locals.

Despite everything, the Tanat Valley Railway managed to open to the public on 6 January 1904. Passenger services started from Oswestry, the route continuing to Llynclys Junction, 3½ miles to the south on the Cambrian Railways' line to Welshpool. From there, Tanat Valley trains took the Cambrian's spur to Porthywaen which had been opened in 1861 to serve the local lime kilns. A plethora of sidings radiated from Porthywaen to serve various quarring and ancillary installations, and TVR metals commenced just beyond Porthywaen station (4¾ miles from Oswestry). The next station was Blodwell Junction (6 miles) where the TVR met up with the Cambrian's line from Llanymynech to Nantmawr Quarries.

Westwards from Blodwell Junction, the intermediate stopping places were Llanyblodwell halt (6¾ miles),

Below: **Under the Cambrian Railways classification system, 2-4-0T No 58 (originally named** *Gladys)* **was a member of the 'Small Side Tank Class'. The locomotive spent a considerable period on the Tanat Valley line, this picture of it at Blodwell Junction having been taken early in 1904.** Real Photographs/Ian Allan Library

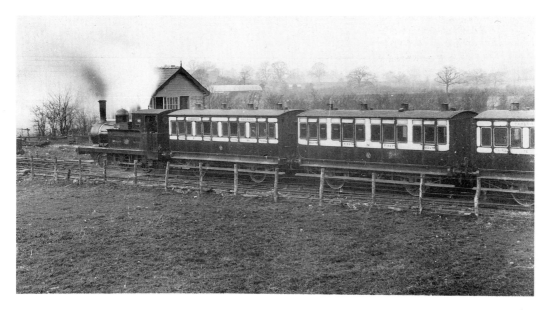

Glanyrafon halt (8 miles), Llansilin Road (9¼ miles), Llangedwyn (10¾ miles), Pentrefelin (12¾ miles), Llanrhaidir Mochnant (14 miles), Pedair Ffordd halt (14 miles) and Penybontfawr (17 miles), the terminus being at Llangynog (19½ miles) where there was a small engine shed. The branch was single track for virtually all of its length, passing loops being provided at all but three of the intermediate stations although, in later years, some of the loops were taken out.

For working the branch, the Cambrian was restricted by the lightly-laid nature of the permanent way. The ideal locomotives were the three 2-4-0Ts which had been built by Sharp Stewart in 1866 for Thomas Savin, the contractor who had originally worked, not only the Cambrian, but also the Brecon & Merthyr Railway and several smaller lines in mid-Wales. Savin had been declared bankrupt in February 1866, but the three 2-4-0Ts had not been delivered until May and had consequently become Cambrian stock. The locomotives were No 57 *Maglona*, No 58 *Gladys* and No 59 *Seaham* although, by the time the TVR opened, the trio had long since lost their names. They had 4ft 6in coupled wheels, inside cylinders of 14in x 20in and weighed 28ton 11cwt apiece. In 1904, the Cambrian purchased three ex-Lambourn Valley Railway 0-6-0Ts from the GWR, and these were deemed suitable for Tanat Valley duties. They became Cambrian Nos 24/26/35, the first having

Below: **After the Grouping, Cambrian 2-4-0T No 58 became GWR No 1196. It is seen with a Llangynog train at Pedair Ffordd on 31 July 1934.** R. W. Kidner

been built by the Hunslet Engine Co in 1903 while the other two, which were slightly smaller, having been built by Chapman & Furneaux in 1898.

The initial service on the line comprised four mixed trains each way on weekdays, an 'as required' freight being introduced soon after the line opened. On the mixed trains, the passenger carriages were a medley of four-wheel and bogie stock, six-wheel coaches being discouraged because of the sharply-curved nature of the line. Two mixed trains were also advertised between Blodwell Junction and Llanymynech in order to provide an alternative connection with main line trains, but the Llanymynech passenger services ceased in 1917, freight lasting only until 1925.

In April 1904, just four months after the TVR had opened its doors to the public, a Receiver had to be appointed. The traffic figures were adequate, although not exactly awe-inspiring, but the financial problems had arisen because the final bill for the line's construction had been double that of the initial estimate. The TVR never recovered and was relieved from insolvency only in March 1921 when it was taken over by the Cambrian Railways. The following year, the Cambrian became part of the GWR empire.

At the time of the Grouping, passenger services on the line consisted of three trains each way on weekdays with an additional one advertised on the first Wednesday of each month. The line's regular locomotives were taken into GWR stock, the 2-4-0Ts becoming Nos 1192/96/97 and the 0-6-0Ts taking Nos 819-21. Authorisation for the use of 0-6-0s on the line had never been officially received, but after

		a.m.	a.m.		p.m.		p.m.					a.m.	a.m.		p.m.	p.m.	
Oswestry	dep.	7 30	7 40		4 35		5 25		Llangynog	dep.		8 50	9 10		5 58	6 55	
Porthywaen	,,	7 32	7 52		4 47		5 37		Penybontfawr	,,		9 4	9 21		6 9	7 6	
Blodwell Junction	,,	7 39	8 0		4 55		5 45		Pedair Ffordd	,,		9 10	9 28		6 16	7 13	
Llanyblodwell	,,	7 44	8 4		4 59		5 50		Llanrhaiadr Mochnant	,,		9 22	9 32		6 20	7 17	
Glanyrafon	,,	7 49	8 9		5 4		5 55		Pentrefelin	,,		9 27	9 38		6 26	7 23	
Llansilin Road	,,	7 54	8 14		5 9		6 0		Llangedwyn	,,		9 35	9 45		6 33	7 30	
Llangedwyn	,,	7 59	8 19		5 14		6 5		Llansilin Road	,,		9 45	9 50		6 39	7 36	
Pentrefelin	,,	8 6	8 25		5 20		6 12		Glanyrafon	,,		9 50	9 55		6 43	7 40	
Llanrhaiadr Mochnant	,,	8 12	8 31		5 27		6 20		Llanyblodwell	,,		9 55	10 0		6 48	7 45	
Pedair Ffordd	,,	8 18	8 37		5 32		6 25		Blodwell Junction	,,		9 59	10 4		6 52	7 49	
Penybontfawr	,,	8 25	8 43		5 37		6 32		Porthywaen	,,		10 5	10 10		6 58	7 57	
Llangynog	arr.	8 37	8 53		5 43		6 44		Oswestry	arr.		10 23	10 23		7 11	8 10	

Above: **The very last GWR timetable was for the period commencing 6 October 1947, this extract referring to the Tanat Valley line.** Author's files

the Grouping the GWR was known to work Nos 898 and 908 through to Llangynog. However, neither of those machines were exactly in the 'heavy freight' league as their respective weights were 27ton and 26ton 16cwt and, furthermore, they were paired with four-wheel tenders.

Over the years, Oswestry shed became known as the traditional home of GWR oddities and, consequently, some of the shed's miscellany of absorbed antiquities were used on the Tanat Valley line. These included ex-Liskeard & Looe Railway 2-4-0T No 1308 *Lady Margaret*, former-Bristol & Exeter Railway 0-6-0T No 1376 and one-time Whitland & Cardigan Railway 0-6-0ST No 1331. During the 1940s, the ubiquitous GWR 0-4-2Ts started to take over on Tanat Valley passenger duties which, by the end of the decade, usually comprised just two trains each way on weekdays. Despite the appearance of the 0-4-2Ts, ex-Cambrian 2-4-0Ts No 1196/97 were

not completely ousted from the line until their withdrawal in April 1948. By then, both were just one month short of their 82nd birthdays.

During the early years of the Nationalisation era, the Tanat Valley line was only lightly used and the coal shortage of 1951 prompted British Railways to withdraw the passenger services as a temporary measure from 15 January. Just weeks later, on 5 February, the closure was deemed permanent. Freight services beyond Llanrhaiadr Mochnant ceased as from 1 July 1952, but the surviving section continued to be used by the occasional goods train until 1960. However, on 4 December that year, flood damage to the bridge over the Afon Tanat west of Llangedwyn resulted in the cessation of the goods workings west of Blodwell Junction. Traffic from Blodwell Quarries continued until 28 October 1988, three trains per week having taken wagon-loads of ballast from the quarries in the years prior to their closure.

Below: **Former Liskeard & Looe Railway 2-4-0T No 1308 *Lady Margaret* shunts an LMSR van and wagons at Llangynog on 31 July 1934.** R. W. Kidner

52 Tickhill Light Railway

The roll-call of British light railways includes some charismatic little lines which became much loved by enthusiasts and, consequently, were extremely well documented, but the Tickhill Light Railway is definitely not one of them. The TLR was originally intended to run from the unbuilt Dearne Valley Railway at Doncaster, via Tickhill, Bawtry and Misson to Haxey, where it would connect with the Great Northern/Great Eastern joint line and also the Isle of Axholme Light Railway (qv). Promoted by the Yorkshire Light Railway Syndicate, the TLR's primary purpose was to serve a proposed colliery at South Carr, near Haxey, but it was considered that welcome bonuses would be realised, firstly by agricultural traffic, and secondly by the establishment of an alternative route to the port of Goole.

Because of various objections, the plans for the northern section of the TLR had to be shelved and so the Light Railway Order which was granted in August 1901 was for a line only from Tickhill to Haxey. Little was done towards constructing the line and so, in July 1908, the Great Northern Railway formally took over the powers for which it paid the light railway promoters the princely sum of £2,300. Earlier, it had been anticipated that the North Eastern Railway would be the main line company which would show the greatest interest in the TLR, but the NER's interest in the Axholme Joint Railway (qv) rendered its involvement with the TLR superfluous.

By the time of the GNR take-over, work was progressing on a joint line between Dinnington Junction (north of Shireoaks) and Kirk Sandal Junction (to the north of Doncaster), and when that line opened on 1 January 1909, it did much to provide an adequate outlet for the potential coal traffic at Tickhill. Consequently, the GNR saw little need for the proposed Tickhill-Bawtry section of the TLR although, at one stage, the company purchased some of the necessary land. Nevertheless, the powers were maintained and passed to the LNER at the Grouping, the land being sold back to its original owner in 1930 after it had been formally decided that the Tickhill-Bawtry section would not be built.

Construction of the Bawtry-Haxey section eventually commenced, and the line opened on 26 April 1912, over 11 years after it had first been sanctioned. It was 7¾-miles long and single track throughout, and was intended solely for freight traffic. Most of the traffic was centred on a goods station at Misson Springs, 2¼ miles from Bawtry, where agricultural produce and sand provided the mainstay; the coal traffic from the Tickhill area, which had featured in

Right: **The imposing station at Bawtry was the point at which the Misson branch diverged from the main line.**
Lens of Sutton

the original plans for the TLR, used the Dinnington-Kirk Sandal line without coming near the Bawtry-Haxey route.

As with one or two other light railways featured in this book, the subsequent history of the line is poorly documented and certainly confused. One well-respected source states that the Bawtry-Haxey line was never even built whereas, in complete contradiction, another source gives an opening date for a non-existent extension to a wharf on the River Trent to the north of Haxey. Such is the sparsity of information. However, the well-respected RCTS book *The Railways of the South Yorkshire Coalfield* suggests that no through traffic ever made the journey between Bawtry and Haxey and, furthermore, that the rails from the central section of the line were lifted during World War 1 and sent to France to help out on the Western Front. That book also suggests that the Haxey end of the line might have been relaid about 1945 for the purpose of storing freight wagons. In the absence of conflicting evidence, this author will not dispute any of those suggestions, particularly as old Ordnance Survey maps mark a ¾-mile stretch near Idestrop merely with a dotted line.

During the early 1960s, a train of about half-a-dozen ventilated vans was hauled to Misson Springs in mid-afternoon each weekday by an ex-LNER 'B12' class 4-6-0, the wagons being required by Notts Crop Dryers. That continued only until 7 December 1964, from which date the line closed completely.

53 Totton, Hythe & Fawley Light Railway

The idea of a railway to Fawley, on the western side of Southampton Water in Hampshire, had first surfaced in the late 19th century, thoughts having been entertained of Fawley becoming the starting point for a ferry service to the Isle of Wight. That came to nothing but the plans for a railway were nevertheless revived and, in 1903, the London & South Western Railway obtained powers for its construction.

The L&SWR was not to have things all its own way as there was considerable local opposition to the line. Things dragged on and on, and by 1920, the railway had still not materialised. In that year, however, Fawley took on a new significance when work started there on the construction of an oil refinery and, as road access to the site was woefully inadequate, the L&SWR looked again at the plans for the railway. This time, the L&SWR took the familiar course of promoting a nominally-independent light railway to undertake the building of the line. The so-called independent concern was the Totton, Hythe & Fawley Light Railway, which was granted the necessary Order in 1921. At first it seemed as if the much-deferred line was never going to arrive as, at the time of the Grouping, construction had still not started,

but after the powers were acquired by the Southern Railway in 1923, things at last got underway.

The line was opened for traffic on 20 July 1925. Single track and devoid of any passing places, it left the SR's Southampton-Bournemouth main line at Totton, 3¼ miles west of Southampton Central, and had intermediate stations at Marchwood (3½ miles from Totton) and Hythe (6½ miles) before terminating at Fawley (9½ miles). The two branch stations and the terminus were all single-platform affairs. The initial passenger service comprised five trains each way on weekdays, but there were many locals who considered that the most convenient route between Southampton and the Fawley area was by means of the ferry to and from Hythe.

The passenger services were usually worked by 'O2' class 0-4-4Ts with 'Jubilee' 0-4-2s looking after most of the freight turns. In later years, mixed-traffic Drummond 4-4-0s took over many of the passenger duties from the 0-4-4Ts, and the SR's rostering lists for 1939 reveal that the seven Eastleigh-based 'L11' 4-4-0s included passenger duties to Fawley among their diagrams. The same lists show one of Eastleigh's 'Jubilees', No 317, as being allotted to the Fawley

Above: **On Sunday 20 March 1966, just five weeks after the cessation of scheduled passenger services on the Fawley branch, an RCTS special conveyed enthusiasts over the line. The locomotives seen near Hythe are 'USA' class 0-6-0Ts Nos 30064/73.** D. E. Canning

Left: **Push-pull fitted 'M7' class 0-4-4T No 30379 waits at Fawley on 22 September 1959.** J. H. Aston

branch, one of its daily turns being the 5.19pm passenger train from Fawley to Southampton Central. The use of tender locomotives on the line was a common feature for many years, despite the fact that there was no turntable at Fawley.

The line was originally worked as one block section with instruments at Totton and Fawley, but it was divided into two blocks during World War 2. The change in arrangements was necessitated by the establishment in 1943 of a network of sidings at Marchwood, these being laid by the War Department to enable Royal Engineers to learn about combined rail and dock operations. Eventually, there were some 30 miles of sidings on which a variety of standard WD locomotives were used and the site became, in a way, a sort of 'Longmoor-by-the-Sea'.

Over the years, the emphasis on the branch veered towards freight, and apart from the military traffic after 1943, much of it was oil from the AGWI refinery at Fawley which was on the south-east side of the railway. In 1951, the new owners, Esso Petroleum, opened what was, at the time, Europe's largest refinery on the west side of the line and this provided even more business for the railway. The construction in the mid-1950s of a large power station near Marchwood and a synthetic rubber factory at Hythe, both of which had their own internal locomotive-worked railways, brought still more traffic to the line. The building of the various industrial premises resulted in the line becoming well patronised by workmen, the train services being, by then, preferred to the ferry crossing from Southampton. In the late 1950s, new factories were being built at Hardley, between Hythe and Fawley, and a concrete platform was provided there for the workers. The platform opened in March 1958 but closed in April 1964. Furthermore, the inward movement of equipment and stores necessitated the laying in 1960 of passing loops at Marchwood and Hythe.

As for motive power, ex-LB&SCR 'E6' class

Above: **'Class 33' or, as it was then, Type 3 No D6539 leaves Fawley with the 3.45pm oil train to Wolverhampton on 22 July 1970.** J. Scrace

0-6-2Ts Nos 32409/12/16 were transferred to Eastleigh in September 1950 to work the goods trains on the Fawley branch, No 32409 soon being replaced by classmate No 32413. Although the new refinery at Fawley had not yet been completed, the loadings of the trains had nevertheless increased and the 23,205lb tractive effort of the 'E6s' was found to be a positive advantage. However, within a few short months of the 'E6s' taking up Fawley duties, it looked as if their reign was going to be brief. Early in December 1950, the powerful 'Z' class 0-8-0Ts Nos 30950/56 were displaced at Eastleigh by a diesel-electric shunter, and the 'Zs' were immediately drafted to the Fawley branch. The 'Zs' could haul trains of 60 or more wagons, but the return of Eastleigh's diesel shunter to Norwood at the end of the month resulted in the 'Zs' being required at Eastleigh once again, and so the 'E6s' were subsequently reinstated on the Fawley line. The 'E6s' held out until the autumn of 1952 when Standard '3MT' class 2-6-2Ts Nos 82012/14/15/16 were drafted in as replacements.

During the 1950s, passenger workings on the line were usually entrusted to 'M7' class 0-4-4Ts, and double-heading was often required to cope with the loadings when huge numbers of construction workers were travelling to and from Fawley. By the 1960s, the massive construction projects had been more or less completed and, of course, many workmen had by then acquired their own cars. Consequently, passenger traffic on the line dwindled and services were ultimately withdrawn on 14 February 1966, public goods facilities formally following suit on 2 February the following year.

Despite the loss of the passenger services, the oil traffic from the Esso refinery at Fawley was more than adequate to secure the line's future. During the 1960s, new loading racks were built at Cadlands sidings at the refinery to handle the white oil traffic for Bromford Bridge near Birmingham. Those trains, which were made up of 64 35-ton railcars, were usually hauled by '9F' 2-10-0s or, later that decade, Class 33 diesels. By 1966, up to 13 heavy trains left Fawley each weekday, but the laying of pipelines in the early 1970s resulted in a temporary drop in rail-borne traffic. In 1979, Esso took over the site of the redundant station at Fawley, and the old signal box was subsequently closed and a ground frame substituted on the BR/Esso boundary. The box and passing loop at Hythe were closed a few years later. December 1985 saw the first of the crude import by rail from Wytch Farm, and although those trains ceased in 1990, crude is now imported by means of a daily train from Holybourne, near Alton.

The outward traffic from Fawley now averages four trains each day, bitumen being taken to Bromford Bridge, Liquid Petroleum Gas to Longport near Stoke-on-Trent and chlorite to Sandbach, a further regular working being to Old Oak. Eastleigh's Class 37 or Class 60 locomotives are the most common forms of motive power, with '47s' available for standby duties.

54 Vale of Rheidol Light Railway

During the latter half of the 19th century Aberystwyth was named in the prospecti of several railway companies. The schemes which came to fruition were the Cambrian's line from Machynlleth, which was completed in June 1864, and the Manchester & Milford's route from Pencader, opened throughout in August 1867. In the Rheidol Valley, near Aberystwyth, there was a thriving mining industry and also considerable farming and forestry activities. Although at least one of the early railway schemes had suggested building a line through the valley to serve those industries, the difficult terrain had done much to dampen the promoters' enthusiasm.

It was 1896 before any really serious proposal was made for a railway through the Rheidol Valley and, sensibly, that scheme was based on the idea of a narrow gauge line. The passing of the Light Railways Act later that year prompted the promoters to apply for a LRO rather than an Act of Parliament, and the necessary Order for the Vale of Rheidol (Light) Railway was granted in August 1897. When it came to raising the necessary funds, however, the local industrialists who had been vociferous in their support of the railway were conspicuously slow to extract their wallets. Consequently, construction of the line was not only protracted but also, in many aspects, haphazard. The line finally opened in 1902, freight traffic commencing without ceremony in August. Special passenger trains operated in November for the benefit of the directors, their staff and local dignitaries but scheduled passenger services did not commence until 22 December.

The single-track line was built to a gauge of 1ft 11½ in. Its original terminus in Aberystwyth was on the southwest side of Smithfield Road (later renamed Park Avenue), but in 1926 the line was extended to the GWR main line station. At Aberystwyth, there was a branch to the harbour, exchange sidings with the standard gauge lines and, alongside the river bank, two single-road engine sheds. Along the route there were stopping places at Llanbadarn (1¼ miles), Glanrafon halt (2¼ miles), Capel Bangor (4½ miles), Nantyronen (6¾ miles), Aberffrwd (7¾ miles), Rheidol Falls (9¼ miles) and Rhiwfron halt (10¾ miles). The terminus at Devil's Bridge was a little over 11¾ miles from Aberystwyth. Lovesgrove (3¼ miles) was added in 1910 to serve a nearby Territorial Army camp but

Below: **The VoR's Bagnall 2-4-0T, No 3 *Rheidol*, became GWR No 1198 at the Grouping but was withdrawn in 1924. Its American-style spark-arrester was dispensed with in 1904.** Bucknall Collection/Ian Allan Library

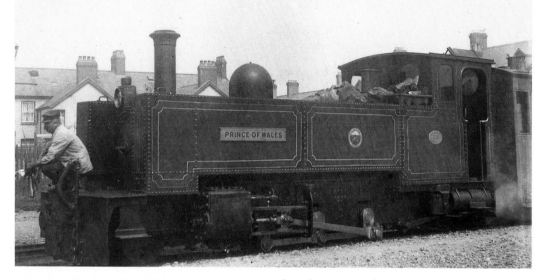

Top: **The terminus of the VoR at Devil's Bridge changed comparatively little over the years. The locomotive on the left is 2-4-0T No 3 *Rheidol*, the one on the right therefore being a Davies & Metcalfe 2-6-2T.**
Bucknall Collection/Ian Allan Library

Above: **Davies & Metcalfe 2-6-2T No 2 *Prince of Wales* waits at Aberystwyth on 30 June 1909.**
LCGB/Ken Nunn Collection

closed in 1914, while there was an unofficial 'halt' at Meithrinfa (8½ miles) where trains would stop for the benefit of children at a nearby nursery school.

Between Aberystwyth and Capel Bangor, the line was gently graded but, eastwards from Capel Bangor, the true nature of the route became evident. The ruling gradient between Capel Bangor and Aberffrwd was 1 in 40, and the last four miles into Devil's Bridge (some 680ft above sea level) required an unbroken climb of 1 in 50. The scenery, particularly on the upper section of the route, was magnificent and the line quickly became popular with holiday-makers. Four daily trains each way were the norm, with journey times of 60min. Nevertheless, one of

the railway's original functions, that of a freight route, was not forgotten as over 7,000 tons of minerals were carried annually during the early years. Even in 1917, when the mining industry was in decline, almost 3,000 tons of freight were transported.

The VoR's first two locomotives, No 1 *Edward VII* and No 2 *Prince of Wales* were Davies & Metcalfe 2-6-2Ts. Built in January 1902, they had 2ft 6in coupled wheels, 11in x 17in cylinders and weighed 22 tons apiece. Locomotive No 3 *Rheidol* was a Bagnall 2-4-0T which had been built in 1896 to the 2ft 3in gauge for use in Brazil. The South American buyer did not take delivery and so the engine was sold, instead, to a Lancashire contractor. It was later regauged for use by the contractors building the VoR line, and the railway company purchased the engine in 1903. Apart from the occasional hirings of the Festiniog Railway's 0-4-0ST No 4 *Palmerston* between 1912 and 1921, the VoR's stud of three engines was sufficient to handle all of the services and provide adequate cover. The VoR's original locomotive livery was olive green with claret lining, while the coaching stock was, from 1904, painted dark chocolate.

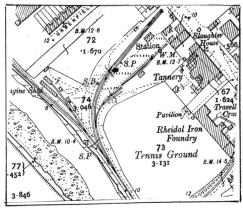

Above: **On 4 June 1963, one month before the VoR line was handed from the Western to the London Midland Region of British Railways, No 9 *Prince of Wales* passes the Crosville bus garage in Aberystwyth.** T. J. Edgington

Left: **The original terminus of the VoR line in Aberystwyth is evident in this 25in Ordnance Survey map of 1911.** Crown Copyright

The Cambrian Railways took over the VoR in July 1913, the new proprietor's first timetables showing a service of eight trains each way every weekday, an additional one on Mondays, Wednesdays and Saturdays, and two each way on Sundays. At the Grouping, the line became part of the GWR empire and the locomotives were renumbered, the 2-6-2Ts Nos 1/2 becoming GWR Nos 1212/13 and the 2-4-0T No 3 taking GWR No 1198. All three had lost their names shortly after the Cambrian take-over in 1913. The VoR line was still doing steady business in the early 1920s and so, in July 1923, the GWR built a pair of 2-6-2Ts to a similar design to the Davies & Metcalfe originals. These were Nos 7/8, and their arrival resulted in the withdrawal in July 1924 of the Bagnall 2-4-0T No 1198. It is on record that 2-6-2T No 1213 was extensively rebuilt at Swindon after the Grouping, but it is strongly suspected that the engine which emerged from the works in 1924 was, in fact, a new one, the alleged rebuilding having been for accounting purposes.

The increasing popularity of mid-Wales as a tourist haunt did not escape the eyes of motorbus operators and, in 1924, Crosville inaugurated routes 601 and 602 between Aberystwyth and Devil's Bridge. Those services were a tremendous blow to the VoR line, and the sharp decline in freight traffic on the route did not help matters. The outcome was the withdrawal of year-round passenger services after 31 December 1930, freight traffic having ceased four years earlier. During the following years, the GWR nevertheless found it profitable to operate passenger services between May and September and, apart from the obvious hiatus during World War 2, that pattern continued virtually unchanged.

On the locomotive front, one of the original 2-6-2Ts, No 1212, was withdrawn in December 1932. Its contemporary, No 1213, the alleged Swindon 'rebuild', became No 9 in March 1949 and, in June 1956, all three locomotives were named, No 7 becoming *Owain Glyndwr*, No 8 *Llewelyn* and No 9 had its original name of *Prince of Wales* restored. Under State ownership, the locomotives were treated to an assortment of liveries, logos and totems. The line passed from the control of the Western Region to that of the London Midland Region in July 1963, and after a few scares about selling-off or even closure, the LMR authorised the laying of a new alignment into Aberystwyth main line station and general improvements which included the provision of a new engine shed.

The new arrangements were unveiled to the public in May 1968. The great irony was that, by the end of the same year, the old VoR route was the only remaining steam-worked line under British Railways ownership. As a tourist attraction, it did good business with some 172,000 passengers being carried during the 1974 season. The conversion of the three locomotives to oil-burners in 1978/80 might have upset the purists, but the economy seemed to make sense although, as if to make a mockery of the costings, BR sold the entire undertaking in 1989 to the Brecon Mountain Railway Co. Under the sixth administrative regime in its 92-year life, the line was given yet another new lease of life and is flourishing once again.

55 Welsh Highland Railway

The Welsh Highland Railway (Light Railway) Company, to give it its full and unwieldy title, was formally incorporated on 30 March 1922, but it had roots which went back to much earlier times. The WHR, which operated on a gauge of 1ft 11½ in, was effectively formed by a merger between the North Wales Narrow Gauge Railway and the Portmadoc, Beddgelert & South Snowdon Railway, both of which had previously acquired LROs for certain extensions.

Of those two constituents, the NWNGR had opened in a piecemeal manner between May 1877 and May 1881, the first passenger services having operated on 15 August 1877. In its entirety, its 'main line' had run for 9¾ miles from Dinas Junction, on the LNWR line south of Caernarvon, to Rhydd-Ddu, on the western side of Mount Snowdon, and there had been a 2½-mile branch from Tryfan Junction to Bryngwyn. For many years, traffic on the NWNGR had been adequate but things had started tailing off early in the 20th century. The first casualty had been the Bryngwyn branch which had lost its passenger services from 1 January 1914, the passenger workings over the 'main line' having continued only until the end of October 1916.

The second constituent company, the PB&SSR, had been incorporated in 1901, primarily to provide a link between the NWNGR at Rhydd-Ddu and the horse-worked Croesor Tramway, which ran north-eastwards from Portmadoc. The PB&SSR had been authorised to use electric traction, the power to be generated by the company's own hydro-electric installations and, in 1904, the PB&SSR and its electrical ancillaries had passed to the control of the North Wales Power & Electric Traction Co. The construction of the PB&SSR's line had eventually commenced, much of the work being under the authority of Light Railway Orders, but the outbreak of war in 1914 had brought an enforced halt to the work. Although the engineering works for the line had made provision for overhead electric cables, electric traction was never used.

Under the new ownership of the Welsh Highland Railway, the old NWNGR section between Dinas

Junction and Rhydd-Ddu was resleepered and laid on fresh ballast which was obtained from a quarry near Salem. That section reopened to passenger traffic on 31 July 1922, although the Bryngwyn branch remained open only for freight. The former PB&SSR section south of Rhydd-Ddu had been partially completed prior to the formation of the WHR, but the new company's plans incorporated several substantial realignments of the original route. Consequently, the work on that section was largely regarded as new construction and, in order to qualify for Government grants, the WHR had to ensure that its contractors drew all of their unskilled workforce from the local area, thereby helping to ease the unemployment problem. In practice, many local labourers proved totally unsuited to the task of railway building but it took extensive negotiations with the Ministry of Labour before the relevant condition could be relaxed.

The 'new' section, which had gradients of up to 1 in 40 and a 300yd tunnel in the Pass of Aberglaslyn, opened to traffic on 1 June 1923. The Board of Trade inspector was far from happy with many aspects of the line but, somewhat remarkably, agreed that the WHR could operate a passenger service provided the company adhered to certain strict conditions. Because of the nearness of the holiday season and the potential traffic, the WHR was more than happy to observe whatever condititions were imposed.

The WHR's route was single track throughout and laid with rails which were around 40lb/yd. At its northern end, it used the old NWNGR facilities at Dinas Junction and, in the station yard, were the WHR's locomotive shed and interchange facilities for freight. After leaving Dinas Junction, the stopping

Right: **An unidentified Festiniog locomotive waits at Dinas Junction with a Welsh Highland train in 1924.**
Bucknall Collection/Ian Allan Library

Above: **The Welsh Highland's 0-6-4T *Moel Tryfan* was one of two similar locomotives inherited from the North Wales Narrow Gauge Railway. Both were cannibalised in 1917 to provide enough parts to construct one useable machine.** Bucknall Collection/Ian Allan Library

Right: **The WHR's 2-6-2T *Russell* (now preserved) was cut down in size so that it could be accommodated by the Festiniog's loading gauge, but is seen here in its unadulterated condition.** Bucknall Collection/ Ian Allan Library

places were at Tryfan Junction (2¼ miles), Waenfawr (4 miles), Bettws Garmon (4¾ miles), Salem halt (5½ miles), Plasynant halt (6 miles), Quellyn Lake (7½ miles) which had originally been called Snowdon Ranger, and Rhydd-Ddu (9½ miles), the last-named being retitled South Snowdon by the WHR to emphasise its usefulness for tourists.

On the 'new' section beyond South Snowdon (formerly Rhydd-Ddu), there were stopping places at Pitts Head halt (10 miles from Dinas Junction), Hafod Ruffydd halt (11½ miles), Beddgelert (14 miles), Nantmor halt (15¾ miles) which was renamed Aberglaslyn in July 1934, Hafodllyn halt (16½ miles), Hafod Garregog halt (17 miles), Ynysferlas halt (17½ miles), Croesor Junction halt (18 miles) where the old Croesor Tramway diverged, Ynysfor halt (18½ miles), Pont Croesor halt (19½ miles) and Port Rhyddin halt (20¼ miles) before the line reached Portmadoc New (21½ miles). Passenger access to the ex-Cambrian Railways station in Portmadoc was by means of a footpath. The WHR's extension to Portmadoc Harbour (22 miles) was first used on 8 June, one week after the rest of the line had opened to passenger traffic, the physical connection with the neighbouring Festiniog Railway being made at Britannia Bridge.

One of the WHR's main promoters was Henry Jack, whose business interests included the North Wales Power & Traction Co, the very concern which had assumed control of the old PB&SSR in 1904. In 1905, permission had been granted for the PB&SSR to lease the NWNGR and so the affairs of the two constituents of the WHR had become intertwined. At the time of the formation of the WHR, Jack was also chairman of the Festiniog Railway (qv) and, despite local caution about the extent of the Henry Jack empire, the futures of the WHR and the FR

were to become inextricably linked.

The administration of the WHR was nominally undertaken from Jack's headquarters in Dolgarrog, across the other side of Snowdonia in the Conway valley, but the mysteries of how to run a railway seemed beyond the grasp of the folk at Dolgarrog. Consequently, much of the workload was unofficially delegated to the Festiniog's offices at Boston Lodge and when the WHR was up and running, the FR men bitterly resented having to look after the affairs of their neighbour. Staff relations were not given an easy start when, in April 1923, the eminently English figure of Lt-Col Holman Stephens was appointed a civil engineer and locomotive superintendent of the WHR and the FR. Within less than two years, Stephens became managing director of both companies, and this did little to improve local morale.

As for locomotives, the WHR inherited two usable steeds from its constituents. One was ex-PB&SSR *Russell*, a Hunslet-built 2-6-2T of 1906 which had 2ft 4in driving wheels and outside cylinders of 10¾in x 15in, although Festiniog records give cylinder dimensions of 9½in x 14in. The other locomotive was former-NWNGR *Moel Tryfan* a Vulcan Foundry 0-6-4T of 1877 which had 2ft 6in driving wheels and 8½ in x 12in cylinders. That engine had been one of a pair supplied to the NWNGR, the other having been *Snowdon Ranger,* and they had been the first

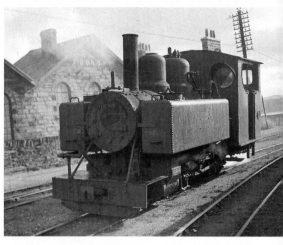

0-6-4s to be used in Britain. In 1917, the pair of 0-6-4Ts had been cannibalised in order to provide one usable locomotive from the two lots of components, the name *Moel Tryfan* being used for the 'rebuild' and *Snowdon Ranger* being nominally withdrawn.

On passing to the WHR, *Moel Tryfan* and *Russell* were cut down in size so that, in theory, they could work over the Festiniog's tracks but, in practice, an adequate reduction in the width of the latter proved impossible. Two other NWNGR locomotives had been retired before the formation of the WHR. Both had been built by the Hunslet Engine Co, one being a 0-6-4ST of 1878 named *Beddgelert* and the other a single Fairlie 0-6-4T of 1908 named *Gowrie*, and they had been withdrawn in 1906 and 1915 respectively.

An additional locomotive was deemed essential for the WHR from the outset and so, in July 1923, an ex-WD Baldwin 4-6-0PT was purchased for £240. Built in 1917, the locomotive had 1ft 11½ in diameter driving wheels, outside cylinders of 9in x 12in and weighed in at 14½ tons; although it had been rebuilt by Bagnall's in 1919, it retained its WD number of 590. The WHR's intention was to use the Baldwin for passenger services but, before long, it was found to be a rough rider, a poor steamer and prone to slipping. On one occasion, wet rails caused the machine to slip so much that, even with a loading of just one bogie coach and a van, it reached its destination 55min late. The WHR had originally planned to purchase a second ex-WD Baldwin 4-6-0PT, but the unhappy experiences with the first one put paid to those thoughts.

The WHR's corporate links with the Festiniog proved fortuitous as, for some time, FR locomotives worked through to Dinas Junction, thereby easing the WHR's motive power shortage. Of the FR's engines, 0-4-0STs *Palmerston* and *Princess* were regular performers over WHR metals and figures for 1927 show that they each covered more miles on the WHR than on their native FR. The FR's famous double Fairlies are also known to have worked through to Dinas Junction although, by the late 1920s, sightings of any FR locomotives north of Beddgelert had become extremely rare.

In the best 'Colonel Stephens' tradition, internal-combustion motive power eventually appeared, although the War Department had beaten Stephens to it when, in 1917, it had used the old NWNGR route for trials of a petrol-electric locomotive. In July 1925, a 20hp petrol-powered Daimler tractor was acquired

and was used on the Croesor Tramway section until being retired in 1929, while a six-wheel diesel tractor arrived in 1928 and was used on the Bryngwyn branch until being transferred to the Festiniog the following year.

The WHR inherited 16 assorted carriages from the NWNGR, most of which were bogie vehicles. The position regarding freight stock is unclear, but it is known that the old NWNGR had, at the end of 1922, some 130 trucks of which the majority were slate wagons; as late as 1933, when the railway was approaching its death throes, the stock list still included over 100 wagons.

Early in 1923, the still-uncompleted WHR considered that tourist traffic could provide a major source of income, and when the line opened to Portmadoc in June that year, four through trains were advertised each way on weekdays with average journey times of 125min. The route through Snowdonia was truly spectacular, and it became customary for trains to slow down through Aberglaslyn Pass so that passengers could take in the scenic delights. However, the anticipation of intense tourist traffic soon proved unfounded as the WHR's returns for 1923 revealed that passenger services contributed just £2,517 for the corporate kitty, that figure being even less than the modest £3,422 receipts from freight traffic. After the end of the 1924 summer season, economies were made and the passenger services usually comprised just one or two through trains daily.

By 1927, things looked very grim indeed as the figures for that year showed receipts of £3,479 from freight but only £686 from passengers. The optimists among the WHR's ranks tried to excuse the sparse passenger returns by citing 'poor summer weather', but that suggestion only amused those who were familiar with the usual climatic conditions encountered in North Wales. The WHR's net loss for 1927 was £3,304, and that was enough to warrant the appointment of a Receiver.

If a miracle had happened and North Wales had become bathed in sunshine it would, arguably, have resulted in the precariously-financed WHR shooting itself in the corporate foot. Even with sparse summer services, the company had to use its three available locomotives for passenger duties during the holiday period, and this failed to impress the freight customers who found that they could not count on the railway company supplying reliable year-round haulage.

Predictably, the WHR's downward spiral became more intense. In 1929, the link between the WHR and the Festiniog at Portmadoc was all but abandoned and WHR passengers had to be led on foot from the WHR station to the FR's premises. That practice might have held a wry appeal for Lt-Col Stephens but it did little for the passengers' tempers. That same year, responsibility for the traffic on the Croesor Tramway section passed from the WHR to the Festiniog but, by then, evidence of the national recession had been reflected in the reduced output from slate quarries throughout North Wales. In the early 1930s, six quarries in the immediate area ceased working, and of the remaining three, only one was a customer of the WHR. Nevertheless, a daily goods working remained until November 1931, although by 1933 the goods service comprised just one train each week.

By 1930, even summer-season passenger services on the WHR ran on only three days of the week. In September of that year, they were suspended and, in subsequent years, were reinstated only between mid-July and mid-September. Largely out of desperation, the WHR courted the GWR and LMSR in turn in the hope of being bought out, but neither of the big boys was remotely interested. However, the Festiniog Railway surprised everybody and, from 1 July 1934, it took a lease on the WHR.

The Festiniog take-over wasn't so much a case of a big fish acquiring a tiddler...it was more like a minnow acquiring plankton. The 'rescue package' was not only rather puny, but also far too late in the day to secure the future of the WHR's line. Passenger services were operated during the next three summers, but the workings of 26 September 1936 were to be the last in WHR history. Despite the small-scale reopening of some local quarries in 1936/37, no realistic hope remained of an adequate flow of freight and the line was officially closed to all traffic on 31 May 1937.

Of the three locomotives, the Baldwin 4-6-0PT and *Russell* were stored at Dinas Junction, whereas the Festiniog claimed *Moel Tryfan* along with one bogie coach and three wagons as compensation for unpaid working expenses. As for the locomotives' subsequent fates, the Baldwin was taken away in 1937 and cut up five years later, *Russell* was requisitioned by the Ministry of Supply in 1941 and put to industrial use, while *Moel Tryfan* remained on the Festiniog, albeit dismantled for much of the time, until being scrapped in 1954. But that was not the end of the story.

A preservation organisation was formed in 1961 with the intention of reopening part of the former Welsh Highland route near Portmadoc. On 2 August 1980, the first short section at Portmadoc was reopened and, since then, services have operated during summer months. A major coup was achieved with the acquisition of *Russell* which had retired from industrial service in 1953 and, after much work, the locomotive was proudly returned to service on 4 April 1987. The preservationists' ultimate aim is to reopen through to Caernarvon, but the neighbouring Festiniog Railway seems to have similar ideas and so the granting of the necessary powers is, it seems, going to require a mutually unhelpful battle.

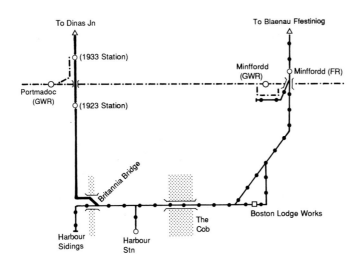

Left: **Diagramatic layout of Portmadoc.**

The communities of Welshpool and Llanfair Caereinion in eastern Montgomeryshire became well-established as market towns during the 18th century. During the 'Railway Mania' of the 1840s, Llanfair found itself on or near the route of more than one proposed line, but Welshpool became the first of the two towns to be rail-connected. In August 1860, the Oswestry & Newton Railway (later part of the Cambrian Railways) opened as far as Welshpool and, predictably, Llanfair was among the surrounding towns which started to clamour for a connection to the new line.

There followed a number of proposals for a railway to Llanfair and, at one stage, it looked as if the Llanfair & Meifod Light Railway was leading the field with its scheme for a line from Llanfair to to the main line at Ardd-lin, north of Welshpool. However, the rival Welshpool lobby put up a strong argument which was supported by Everard Calthrop, one of the best-respected names in light railway engineering, and it was the Welshpool & Llanfair Light Railway which eventually won the day.

With the backing of the Cambrian Railways, which undertook to construct and work the W&LLR, the building of the line formally commenced on 30 May 1901. By the early part of 1903, the line was near enough to completion to permit the working of some unscheduled freight services, but the official opening for freight traffic did not take place until 9 March of that year. Passenger services were inaugurated on Saturday 4 April. The W&LLR cost £47,900 to construct and was built to a gauge of 2ft 6in. It started adjacent to the Cambrian Railways' coal sidings at Smithfield Road in Welshpool, and there were intermediate stopping places at Seven Stars (half a mile), Raven Square (1 mile), Golfa (2¾ miles), Sylfaen (3¾ miles), Castle Caereinion (4¾ miles), Cyfronwydd (6¾ miles) and Heniarth (7¾ miles), before the terminus at Llanfair Caereinion (9 miles) was reached. An unadvertised halt at Dolrhyd Mill, half a mile west of Castle Caereinion, was added later.

The stations had low platforms which were faced in gravel and, although the line was worked on the 'one engine in steam' principle, passing loops were provided at all intermediate stopping places except Seven Stars and Raven Square. Those two were in the town of Welshpool itself, and the former was named after a pub which, ironically, had to be demolished to make way for the railway. For some of its route through

Above: **At Welshpool, part of the W&LR's route threaded between the rear of houses and, clearly, the novelty value still remained for the locals.** Montgomeryshire Express

Left: **The W&L's 0-6-0T No 1 *The Earl* provides a suitable prop for the station staff at Llanfair.** Bucknall Collection/Ian Allan Library

Welshpool, the railway wound between the back yards of cottages but it remains unrecorded just what effect the locomotives' exhaust had on washing which was hung out to dry. Westwards from Welshpool, the railway's route between the hills was very scenic, but the earthworks were not as extensive as might have been imagined for a North Wales narrow gauge railway. Nevertheless, there were some severe gradients including the 1 in 29 of Golfa bank and a short stretch of 1 in 25 west of Cyfronydd.

The Cambrian Railways ordered two locomotives for the W&LLR. They were identical Beyer Peacock 0-6-0Ts which became No 1 *The Earl* and No 2 *The Countess*; they had outside frames, 2ft 9in diameter wheels, Walschaerts valve gear and outside cylinders of 11½in x 16in. Finished in the standard Cambrian livery of gloss black, it was often remarked that their

stovepipe chimneys spoilt their otherwise smart appearances. The passenger rolling stock consisted of three oil-lit bogie coaches which had gated balconies at each end, while freight stock originally comprised a mixture of four-wheel opens and vans, although timber bolster trucks, sheep and cattle vans, and a number of private-owner wagons appeared on the line in later years. The W&LLR's locomotive and carriages were accommodated in sheds at Welshpool.

Much of the W&LLR's traffic depended on the farming community, agricultural produce and livestock forming the mainstay of freight with passenger traffic enjoying a significant boost each Monday when there was a market at Welshpool. Before very long, however, the company found that non-agricultural freight traffic was failing to materialise in anything like the quantities which had been, not only anticipated, but almost relied on. The dilemma was that its freight charges were higher than those for road transport but it could not afford to lower the rates, and even had a reduction been possible, the company could not afford to purchase additional rolling stock to accommodate the extra traffic generated. The cash-flow problem was illustrated by the fact that the W&LLR's 40% share of receipts was, on occasions, greater than the Cambrian's

Above: **After the Grouping, W&LR No 2 became GWR No 823, albeit with an abbreviation of its name to *Countess*. It is seen at Welshpool on 6 April 1926.**
LCGB/Ken Nunn Collection

net profit from working the line. Nevertheless, additional traffic was gradually secured, some being in the form of timber from Jones' sawmill at Llanfair and stone from the Standard Quarry in Welshpool.

Until 1908, services on the W&LLR usually comprised four trains each way on weekdays. Most were mixed but there was an additional freight-only train in the down direction on three days of each week, a passenger carriage being attached for the return trips. Cuts were made in the timetables after 1909, although by the time of the Grouping, there were three down and four up trains on weekdays, with an additional service in each direction on Tuesdays, Wednesdays and Saturdays. To the locals, each working was known as 'Llanfair Jinny', irrespective of the locomotive or the rolling stock formation. The W&LLR passed to the Great Western Railway at the Grouping, the two locomotives becoming GWR Nos 822/23 and receiving liveries of unlined green. The GWR repositioned the locomotives' nameplates by the cab side-sheets but, because of the restricted space, the name of *The Countess* had to be abbreviated to plain old *Countess*.

By the mid-1920s, freight traffic on the W&LLR route was steady, if not exactly spectacular. However, the GWR realised that locally-operated bus services could provide stiff competition for the passenger traffic and so, rather than lose out, the GWR introduced its own single-deck buses on the Welshpool-Llanfair route in July 1925. At first, the GWR routed its buses via the hilly roads to serve the centres of the villages along the journey, but while that might have seemed sensible, the gradients had such a damaging effect on the vehicles that, by the beginning of 1926, the company chickened out and used the road which ran almost parallel to the railway. Despite the less-useful rerouteing of the buses, many passengers defected from the trains. By 1930, some of the market day trains carried 80 or 100 passengers but, for the rest of the week, completely empty trains were not uncommon. As if to set a precedent for the 1960s, the 'arm-

chair' passengers kicked up a rumpus when the GWR announced that passenger services were to be withdrawn, but the protests were to no avail.

The last passenger trains ran on 7 February 1931 but a freight service was retained and, on most weekdays, there was one return working. During World War 2, railways everywhere saw additional traffic as petrol rationing affected road transport, and the W&LLR route was no exception. By 1942, two daily freight workings were being undertaken on weekdays and, during the 'sheep month' of September, up to five trips were needed each day. Happily for the GWR, if not the animals, the extra livestock traffic continued for a while after the war but, before long, road transport resumed its former dominance. At the time of Nationalisation, the only real remaining traffic was coal and coke to Llanfair, the outward traffic having all but vanished. Predictably, British Railways did not let that situation persist for too long and, after a few false alarms, total closure took place on 5 November 1956, the last revenue-earning freight train having run three days previously. The line had a handsome send-off and on 3 November, the day after the last regular freight working, No 822 *The Earl* proudly hauled the obligatory enthusiasts' special.

Fortunately, the line and the two locomotives were rescued by preservationists and on 6 April 1963, exactly 60 years after the first opening ceremony, the W&LLR was formally reopened to the public. The site of the original terminus at Welshpool was acquired by the local council soon afterwards and so the line had to be truncated at Raven Square where a new station was subsequently established. Today, the 'new' Welshpool & Llanfair Light Railway is a deservedly successful tourist attraction.

57 Weston, Clevedon & Portishead Light Railway

There is a popular, albeit unconfirmed, story about this little line which concerns a refined female passenger who was waiting at the Great Western station at Weston-super-Mare. She asked an official about connections to Portishead, and the latter considered that the nearby Weston, Clevedon & Portishead Light Railway would offer a more direct service. His reply, which resulted in his subsequent sacking, was 'Well madam, I suggest you go to the WC&P'.

Whether or not that tale is true, the WC&PLR *did* offer a more direct service between Weston and Portishead, in northwest Somerset, than the mighty GWR. The Weston, Clevedon & Portishead Tramway, as it was originally titled, was founded by local businessmen to establish a direct line between the communities of its title. In true Brunellian fashion, the GWR's predecessor, the Bristol & Exeter Railway, had initially served the three towns only by means of branches from the main line, although a loop into Weston itself had condescendingly been provided by the GWR in 1884. Weston and Clevedon were holiday resorts which had grown after the arrival of the B&ER branches, but it was felt that a connecting railway would improve local fortunes even more.

The first section of the WC&P to open was that between Weston and Clevedon. It had been authorised as a tramway in 1885, 11 years before the coming of the Light Railways Act, but it was 1 December 1897 before the line opened to the public. The line started at Ashcombe Road station in Weston, ¾-mile from the GWR station in the town, and there were intermediate stopping places at Milton Road halt (1 mile), Worle Town (2 miles), Ebdon Lane halt (3¼ miles), Wick St Lawrence (4 miles), Ham Lane halt (5 miles), Kingston Lane (6¼ miles) and Colehouse Lane (7¼ miles) before reaching Clevedon (8¼ miles). As if those stopping places weren't enough, halts were added at Bristol Road (1½ miles) and Broadstone (5¾ miles) in 1912 and 1918 respectively. At Wick St Lawrence, a spur was laid in 1915 to a wharf on the River Yeo from where sailing barges arrived from South Wales with cargoes of coal.

Clevedon was the WC&PLR's headquarters, and in the yard opposite the single platform station were the company's engine and carriage sheds. Behind the sheds, a tightly-curved loop was laid to provide a link with the GWR's branch from Yatton, but the GWR insisted that any movement on the loop had to be at the WC&PLR's own risk. Although, in later years, the WC&PLR was known to remove the rear coupling rods from an 0-6-0T in order to ease its passage over the loop, the little company took the safest option and hardly used the track at all.

Left: **The WC&P's well-groomed ex-Furness 2-2-2WT perches on the bridge at Wick St Lawrence, undoubtedly for a posed publicity shot.** Bucknall Collection/ Ian Allan Library

Top: **The WC&P's Manning Wardle 0-6-0ST, No 3 *Weston*, stands outside the engine shed at Clevedon and, judging by the locomotive's pristine condition, the picture could well have been taken very shortly after its purchase in 1930. The carriage on the left of the frame is on the platform road of Clevedon station.**
Bucknall Collection/Ian Allan Library

Above: **Despite the absence of a platform, this is, in fact, Ebdon Lane halt on the WC&P's southern section in September 1936. The locomotive is Manning Wardle 0-6-0ST No 5 and the seemingly extravagant carriages are those originally destined for work in South America.**
R. W. Kidner

So far, the railway company has been referred to as the Weston, Clevedon & Portishead Light Railway but, to be precise, it was not until 1899 that the company was formally reincorporated as a light railway. By then, virtually nothing had been done towards the extension to Portishead and, ominously, the following years saw a nosedive in the company's financial fortunes. Despite all sorts of problems, the Portishead section was nevertheless completed and it opened to the public without any formal ceremony on 7 August 1907.

The new section had intermediate stopping places at Clevedon East halt (9 miles from Weston), Walton Park (9¾ miles), Walton-in-Gordano halt (10¼ miles), Cadbury Road (11¾ miles), Clapton Road (13 miles) and Portishead South (13¾ miles) on its route to the terminus at Portishead (14¼ miles). In 1917, All Saint's halt (9¼ miles) was added to the seemingly impressive roll call but, in fact, almost all of the stopping places were no more than roadside halts which were devoid of raised platform.

At the Clevedon end of the extension, trains crossed a road junction in the centre of the town, the Board of Trade stipulating that each train should travel at no more than 4mph over the roadway and be preceded by a railway official carrying a red flag. At Walton Park, a siding led to Conygar quarry while, between Cadbury Road and Clapton Road halts, interchange sidings were later laid to connect with the 2ft gauge tramway system at Black Rock quarry which opened in 1919. Beyond the station at Portishead, a line continued to a steamer pier but there is no record of the WC&PLR ever having graduated to the running of boat trains. Apart from a passing loop at Wick St Lawrence, the WC&PLR's route was single track throughout; the Weston-Clevedon section was laid with 56lb/yd flat-bottomed rails 60lb/yd

Above: **The WC&P's tracks crossed the roadway on their approach to Clevedon station from the north. However, No 2 *Portishead,* one of the ex-LB&SCR 'Terriers', seemed to attract little attention from residents and holidaymakers on 10 August 1935.** R. W. Kidner

being used on the Clevedon-Portishead section. The entire line was subjected to a punitive axle-weight limit of 12tons, and the signalling apparatus was supplied by Saxby & Farmer.

As one of the contractor's 0-6-0Ts, *Clevedon,* was away for repair at the time the first section of line opened, the inaugural services were entrusted to a hired Kitson 0-6-0ST named *Harold.* The first locomotives which the WC&PLR could call its own were a Stephenson 0-6-0T named *Portishead,* purchased from contractors in 1898, and a pair of outside-framed 2-2-2WTs, which were purchased from the Furness Railway in 1898/99 and subsequently christened *Weston* and *Clevedon.* Of those three *Portishead* worked only briefly on the WC&PLR before being sold for £950 to the Renishaw Iron Co while the two ex-Furness engines were scrapped in 1904/06.

From then on, the WC&PLR's locomotive lists take a little sorting out as the same names were used on a different locomotives while, from 1906, numbers were also used. It seems that the first WC&PLR locomotive to carry a number was a Dubs 2-4-0T. Purchased in 1901, it had started life on the Jersey Railway but when, in 1884, that company had converted to narrow gauge, the locomotive had been sold to

contractors. The WC&PLR released it from industrial slavery and treated it to an overhaul at the Avonside Engine Co in Bristol before letting it perform its new tasks. It arrived in Somerset wearing the name *General Don* but, in 1904, was renamed *Clevedon* following the demise of the ex-Furness engine of the that name; in 1906, *Clevedon* became WC&PLR No 1.

An acquisition of 1903, a former-LB&SCR 2-4-0T, was retired in 1906 before the WC&PLR's numbering scheme was introduced; the locomotive was allegedly named *Portishead* but there is no photographic evidence to support that claim. The name *Portishead* was, however, applied to a secondhand Manning Wardle 'M' class 0-6-0ST which was purchased in 1907, that engine being designated No 2. Under WC&PLR ownership, it had the distinction of hauling the inaugural train on the Portishead extension. Another Manning Wardle 0-6-0ST arrived in 1907 to become No 3 *Weston;* it had been built for a contractor but, between 1894 and 1904, had worked on the Burry Port & Gwendraeth Valley Railway where it had been named *Cwm Mawr*.

New and adventurous ground was broken in 1908 when a brand new 0-6-0ST was purchased from Hudswell Clarke. Named *Walton Park*, the locomotive was a bit too close to the weight limits for comfort and was transferred in 1912 to the Bere Alston & Calstock Light Railway, then to the Shropshire & Montgomeryshire Light Railway (qv) and, in 1916, moved to the East Kent Light Railway (qv). The only other brand new steam locomotive ever purchased by the WC&PLR was the unnamed No 5, a Manning Wardle 0-6-0ST which arrived in 1919. Between the arrival of the two new locomotives, a 35-year old Sharp Stewart 2-4-0T was purchased in 1911 and became No 4 *Hesperus*. It had been built for the Watlington & Princes Risborough Railway and had passed to the GWR to become No 1384. It had subsequently worked on the Lambourn Valley and the Wrington Vale Light Railways, and later in Devon, before arriving at the WC&PLR. Its maximum axle weight was only 8tons 8cwt, but the timber bridge at Wick St Lawrence collapsed under it in 1934. After that escapade, it was seldom used until its withdrawal in 1937.

At first, the WC&PLR's coaching stock comprised six bogie carriages which were part of a cancelled order from an Argentinian railway company. They had clerestory roofs and, at each end, open platforms which were fitted with steps; in view of the plethora of roadside halts on the WC&PLR's route, the steps were very useful extras. When the Portishead extension opened, seven four-wheeled coaches were purchased from the Metropolitan Railway. In 1924, three ex-L&SWR four-wheel coaches were purchased but these were close-coupled and, consequently, were regarded as one set; the only other coach owned by the WC&PLR was an ex-GER four-wheel brake. The official livery for coaching stock was crimson, the same as that for the locomo-

Right: **One of the WC&P's trio of Manning Wardle 0-6-0STs, No 5 of 1919, is seen at Clevedon.** Real Photographs

Below: **Bradshaw's, March 1940, one of the very last issues in which the WC&P appeared.** Author's files

Portishead and Weston-super-Mare] 1085 [Kensington and Clapham Jn.

PORTISHEAD and WESTON-SUPER-MARE.—Weston, Clevedon, and Portishead.

Miles	Down.	Week Days only. mrn	mrn		aft	aft		
	Portishead .... dep.	..	1015	..	1 35	4 45	..	..
½	Portishead South **D**	....	1018	....	1 38	4 48	....	....
1¾	Clapton Road	..	Aa	..	Aa	Aa	..	..
2¾	Cadbury Road **C**	....	1025	....	1 42	4 52	....	....
4	Walton-in-Gordano	..	1029	..	1 46	4 56	..	..
4½	Walton Park	....	Aa	....	Aa	Aa	....	....
5	Clevedon (All Saints') ...	..	1033	..	1 50	5 0	..	..
5½	Clevedon East	....	1034	....	1 55	5 5	....	....
6	**Clevedon F 53**	7 50	11 0	..	2 15	5 20	..	..
7	Colehouse Lane	Aa	Aa	....	Aa	Aa	....	....
8	Kingston Road	7 56	11 6	..	2 21	5 26	..	..
8½	Broadstone	Aa	Aa	....	Aa	Aa	....	....
9	Ham Lane	7 59	11 9	..	2 24	5 29	..	..
10½	Wick St. Lawrence	8 5	1113	....	2 28	5 33	....	....
11	Ebdon Lane	Aa	Aa	..	Aa	Aa	..	..
12¼	Worle Town	8 13	1121	....	2 36	5 41	....	....
12¾	Bristol Road	8 16	1124	..	2 39	5 44	..	..
13¼	Milton Road...[**Mare H**	Aa	Aa	....	Aa	Aa	....	....
14¼	**Weston-super-** arr.	8 35	1130	..	2 45	5 55	..	..

Miles	Up.	Week Days only. mrn	mrn		aft	aft			
	Ashcombe Rd. Sta. **Weston-super-** dep.	8 55	1145	..	3 0	6 0	..	..	..
1	Milton Road...[**Mare** ..	Aa	Aa	....	Aa	Aa	....	....	....
1½	Bristol Road	9 1	1151	..	3 6	6 6	..	..	..
2	Worle Town	9 4	1154	....	3 9	6 10	....	....	....
3¼	Ebdon Lane	Aa	Aa	..	Aa	Aa	..	..	..
4	Wick St. Lawrence	9 12	12 2	....	3 17	6 18	....	....	....
5	Ham Lane	9 16	12 6	..	3 21	6 22	..	..	..
5¾	Broadstone	Aa	Aa	....	Aa	Aa	....	....	....
6¾	Kingston Road	9 19	12 9	..	3 25	6 25	..	..	..
7¼	Colehouse Lane	Aa	Aa	....	Aa	Aa	....	....	....
8½	**Clevedon F 53**	9 30	1215	..	3 30	6 30	..	..	..
9	Clevedon East	9 33	1218	....	3 32	....	....	....	....
9¼	Clevedon (All Saints') ..	9 34	1219	..	3 33	..	..	..	..
9¾	Walton Park	Aa	Aa	....	Aa	....	....	....	....
10¼	Walton-in-Gordano	9 38	1223	..	3 37	..	..	..	..
11¾	Cadbury Road **C**	9 42	1227	....	3 41	....	....	....	....
13	Clapton Road	Aa	Aa	..	Aa	..	..	..	..
13¾	Portishead South **D** ...	9 46	1231	....	3 45	....	....	....	....
14¼	**Portishead J 52** .. arr.	9 55	1245	..	4 0	..	..	..	..

Aa Stops when required. **C** Cadbury Road (Walton-in-Gordano). **D** Portishead South (Portboy Road).
F Adjoining Great Western Station. **H** Ashcombe Road Station. **J** ½ mile to Great Western Station.

Steam Locomotives of the Weston, Clevedon & Portishead Light Railway

No	Name	Type	Builder	Built	Bought	Origin	Wheels	Cyls	Weight	Disposal
-	Portishead	0-6-0T	Stephenson	1880	1898	Contractors	4ft 6in	16in x 20in	21t 0c	Sold 1900; scr 1939
-	Weston	2-2-2WT	S/Stewart	1866	1898	FR No35	5ft 6¼in	15in x 18in	30t 10c	Scr c1906
-	Clevedon	2-2-2WT	S/Stewart	1857	1899	FR No12	5ft 6¼in	14in x 20in	30t 2c	Scr c1904
1	Clevedon*	2-4-0T	Dubs & Co	1879	1901	Jersey Ry	4ft 0in	10in x 19in		Scr 1940
-	†	2-4-0T	S/Stewart	1872	1903	LBSC No 53	4ft 0in	12in x 17in		Scr 1906
3	Weston	0-6-0ST	M/Wardle	1881	1906	Contractors	3ft 0in	13in x 18in	19t 10c	Scr 1940
2	Portishead	0-6-0ST	M/Wardle	1890	1907	Contractors	3ft 0in	12in x 17in	18t 10c	Sold 1926
-	Walton Park	0-6-0ST	H/Clarke	1908	new	new	3ft 7in	14in x 20in	29t 10c	Sold 1912; scr 1947
4	Hesperus	2-4-0T	S/Stewart	1876	1911	W&PR No2	4ft 2in	12in x 17in	24t 7c	Wdn 1937
5	-	0-6-0ST	M/Wardle	1919	new	new	3ft 0in	12in x 18in	20t 0c	Scr 1940
2	Portishead	0-6-0T	Brighton	1877	1926	LBSC No 43	4ft 0in	12in x 20in	28t 5c	To GWR; wdn 1954
4	-	0-6-0T	Brighton	1875	1937	LBSC No53	4ft 0in	12in x 20in	28t 5c	To GWR; wdn 1948.

*Retained former name of *General Don* until c1904
†Designated name *Portishead* seemingly not carried
NB: Hired locomotives not included, Apart from contractor's locomotives, these were 0-6-0STs hired from Philips' of Newport in 1903/05, and Kent & East Sussex No 2 *Northiam* on loan c1917-21.

tives, but as the years progressed neither cleaning nor repainting were top of the company's priorities and so, to most observers, the livery of later years invariably appeared somewhat indistinct.

Returning to the early years of the WC&PLR, in 1909, only two years after the line had opened through to Portishead, the company went into receivership, its major creditor being the Excess Insurance Co which had provided most of the finance for the Clevedon-Portishead section. The creditor decided to keep the railway running in the hope that at least some of the debts might be repaid and, in 1911, our old friend Holman Stephens was appointed as general manager of the line.

In his time, Stephens had become used to seeing disadvantaged little railways, but he didn't fancy the WC&PLR's chances one iota. First, he tried to negotiate a sell-out to the GWR, but when the laughter had subsided at Paddington, he turned to the Midland Railway. That was not as daft as it seemed, as the Midland was active in Bristol, 11½ rail-miles east of Portishead and, courtesy of its share in the Somerset & Dorset Joint Railway, also at Highbridge, not too far to the south of Weston. The Midland expressed vague interest, but required the WC&PLR to build an extension from Weston to Highbridge. Financially, that idea was a complete non-starter and so the talks came to nothing.

At the Grouping, the GWR fought tooth and nail not to be lumbered with the impecunious WC&PLR, and so the little company was left to struggle on as an independent concern. In the early 1920s, the weekday services usually consisted of three or four trains each way between Weston and Portishead with an additional four or five each way on the Weston-Clevedon section. The siting of the engine and carriage sheds at the mid-point of Clevedon meant that a considerable amount of empty

running had to be undertaken at the start and finish of each day, but that situation had been inherited from the line's original promoters and there were no funds to rectify it. In an attempt to reduce overheads to the barest minimum, a four-wheel 30hp Drewry petrol railcar was purchased in 1921; with its three gears, it could manage 25mph and return over 15mpg. Nicknamed the 'Flying Matchbox', a trailer was purchased for it in 1923. In 1934, a six-year old 22-seat Drewry car was purchased from the Southern Railway for £272.

During the 1920s, an average of 90,000 passengers used the line annually to provide receipts of around £9,000 but, mysteriously, other light railways in Britain had greater revenue from less than half the number of passengers. Perhaps surprisingly, freight contributed only a little less to the WC&PLR's coffers than the passenger traffic. Stone from the Conygar and Black Rock quarries accounted for much of the freight traffic, but coal for the gas works at Clevedon and Worle also contributed. An economy in the method of working the Wick St Lawrence jetty was made in 1921 with the purchase of a Muir-Hill rail tractor. The Fordson-powered machine had 40in diameter flanged wheels and was capable of moving 60tons on the level. A derailment resulted in it being damaged beyond repair but a more powerful replacement was bought in 1926.

The only other additions to the WC&PLR's motive power fleet were two ex-LB&SCR 'Terrier' 0-6-0Ts, one being purchased in 1926 and the other in 1937, to become No 2 *Portishead* and No 4 (unnamed) respectively. The first 'Terrier' was allegedly painted black before being released by its previous owner, but the second definitely retained its green Southern Railway plumage during its WC&PLR days. From the mid-1920s, green had, in fact, replaced crimson as the WC&PLR's standard liv-

Above: **Although 62 years old when purchased by the WC&P in 1937, the ex-LB&SCR 'Terrier' looked very smart in its new livery.**

Right: **The WC&PLR's petrol-driven Drewry Railcar was photographed at Clevedon on 25 June 1938.**
H. C. Casserley

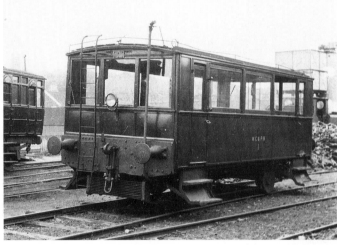

ery but expenditure on paint was not exactly high on the company's list of priorities and, consequently, the casual observer was often hard-pressed to find evidence of a definitive colour scheme.

The 1930s saw a continuing decline in the WC&PLR's traffic and, when war broke out in 1939, the line escaped being brought under Government control. By then, the WC&PLR had been in receivership for 30 years. Although economies had been made, they had not performed the miracle that had been required and as the company had inadequate funds to bring the permanent way up to the required standard, a Court Order was made for the line to close. The last services operated on 18 May 1940, with 'Terrier' No 4 in charge of the final working.

The Great Western Railway, which had previously laughed off any suggestions that it should purchase the WC&PLR, readily paid £10,000 for the remnants.

The GWR wanted to use the tracks for storing loaded coal wagons which had been held up at ports in South Wales but it seems that no such useage was ever made of the line and the tracks were lifted in 1942/43. As for the WC&PLR's rolling stock which passed to the GWR, the folks at Swindon demonstrated their opinion of the inheritance by selling or scrapping everything except the two ex-LB&SCR 'Terriers'. They were absorbed into GWR stock and became Nos 5 and 6, the former still retaining its name of *Portishead*. No 6 was withdrawn from St Philip's Marsh shed in Bristol in January 1948 but No 5 hung on until February 1954 when it was withdrawn after spells at Bristol, Bridgwater and Newton Abbot.

58 Wick & Lybster Light Railway

The absolute extremity of Britain's main line railway network was at Wick, a mere 14 miles as the crow flies from John o'Groats. The Highland Railway reached Wick as early as 28 July 1874 and considering that other railway companies elsewhere in Britain were, at that time, struggling to overcome far less challenging terrain, the Highland's achievement should never be underestimated.

South of Wick, but well away from the route of the railway, was the fishing village of Lybster which, at one time, was acknowledged as the third most important herring port in Scotland. In the 1890s, it was considered that a line to Lybster would benefit the local fishing industry, and so the Wick & Lybster Light Railway was formed. The W&LLR was an independent concern and it took full advantage of the Light Railways Act. Of the £71,000 required for its capital, £25,000 was obtained by means of a Treasury grant and, as permitted by the Act, the Caithness County Council took a significant stake. The other major financier was the Duke of Portland who owned a medium-sized chunk of Caithness. After the Duke had overcome an initial bout of cold feet, he became keen to ensure that the railway got off to a flying start and he consequently spent a considerable amount on improving the harbour at Lybster.

The railway opened on 1 July 1903 and boasted impressive Norse names for four of its five stations.

After leaving Wick, there was Thrumster (4¼ miles), Ulbster (7¼ miles), Mid Clyth (9½ miles) and Occumster (12¼ miles) before the line reached the terminus at Lybster (13½ miles). On 27 January 1936, halts were added at Welsh's Crossing (6½ miles), Roster Road (10 miles) and Parkside (13 miles). According to official records, the cost of constructing the line worked out at a remarkably low £3,372 per mile.

The Highland Railway worked the line from the outset, and the locomotive in charge of proceedings on opening day was 0-4-4T No 53 *Lybster*. Designed by David Jones of 'Jones Goods' fame, it had been built as a 0-4-4ST at Lochgorm Works in Inverness in 1890 for working the Strathpeffer branch and, accordingly, had been named *Strathpeffer*; originally No 13, it had been renumbered in 1899, rebuilt with side tanks in 1901 and, just prior to the opening of the W&LLR, had been renamed *Lybster*. Apart from occasional duties on the Dornoch Light Railway, No

Below: **Highland Railway 0-4-4T No 53 *Lybster* did the honours on the opening day of the Wick & Lybster Light Railway. Although the locomotive was made extremely presentable for the auspicious occasion, little attention seems to have been paid to the modernity of the rolling stock.** Bucknall Collection/Ian Allan Library

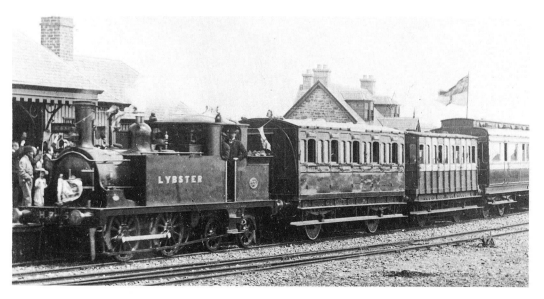

Above: **Drummond 0-4-4T No 15053 prepares to take on water at Lybster in July 1931.** Rail Archive Stephenson

Above right: **25in Ordnance Survery map of Wick station and surrounds, 1906.** Crown Copyright

Right: **Five 4-4-0Ts were built in 1892 by Dubs & Co for the Uruguayan Eastern Railway but, when the order was cancelled, the Highland Railway stepped in and purchased all five for £1,500 apiece. After the Grouping, they were allotted LMSR Nos 15013-16, the first of the class being photographed entering Lybster on 19 May 1928.** H. C. Casserley

53 spent the rest of its life on the Lybster branch and was finally withdrawn in 1929, by which time it wore LMSR No 15050, albeit without a name. The branch locomotive was accommodated in a small engine shed at Lybster which, until after nationalisation, was regarded as a sub-shed of Inverness. However, the importance of Wick depot as a motive power centre can be gauged by the fact that its allocation at the end of 1922 comprised just six locomotives.

Over the years, the other locomotives used on the Lybster branch included Stroudley-designed 0-6-0T No 57 (later LMSR No 16119) *Lochgorm*, one of a class of three which later became acknowledged as the forerunners of the famous London, Brighton & South Coast Railway 'Terriers'. An occasional guest during the mid-1920s was 'Yankee' 4-4-0T No 15 (later LMSR No 15016) *Fortrose*. For much of the Lybster branch's existence, there were three services each way on weekdays, most of which operated as mixed trains. Seemingly, there were few comments from passengers about the vans of fresh Lybster fish which were within sniffing distance behind the carriages. The times for the 13½ -mile trip were usually between 40 and 50min.

During the early years, relations between the W&LLR and the Highland Railway were not always idyllic, the former being distinctly unimpressed by the latter's unannounced charges for depreciation on the rolling stock and for administrative staff at Wick and Inverness. The W&LLR subsequently negotiated alternative conditions but those turned out even more expensive than the original ones, although a reasonably amicable compromise was eventually reached.

Like most of the other railway companies in Britain, the W&LLR came under Government control during World War 1. The little company tried to make the most of the Government's financial arrangements for compensation, and correspondence regard-

ing the W&LLR's creative accounting bounced back and forth between Whitehall and Wick until 1919. By then, the company found itself under the scrutiny of, not only Treasury accountants, but also the Highland Railway, the latter once again trying to impose stiffer terms for working the line. As things turned out, the hypothetical problems took second place in 1921 when the plans for the Grouping were announced. In 1923, the W&LLR was swallowed up by the mighty LMSR.

By the time of the Grouping, traffic figures on the Lybster line had already started to decline. This was despite the 'Saturday specials', which had started to be operated to Lybster in 1921 after the councillors of Wick had decided to close all the town's licensed premises. For thirsty fishermen, the nearest sources of refreshment were Thurso or Lybster, and the latter was more easily accessible by rail. During the 1920s and 1930s, however, road transport gained an increasing share of the remaining passenger and goods traffic from Lybster.

The outbreak of World War 2 saw the line return to Government control. A military camp was established just to the north of Lybster, but although that

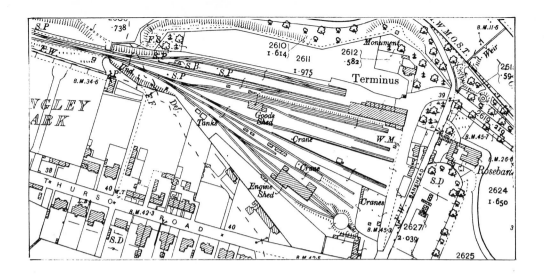

generated a small amount of traffic for the railway, the line's other usage was negligible. Matters were not helped by the opening of a new main road over the Ord of Caithness which did much to improve alternative communications in the area, and it came as little surprise when it was announced that the services on the Lybster branch were to be suspended as a war-time economy. The suspension became effective on 1 April 1944. When peace was restored it was evident that, within two years, some £27,000 would have to be spent on relaying the line and, as there were few realistic hopes that a worthwhile amount of traffic could be attracted, the line was never to reopen.

As for the post-Grouping motive power situation on the Lybster branch, the 1920s and 1930s usually saw a Drummond 0-4-4T in charge with Nos 15051/53 being the most regularly-photographed occupants of Lybster shed during those decades. Those locomotives survived until 1956/57, by which time they were employed on the Dornoch branch. There are reports that an ex-LB&SCR 'D1' class 0-4-2T worked on the Lybster line during World War 2, but although it is known that seven members of the class worked in Scotland between 1941 and 1944 and that No 2699 had a spell at Wick, this writer can find no official confirmation that a 'D1' was actually engaged on Lybster duties.

By the mid–1890s, Bristol Waterworks was ready to start building its new reservoir near Blagdon, at the foot of the Mendip Hills in north Somerset. When local businessmen formulated a proposal for a railway to Blagdon, the folks at the waterworks were quick to support the scheme as the prospect of a railway link to the construction site was a rosy one indeed. The incorporation of the Wrington Vale Light Railway was a remarkably swift procedure, but although the backing of Bristol Waterworks had helped matters, the support of the Great Western Railway had played an even greater part. Nominally, the WVLR was an independent concern but it was to be largely financed and constructed by the GWR which, of course, intended to work the line.

The line opened to the public on 4 December 1901. It started at Congresbury station on the GWR's Yatton-Wells-Witham branch, and a second through platform was constructed there. The reason for the provision of a through platform rather than a bay was

that trains on the WVLR were intended to start and finish at Yatton station, on the main Bristol-Weston line, rather than at Congresbury itself. Along the WVLR there were stopping places at Wrington (3 miles from Congresbury), Langford (3½ miles) and Burrington (5¼ miles) before the terminus at Blagdon (6¾ miles) was reached. At first, Burrington was little more than a halt and it was the only station on the line without separate freight facilities. About ¾-mile before the line reached Blagdon, two spurs diverged, one being a quarter of a mile long and leading to Bristol Waterworks's new pumping station at the Yeo Valley Reservoir, the other running into the grounds of Coombe Lodge, the home of Baron Winterstoke whose family, the Wills's, had done rather nicely from the tobacco industry in Bristol.

At one stage, it seemed possible that Blagdon might become a junction. In 1906, a Light Railway Order was obtained for the construction of the Blagdon & Pensford Light Railway which was intended to tap

J W Pitt

Left: **Congresbury was the point at which the Wrington Vale line left the Yatton-Wells-Witham branch. The two lines diverged a little beyond the station.** Lens of Sutton

Above: **The term 'typical GWR country branch terminus' is something of a cliche, but it fits this scene very well indeed. The date is May 1929 and the locomotive is '517' class 0-4-2T No 540.** Rail Archive Stephenson

the coal traffic around Pensford and, hopefully, develop into a commuter line for nearby Bristol. However, after the initial enthusiasm for the railway had subsided, the plans passed into oblivion.

For working the WVLR line, the GWR was faced with the restriction of a 14-ton axle-weight limit and, after scouring its lists for suitable lightweight steeds, brought in Sharp Stewart 2-4-0T No 1384. That locomotive had led a peripatetic life. It had started out in 1876 as Watlington & Princes Risborough Railway No 2 and, after that company had been absorbed by the GWR in 1883, had been used on the construction of the Bodmin branch in Cornwall and, later, on the Lambourn Valley Railway. After being 'Swindonised' in 1899, it had 4ft 2in diameter driving wheels and 12in x 17in cylinders. Even after it departed from the WVLR, its travels were not over as it was used on the Tiverton Junction-Hemyock

branch in Devon and, after being sold by the GWR in 1911, re-emerged on the Weston, Clevedon & Portishead Light Railway (qv) in the guise of No 4 *Hesperus.*

The GWR intended to replace No 1384 with an oil-burning 0-4-0T. The latter, which went down in the annals as the only 0-4-0T to be built at Swindon, was constructed in 1902 and had 3ft 8in diameter wheels and outside cylinders of 13in x 22in. Carrying No 101, it was very much an experimental locomotive and so there were no qualms about replacing its original boiler with one of a Lentz design after only a year. The Lentz boiler failed to work wonders, and so No 101 was converted to a conventional coal-fired machine in 1905. It was withdrawn in 1911 without having set foot on its intended stomping ground of the WVLR. Instead, it had spent all of its brief working life shunting at Swindon.

As things turned out, the usual replacements for 2-4-0T No 1384 on the WVLR line were, at first, a '517' class 0-4-2T although 'Metro' 2-4-0Ts occasionally crept in during the 1920s. However, no one locomotive was allocated to the line as the shed at Yatton invariably had two or three members of each class on its books, and the Blagdon duty was just one of three branch turns serviced by that shed. Nevertheless, the GWR's allocation lists for January 1921 actually show '517' class 0-4-2T No 837 as being outstationed at Blagdon. It would be incorrect to use the

term 'shedded at Blagdon' in those days as the single-road timber-built engine shed had burned down in October 1912, but Blagdon nevertheless remained in the official shed lists until March 1924. It cannot go unmentioned that, in the early 1920s, the line's regular driver was one Oliver Oliver who was usually referred to as 'Oliver Twice'.

For its first 20 years, the WVLR was reasonably well patronised. The passenger services usually comprised four trains each way on weekdays with journey times of 30-45min for the 8¼ -mile trip to or from Yatton. During the peak summer periods, the branch services to Clevedon and Wells sometimes caused considerable congestion at Yatton station and, to avoid adding to the chaos there, services from Blagdon often terminated at Congresbury, where passengers were transferred to a train from Wells. The WVLR's outwards freight traffic was mainly agricultural produce while most of the goods inwards was coal; for many years, some 2,000 tons of coal was brought annually to the waterworks pumping station near Blagdon.

Throughout this book, there have been numerous examples of railway lines which were affected during the 1920s by the competition of road transport, and the WVLR is yet another to add to the list. In an attempt to reduce overheads on the under-used line, the GWR occasionally used the Clevedon branch

railmotor on the WVLR route, but that was not considered to be a long-term option as the machine had an exceptional appetite for water and, between Yatton and Blagdon, there were no watering facilities. Despite other efforts to economise, the branch became less and less viable and passenger services were withdrawn on 14 September 1931.

The branch remained open for freight traffic, but that also declined. Nevertheless, it was 1 November 1950 before the section beyond Wrington station was closed completely, the Congresbury-Wrington section being retained for another 13 years for use by a daily coal train. The official closure date of that last section was 15 July 1963, but it is believed that the final coal train to Wrington had run at least one month previously. After the withdrawal of scheduled passenger services in 1931 three special workings had been accommodated on the line, the last having been an RCTS special on 28 April 1957 when ex-LMSR class '2P' 2-6-2Ts Nos 41202/03 had hauled an eight-coach train.